Nocturne:
A Life of Chopin

RUTH JORDAN

Nocturne:
A Life of Chopin

Taplinger Publishing Company
New York

First published in the United States in 1978 by
TAPLINGER PUBLISHING CO., INC.
New York, New York 10003

Library of Congress Catalog Card Number: 78–53797
ISBN 0–8008–5593–0

Contents

List of illustrations

A note on sources

The originals of the frontispiece and nos. 1, 2, 4, 5, 6, 7, 10 and 13 have either been lost or destroyed, and are copies of reproductions published before the Second World War, made available by courtesy of the Chopin Society in Warsaw.

Acknowledgments

The time I spent in Poland as the guest of the Frederick Chopin Society was one of the most exhilarating periods in my research for this new life of Chopin. I am indebted to the Director General, Mr Wiktor Weinbaum, for enabling me to work at the Society's beautiful headquarters at Ostrogski Castle in Warsaw; to the Curator, Mrs Hanna Wroblewska-Straus, for opening the Society archives to me; to Miss Janina Ohrt for her assistance with the use of the library; and above all to Dr Dalila Teresa Turlo for her invaluable help with sources, illustrations and general information. I am also grateful to Miss Krystyna Kobylanska for showing me some of her personal *Chopiniana*; to Irena for her help with Polish texts and to the staff of the British Council in Warsaw for their kindness; to M. Georges Lubin for his interest and encouragement; to Miss Rosemary Loxton for putting at my disposal an unpublished letter by George Sand; to Mr Lance Thirkell for reading my typescript; and to my husband for driving me round Poland, France and Majorca on the trail of Chopin.

Foreword

When Berlioz read Stendhal's *Life of Rossini* he criticized it for being full of irritating misconceptions resulting from the writer's pretension to know all about music.

Hoping to avoid such a pitfall, I have confined myself to Chopin's life without trespassing on the musicologist's preserve. On the other hand it would have been impossible to try to recreate his life without a deep empathy with his music. Indeed my interest in Chopin as a person had first been roused by my love for his music which to me, a marvelling layman, is as gripping and poignant as love itself.

The number of works which have been written about him is literally countless. Sydow's *Bibiliografia F. F. Chopina*, published in 1949 with a later Supplement, lists nearly ten thousand items, while the more selective *Bibliografia Chopinowska* by Michalowski, published in 1970 and still continuing, has some four thousand entries. The remarkable thing is that although Chopin is probably one of the most written-about composers who ever lived, his life has still some surprises to offer.

The most controversial came in 1945, when letters alleged to have been written by him to Countess Delphina Potocka were uncovered, showing him in an entirely new light; no longer the diffident admirer of Constance Gladkowska or the repressed son-figure of George Sand, but a flesh-and-blood lover expressing himself in the most unrestrained of colloquial terms. That verbal licence, so different from his written communications to parents and sisters, has shocked traditionalists who will not see in him anything but an ethereal romantic and started a storm which has not yet subsided.

At the root of the controversy is the fact that nobody has seen the originals. Some letters exist in photostats, the majority only in the hand of a copier. There are over a hundred of them, mostly in fragments, without conventional beginning or end. The Frederick Chopin Society in Warsaw, which is now in possession of the copier's text, is of the opinion that the letters cannot be authentic. The late Arthur Hedley firmly upheld this view, and the late J. M. Smoter, in the 1976 edition of his *Spor o 'listy' Chopina do Delfiny*, published the first unexpunged text of the copier only to suggest that it was based on some sort of forgery. Other Chopinologists, like the late B. E. Sydow and the late M. Glinski, believed them to be authentic. So does Mr A. Harasowski, who, to support his theory that at least some of the letters are authentic, had some photostats in Chopin's own hand reproduced in the March 1973 issue of *Music and Musicians*. Still the controversy goes on.

Having given much thought to the arguments for and against the authenticity of the letters and seen the photostat reproductions in Chopin's hand as well as the text in the hand of the copier, my feeling is that the ayes have it. In the following chapters I have therefore included the text, translated into English for the first time *in extenso*, of two of Chopin's most controversial letters to Delphina Potocka, as well as a selection of fragments. His Polish style, as distinct from his French, was chatty and uncontrived, as natural as colloquial speech and often as repetitive and unpolished. His letters to Delphina possess these qualities in abundance, showing him aglow with intimate recollections, writing the first thing that came into his head. They also contain his unrepressed views on music and musicians.

To those who might find the image of an earthy Chopin somewhat disconcerting, may I quote what James Huneker, one of the composer's earliest biographers, wrote in 1899. 'The real Chopin life', Huneker wrote, 'shall embrace his moral and physical nature, will not shirk his marked abnormalities of vision, of conduct, and will not bow down before that agreeable fetish of sawdust and molasses called *Frederick Chopin*, created by silly sentimentalists and rose-leaf poets. Chopin with all his imperfections full blown; Chopin with his consummate genius for giving pain as well as taking pain; Chopin the wonder-maker.'[1]

Another controversy, although by now of no real importance

except perhaps to horoscope casters, has centred around Chopin's date of birth. His birth certificate, which is extant, gives it as 22 February 1810; on the other hand there are some grounds to suspect that both year and day may have been wrongly entered. Some therefore believe that he was born in 1809; his mother used to celebrate his birthday on 1 March. Here I must digress for a moment. My own mother used to celebrate my birthday on 19 April whereas my birth certificate shows me to have been born on 19 June. My point is that while mothers know best, it is more convenient to make one's peace with the superior authority of the official document and accept what it states. This, I need hardly add, is no scholarly argument in favour of any given date, only an observation on the margin of error in anyone's personal documentation. The Frederick Chopin Society formally accepts the date stated in the birth certificate and marks it every year with a concert held at the Church of the Holy Cross in Warsaw, where Chopin's heart had been laid to rest.

Errors apart, much of the Chopin documentation has been lost over the years. Many of his letters to his family, kept by one of his sisters after his death, were destroyed in 1863 during a Russian punitive action; other letters, and many documents besides, were lost during the Second World War and are now available only in pre-war reproductions. No love letters of his to George Sand have ever come to light, and her own love letters to him, strangely discovered and returned to her by Alexandre Dumas the Younger, were apparently burnt by her own hand. The Frederick Chopin Society is leaving no stone unturned in the hope of retrieving some of the vanished documentation and finding out the truth about the lacunae in his life.

Truth, however, is something which even the fullest documentation cannot guarantee. There is nearly always room for deduction, conjecture, search for motivation and finally interpretation. This is surely the case of Chopin's relations with George Sand. Having once told the story from her point of view, I have now tried to tell it from his. If the two accounts differ in emphasis, though not in factual detail, the reason is that no man views his relationship with a woman in the same way that she views hers with him.

Another case in point is Jane Stirling. Chopin's early biographers saw her as his guardian angel; later ones as a gentle vampire. The first claim is based on the fact that she discreetly supported him during the last year of his life; the second on the fact that she imposed on him an exhausting social itinerary when he was already a dying man. There are not much data to go by. At one time she used to write to him every day. Presumably he did not keep any of her letters and, apart from a non-retrieved note he once enclosed for her in a letter to a mutual Polish friend, he never answered them. Yet she had a hold over him and after his death became the unchallenged dispenser of Chopin mementoes. Only a degree of inference can throw more light on the nature of their relations.

The margin of uncertainty in Chopin's life seems to extend even to such apparently ascertainable facts as the colour of his eyes. Some of his friends, like Liszt, put on record that they were blue; his second French passport, issued on 7 July 1837, stated that they were blueish-grey; but his Anglophile acquaintance Count Wodzinski remembered them as the colour of beer best described by the English word *auburn* (*sic*). Contemporary portraits, of which there are so many, only add to the confusion. In some the eyes appear to be dark brown, in others a shade of grey. A definite verdict seems to be impossible.

Yet another uncertainty concerns the object of Chopin's visit to Great Britain in 1848. The tendency has been to see it as a tour, but there is enough evidence to suggest that, for a time at least, he toyed with the idea of making London his permanent home. It is therefore all the more pleasing to record that, thanks to the initiative of the late Arthur Hedley, his first public appearance in London, at 99 Eaton Place, has been commemorated by a Blue Tablet.

The Tablet spells his Christian name Fryderyk, in the Polish way. For the sake of simplicity and familiarity I spell Polish given names as we know them in English: Frederick rather than Fryderyk, Constance rather than Konstancja, Louisa rather than Ludwika but, departing from my own rule, Jan rather than John. Surnames are spelt in the Polish way, though not names of well-known towns. In my rendering of Polish texts I tried, on the advice of Polish-speaking colleagues, to keep to Chopin's staccato style. For their advice and help I am tremendously grateful; for my aberrations I crave forbearance.

R.J.
1978

1

A Frenchman in Warsaw

In late 1787 or early 1788 a young village lad from Lorraine was taking his first look at Warsaw, where he was hoping to embark on an exciting commercial career. Nicholas Chopin, Frederick Chopin's future father, was seventeen at the time.

The choice of Warsaw as a starting point was no accident; indeed a twist of history had brought the distant Polish capital well within the consciousness of the natives of Lorraine. The Duke of Lorraine and Bar was Stanislaus Leszczynski, the twice deposed king of Poland, who was given a life dukedom by his son-in-law Louis XV. Even before his arrival the region had harboured a growing number of Polish aristocrats fleeing from their native land in the wake of political upheavals. They brought some of their wealth with them, bought land and in due course formed a court round their former king. Stanislaus, as Duke of Lorraine, ruled benignly over native Frenchmen and Polish exiles, founded schools and published learned works on the nature of philanthropy. When he died at eighty-nine, of a riding accident, the Polish community had become part of the Lorraine scene. A Polish count was lord of the manor at Marainville, Nicholas Chopin's birthplace.

It was a typical Vosges village with a total population of one hundred and thirty. Some of the villagers were vine growers; Nicholas' father was the local wheelwright. There were other Chopins scattered in the neighbouring villages, hard-working peasants who cultivated the land and sold its produce to the well-to-do Poles in their midst. When Nicholas was born, on 15 April 1771, a young relative called Thérèse Chopin stood godmother to him. While the godfather, a relative on the mother's side, was literate enough to sign his name on the infant's baptismal certificate, Mlle Chopin could only trace a cross by way of signature.

Of Nicholas' life at Marainville little is known beyond the fact that he was exceptionally bright. His two sisters—Frederick Chopin's future aunts—were taught domestic skills rather than book learning; but he, the only son in the family, was given an education which went well beyond the traditional village standards. He may well have attended one of the schools founded by the late Stanislaus Leszczynski and acquired not only a solid grounding in the general curriculum of the day, but also some familiarity with the Polish language and way of life. He probably carried off some school prizes and he certainly set his sights higher than the rest of the village boys. He was ambitious and, in his small community, quite out of the ordinary. By the time he was seventeen he had brought himself to the notice of the Polish Count Pac, lord of the Marainville manor, and asked to be taken into his employ. When shortly afterwards the count sent his steward to Warsaw to see to his Polish estates, it was agreed that young Nicholas should accompany him as a clerk and business apprentice. For a village lad it was a brilliant opening.

Nicholas was no stranger to Poland's recent history. Through their business and social contacts with the local Polish community, the natives of Lorraine were more familiar with Poland's political vicissitudes than was the average Frenchman of the day. The elder Chopins would have heard that in 1772, a year after their son's birth, large slices of Poland were annexed by Russia, Prussia and Austria through a process which later came to be known as the First Partition. They would also have learnt that the much shrunken country was valiantly progressing towards constitutional changes and economic rehabilitation. Under the patronage of a Polish gentleman like M. Weydlich, the count's steward and envoy, a bright young lad from Lorraine could well make his way in Warsaw and return home laden with honours and wealth. On the day of departure friends and relatives from Marainville and the adjoining villages turned out in force to bid Nicholas goodbye. The parish priest gave the young man his blessing. The parting from parents and sisters was not sad; nobody could have foreseen that Nicholas would never return. M. and Mme Chopin entrusted their son to the good care of M. and Mme Weydlich and enjoined all three to send them news as often as possible.

There is no knowing what Nicholas' first impressions were of the Polish capital, but an eye-witness account by the English clergyman William Coxe gives an idea of what it looked like to an older contemporary. 'The situation of Warsaw is not unpleasant,' Coxe wrote, then went on to describe it in detail:

It is built partly in a plain, and partly on a gentle ascent rising from the banks of the Vistula, which is about as broad as the Thames at Westminster Bridge, though very shallow in summer. The city and suburbs occupy a vast extent of the ground; but contain no more than between sixty and seventy thousand inhabitants, among whom are numerous foreigners. The whole town has a melancholy appearance, exhibiting that strong contrast of wealth and poverty, luxury and distress, which pervade every part of this unhappy country. The streets are spacious, but ill-paved and scarcely lighted with a single lamp; the churches and public buildings large and magnificent, the palaces of the nobility numerous and splendid; but the greater part of the houses, particularly in the suburbs, are mean and ill-constructed wooden hovels.[1]

To a sophisticated observer like William Coxe Warsaw was a sad example of Poland's general state, but to an inexperienced village lad like Nicholas the Polish capital was a wonder. It was the most colourful and cosmopolitan place he had ever seen. Proud-looking noblemen went about in traditional caftans with belted swords and bright boots; young sparks sported the latest fashions from Paris; long-bearded Jews rubbed shoulders with monks in every conceivable habit. There were Turks wearing oriental turbans, Greeks and Italians conducting business in street corners, Russian soldiers ogling passing girls, French traders discussing aloud the latest import dues. In the paved squares beautiful ladies clad in silk strolled side by side with veiled nuns. On fine summer days the townsfolk took the ferry to the other side of the Vistula and picnicked on its wooded banks. It was impossible not to be enthralled.

For a year or two all went well. Nicholas showed that quality of conscientiousness which was to stand him in good stead all his life, and was entrusted with money transactions connected with Count Pac's Polish estates. The Weydliches tried to keep the Chopins informed of their son's progress and once or twice asked them to undertake business commissions on their behalf at nearby Strasbourg. The correspondence was sparse and what letters were written often failed to reach their destination: the French Revolution had begun.

In a comparatively peaceful Warsaw, nineteen-year-old Nicholas was pursuing his career and prudently weighing the risks of a return visit to France. On 15 September 1790 he wrote his only known letter to his parents in Lorraine:

Dear Father and Mother,

Not knowing whether any of my letters have reached you I am writing a word or two to enquire after your health and show my respect and affection for you. It is two years since I have last heard from you, I do not know why, yet, dear parents, the distance only increases my respect for you as it makes me realise all the more what happiness I am being deprived of when I have no News of you. . . .

Count Pac's affairs have not yet been wound up, and as he requires an account of his revenues from his Marainville property, I was instructed by M. Weydlich to go to Strasbourg to settle up in his name. But since we understand that France is not quiet yet after the revolutions which have taken place there, I have put off my departure, still I hope to be able to leave very shortly because M. Weydlich has already made arrangements with a banker who is about to leave for France.

However before I set out I would like you to find out for me whether the militia is not stricter than it used to be, for we hear that all young men from the age of eighteen upwards are soldiers; this is what we are anxious to know for, being as I am in a foreign country where I can make my way I would be loath to leave here in order to become a soldier even in my own country considering that M. Weydlich had been most kind to me and I can foresee excellent opportunities opening up before me. I therefore beg of you dear parents to reply as soon as possible so that I can set out fully reassured and enjoy the pleasure of seeing you and all my dear relatives.[2]

Nicholas' word or two stretched to four pages, neatly written in a small, beautiful, legible hand. His calligraphy was more orderly than his thinking, for he was much disturbed by the prospect of being called up. He kept repeating himself, asked to be remembered to friends and sisters, sisters and the parish priest, friends and relatives. In conclusion he reiterated his dismay at not having had any news from home for two years and gave his address as Monsieur Chopin, Warsaw via Dresden, Poland, poste restante.

Whatever his parents may have reported about the strictness of the French militia, if indeed they answered the query, the young man stayed put. In his old age Nicholas Chopin used to say that twice during his youth he had intended to go back to his homeland and had twice been prevented by sudden illness. By that time there was nobody in Warsaw who could either verify or question that statement. Be this as it may, Nicholas Chopin never returned to France. The sparse correspondence with his family petered out and, as the years went by, he dissociated himself altogether from a country he had consciously renounced and a background which would have impeded his social advancement.

When Nicholas was seeking his parents' guidance about military service in France, he little imagined that within a year Poland too would call her men to arms.

The unrest had started long before he was born. In 1764 Stanislaus Poniatowski, a favourite of Grand Duchess Catherine, later Catherine the Great, was elected King of Poland and ascended the throne as Stanislaus II. Eight years later he had the mortification of seeing large areas of his kingdom seized by Russia, Prussia and Austria in order to preserve what the three powers were pleased to describe as the equilibrium of Europe. That was Poland's first partition.

After the partition of 1772 Stanislaus directed his energies towards improving the domestic situation. Local industries were established, the arts were encouraged, constitutional amendments were put forward. While France was in the throes of a revolution, Poland seemed to be peacefully progressing towards evolution. On 3 May 1791, when Nicholas had been living in Warsaw for three years or so, a new Polish constitution was ratified, converting the elected monarchy into a hereditary one with ministerial powers and a chance of stability, abolishing the *liberum veto* which had frustrated past attempts to improve legislation, and officially ending invidious class distinctions.

Hardly had the constitution been signed when three of its main opponents entered into secret negotiations with the court of St Petersburg and persuaded Russia to present Stanislaus with a formal declaration of war. The small Polish army fought valiantly under the veteran war hero Tadeusz Kosciuszko and the king's nephew Prince Joseph Poniatowski; but in spite of initial successes the king lost heart and accepted the Russian peace terms. In the autumn of 1793 Poland was partitioned for the second time. The country was reduced to a third of its original size and its estimated overall population of nine million shrank within the new boundaries to a mere three and a half. Earlier that year, in France, Louis XVI was sentenced to death by the republican Convention and publicly guillotined on the Place de la Révolution.

In Poland a patriotic movement refused to accept the humiliating mutilation and the spirit of resistance spread like wildfire. The following year Kosciuszko assumed the powers of dictator and called for national insurrection. Now it was an all out war against Russia and against King Stanislaus who had control of Warsaw. At first the insurgents won spectacular victories. Three quarters of the ancient territory were recovered, Warsaw was taken, King Stanislaus had to beg Kosciuszko for his life. Then the Empress Catherine ordered General Suvorov to the Polish front.

While the Russians were pushing forward, Kosciuszko and his troops retreated to Warsaw and mobilized all able-bodied men to its defence. Nicholas Chopin, who had had no work since the beginning of the insurrection, joined the Home Guard and within weeks, so tradition has it, rose to the rank of captain. The rest of that sad chapter in the history of Poland hardly needs retelling. Kosciuszko was defeated on the battlefield and taken prisoner, Suvorov's troops poured into the Warsaw suburb of Praga, on the right bank of the Vistula, and massacred ten thousand men, women and children. Nicholas was not among them. Just before the beginning of the Russian onslaught his unit was relieved and ordered back into the centre of the city.

A few weeks later the rest of Warsaw capitulated. King Stanislaus was conducted to St Petersburg, and in 1795 Poland was partitioned for the third time. Again the three old allies shared the spoils of war, with Warsaw being conceded to Prussia. Poland was no more.

After the suspension of hostilities Nicholas had to re-appraise his position. He had escaped the massacre at Praga and come to no harm when the rest of the capital fell to the Russians, but he had nothing to live on. His hopes of making his way in the world of commerce through his contacts with the Weydliches and Count Pac had come to nothing even before the Kosciuszko insurrection. So had a modest clerical post in a tobacco business run by a fellow countryman. He was twenty-four and hardly better off than when he first set foot in Poland. In the general depression that followed the Third Partition there was little a hard-up foreigner could do except give lessons in his native language. Nicholas became a teacher of French.

He was sufficiently well-connected to secure a resident post with a noble family. In Prussian-occupied Warsaw the Polish aristocracy looked to France for help and sympathy, and French was in great demand. Nicholas proved to be a good language teacher and his pupils, like most of the Polish intelligentsia, became fluent French speakers. One of them, Maria Laczynska, was later to marry Count Walewski and as Maria Walewska played a part in Napoleon's romantic history.

The six years Nicholas spent in the country house of the Laczynskis near Warsaw brought out in him those qualities for which he was to be best remembered. Steadfast and thorough, he took his profession seriously and while teaching others, found time to pursue his own education. One of his charges later described him as a reader of Voltaire and no mean player of the violin and flute. His qualities were recognized and when the last of the young Laczynskis reached the age when he no longer required a tutor, Nicholas had no difficulty in obtaining a resident post in another country house. In 1802 he was engaged by Countess Skarbek as tutor to her ten-year-old son Frederick, the eldest of five brothers and sisters all of whom were in due course going to need some home instruction. By then

Nicholas had been living in Poland for fourteen years. He was thirty-one and still unmarried.

The move to Zelazowa Wola, the Skarbek estate west of Warsaw, was the turning-point in his life. The count was living abroad to escape his creditors and the countess came to regard her children's tutor as a reliable and worthy person, fit to join the family circle. It was thanks to her benevolence and approval that four years later he married her young kinswoman and housekeeper Justina Krzyzanowska.

In those days it was customary for the lesser gentry of Poland to send their sons and daughters to the houses of the great to serve and earn a living. Justina, who had a Countess Justina Skarbek for a godmother and a Count Eugenius Skarbek for a godfather, was no exception. Although poor, she had been given the education considered proper for a young lady of her class. She could run a large house, sew, play the piano, sing and speak French. She was twenty-four, her bridegroom thirty-five.

The marriage was solemnized on 2 June 1806 in the nearby Roman Catholic church at Brochow and a marriage certificate was issued by the officiating priest in the customary Latin, saying:

> I, Ignatius Maryanski, curate of the church, having called the bans on three Sundays in the presence of the congregation at Divine Service and having found no impediment to the marriage of Nicholas Chopin, gentleman, tutor at Zelazowa Wola, bachelor, to Justina Krzyzanowska, spinster, have blessed and legally confirmed the contract according to the rites of the church in the presence of Franciszek Grebecki, gentleman, and Karol Henke, gentleman[3]

For the wheelwright's son to have married a gentlewoman, even a poor one, was a social achievement he could hardly have attained without a white lie or two. Fortunately in Zelazowa Wola he was a foreigner whose personal merit was taken as sufficient proof of an acceptable background. For his part Nicholas had taken trouble to diffuse the truth about his parentage and discreetly elevated himself to the rank of gentleman. To avoid an embarrassing confrontation with the past he had long shed his family and may not even have known that his mother had died in 1800 and that his widowed father, at sixty-two, had married a vine-grower's widow and taken to vine growing. He may well have given his in-laws to understand that his kith and kin had all perished in the aftermath of the French Revolution; after that nobody could probe into his antecedents without seeming heartless. Indeed nobody attempted to. It was just as convenient for Krzyzanowskis and Skarbeks to accept Justina's husband for a gentleman as it was for Nicholas Chopin to pass himself off as one. Countesses, in-laws, wife and finally children took him for what he chose to be, a Frenchman without ties who made Poland his adopted country.

2

Child prodigy

In 1806, even as the Zelazowa Wola household was preparing for the forthcoming wedding festivities, Poland was again under crossfire. Napoleon's *Grande armée* was on the march against Prussia and Russia, and Polish volunteers were fighting on their own soil under French command in the hope of winning back their country's independence. In November of that year, when Justina Chopin was already expecting her first baby, Prussian-held Warsaw fell to the French.

The Peace of Tilsit, concluded in 1807, only partially satisfied Polish aspirations. The name Poland was not officially restored; instead the Grand Duchy of Warsaw was created, encompassing the territories annexed by Prussia during the Second and Third Partitions. Napoleon dictated a constitution modelled on French lines and granted the Duchy autonomy in internal affairs. His staunch ally Frederick Augustus I, King of Saxony, was created Grand Duke of Warsaw, and Prince Joseph Poniatowski, a general in the French army and previously Kosciuszko's ally against the Russians, was made Minister of War. There were no new fronts as yet, but the Duchy was put on a war footing. Napoleon's generals were preparing the army's supply lines to Russia and commandeered all available resources.

Zelazowa Wola, twenty-eight miles west of Warsaw on the main road to Poznan, was right in the path of troop movements. Advancing Frenchmen, retreating Prussians, fleeing peasants, straggling convoys of requisitioned ponies, all passed through the Skarbek land. Life on an unprotected country estate was becoming increasingly hazardous. The visitations became so menacing that for greater safety the household moved to the capital where, in April 1807, Justina was delivered of a baby girl. Chopins and Skarbeks came even closer together when the countess stood godmother to the baby and graciously agreed to her being named Louisa after her. By the end of the following year the national situation seemed more settled and both families returned to the country.

Of the three country seats owned by the Skarbeks, Zelazowa Wola was the most modest, consisting of an unassuming manor-house and two cottages. The countess and her children occupied the main building, the Chopins one of the cottages. It was there, on 22 February 1810 that Frederick Chopin was born.

For one reason or another the birth was not registered until two months after the event, when it was recorded in the same church where the parents' wedding had taken place four years earlier. The birth certificate retraced every stage of the unhurried proceedings.

Given in the year One Thousand Eight Hundred and Ten on the Twenty Third day of April at Three in the afternoon. I the undersigned, Parish Priest and Acting Registrar of Brochow, in the district of Sochaczew in the Department of Warsaw, confirm that Nicholas Chopyn [*sic*] of Zelazowa Wola, aged forty, presented himself to me and showed me a Male Child born in his house on the Twenty Second of February of this year at Six in the evening, declaring that it was born of him and of Justina Krzyzanowska, his Wife, aged twenty-eight, and that he desired the boy to be christened Fryderyk Franciszek. While making his declaration he showed me the Child in the presence of Joseph Wyrzykowski, Bailiff, aged thirty-eight, and Frederick Gerszt, aged forty, both from the village of Zelazowa Wola. Having read the Birth Certificate, father and witnesses declared that they were able to sign their names. We have signed this document: Jan Duchnowski, Parish Priest and Acting Registrar of Brochow, Nicholas Chopin, father[1]

The registration formalities over, the child was baptized and a baptismal certificate in Latin duly issued, in which the father was described as 'The Honourable Nicholas Choppen [*sic*], a Frenchman'.[2] The godparents were both former pupils:

eighteen-year-old Count Frederick Skarbek who was away but who had given his consent to be represented by proxy, and his seventeen-year-old sister Countess Anna. In accordance with the father's wish the boy was christened Fryderyk Franciszek; Fryderyk after the official godfather, and Franciszek after the old family friend Franciszek Grembecki who had witnessed the parents' wedding and who now stood proxy for the absent godfather; or so the family thought. In fact François, the French form of Franciszek, was the name of Nicholas' own father, still alive in Lorraine though long made out to be dead. Choosing François as his son's middle name may well have been Nicholas' unsuspected response to the call of the blood.

While Zelazowa Wola was enjoying a relative calm, Warsaw suffered another upheaval. In the spring of 1809 the Austrians invaded the capital and occupied it for several weeks before being driven out by Napoleon's army. After this further French victory the territories seized by Austria during the Third Partition were ceded to the Grand Duchy. Even so it extended only to one fifth of Poland's original area.

Although severely handicapped by heavy contributions towards Napoleon's war budget, the Duchy made the most of its autonomy and introduced much needed administrative reforms. Culture and education flourished. Polish letters and scholarship were encouraged as well as the study of French language and literature. For Nicholas it was a time of decision. Count Frederick, the eldest of his Skarbek charges, had already left home to study in Paris. The other brothers and sisters were also nearing an age when they would no longer require a tutor. With a wife and two young children the chances of another residential post were negligible. Fortunately a vacancy occurred for the post of an assistant master of French at the Warsaw Lyceum, a newly-founded school where the sons of the gentry were being educated. In October 1810 the family bade farewell to the Skarbeks and moved to Warsaw. Frederick Chopin was seven months old.

The school was housed in the former Saxon Palace and the masters were allotted living quarters in the wings. The Chopins' apartment had ample room for nurseries. Within the next two years Justina gave birth to two more daughters: Isabel, born in July 1811, and Emily, born in November 1812. That year Nicholas obtained an additional part-time post as master of French at the Warsaw School of Artillery and Military Engineering. To help with the budget Justina took in boarders from among the schoolboys whose parents lived outside the capital. Countess Skarbek was one of the first to place her young with the Chopins, as Zelazowa Wola had again become unsafe. Napoleon's Russian campaign was going against him and Poland was overrun by foreign troops.

The Grand Duchy stood loyally by Napoleon and drained its resources to supply the men he needed. Ninety thousand Poles joined the ranks of the *Grande armée* only to lose their lives. Between 1812 and 1814 the French army was routed and the heroic Prince Joseph Poniatowski, by then a field-marshal, perished with his Polish troops while covering the Emperor's retreat. The Grand Duchy was occupied by the Russians.

When hostilities ceased Poland suffered a further blow. The congress of Vienna allowed Austria, Prussia and Russia to keep the Polish territories they had occupied during their earlier invasions and turned the much diminished Grand Duchy into a kingdom under Russian tutelage. Tsar Alexander I was proclaimed King of Poland and his brother, Grand Duke Constantine, was sent to Warsaw as Commander-in-Chief of the Polish army.

In spite of the blow to national aspirations the cultural revival which had begun during the short-lived Grand Duchy forged ahead. Letters, education and music reflected the national awareness. Polish became the official language of the law-courts and the civil administration, Polish-language journals were founded. The National Opera which since its foundation in 1778 had been drawing heavily on Czech, Hungarian and German composers, gave encouragement to Polish works and Linde, the Warsaw Lyceum headmaster, was working on his great Polish dictionary which was to become a classic.

In his modest way Nicholas Chopin was contributing to the cultural revival by educating the sons of the Polish gentry. He was in charge of the Lyceum's French curriculum and once a year put on a French play which was open to the public and commented on in the press. He became a well-known figure in educational and parental circles. Dark, severe-looking, his sober clothes relieved by a white shirt carefully starched under Justina's supervision, he was respected by his colleagues and feared by his pupils. He was a great disciplinarian. A former boarder, who at the age of twenty called on Nicholas to pay his respects, found himself trembling and desperately wondering what he had done wrong when he heard the familiar old voice call out his name.

At home Nicholas was a conscientious *pater familias* who exerted himself to give his children the opportunities and background he had lacked in his own childhood. He had them taught early how to read and write and encouraged them to speak French as well as Polish. In due course he would see that they were taught how to play the piano, as their mother had been and as was the custom among the educated gentry.

The children fell into two age-groups; the elder ones, Louisa and Frederick, being as thick as thieves, the little ones turning to each other. All four were to prove many-sided, taking pleasure in singing, reciting, playing charades, making up stories and composing verse. Family birthdays and namedays provided regular opportunities for a display of creativity. On 6 December 1816 a six-and-a-half-year-old Frederick handed his father a poem in Polish which he had composed and written down in his own hand:

When the world celebrates your nameday
It gives me joy too, dear Papa.
May you live in happiness
And know no care.
May you have your heart's desire
This is my wish for you today.[3]

Round the poem the boy had drawn a semi-circle of laurel leaves. At six and a half he was not only a fluent versifier but in perfect command of his hand, and his still unformed writing was beautiful and ornate in the style of the day. His signature, even to Papa, was formal: F. Chopin.

From his very first years it was evident that music had a hold over him. As a toddler he used to throw a tantrum when-ever his mother attempted to play the piano to him, until he learnt to climb the stool and produce sounds of his own. In no time he was playing duets with his sister Louisa who was three years older and a competent performer for her age. The parents were quick to realize that their son's playing was exceptional and agreed that no run-of-the-mill piano mistress would do for him. Frederick had hardly passed his sixth birthday when he began to take lessons with Albert Zywny, a somewhat eccentric musician noted for his life-long services to Warsaw's musical life.

Gaunt, unkempt and exhaling a strong smell of tobacco, sixty-year-old Zywny was a familiar figure in the aristocratic drawing-rooms of the capital. As a young man he had left his native Bohemia in the hope of conquering Poland with his violin, only to be jostled and frustrated by the adversities of war. He fell back on teaching, and since genteel young ladies were expected to play the piano rather than the violin, a piano teacher he became. His frivolous young pupils sometimes made fun of his unmatching yellow trousers, yellow vest and yellow cloak, all frayed and tobacco stained, but their mothers had faith in him. He composed and sometimes conducted, and had a say in the arrangements of musical evenings in the palaces of titled patrons.

The sixty-year-old teacher and his six-year-old pupil got on well. Zywny guided rather than taught and the virtuosity which the boy soon acquired was due to his natural ability rather than instruction. Frederick possessed perfect muscular control and coordination which enabled him to sight-read the most difficult pieces and spared him the drudgery of continued exercising. Furthermore, his manual dexterity was matched by mental alertness and sensitivity. Under Zwyny's guidance he played his way through Haydn, Mozart, Beethoven, Bach and a host of contemporary composers like Ries, Hummel and Kalkbrenner. The Chopins acquired a grand piano made by one of Warsaw's leading piano makers and Frederick was not subjected to the musical frustration of the proverbial child prodigy when confronted with an inferior instrument. In his keenness to master difficult works he took to going to bed with wooden wedges between his fingers hoping to have the span of his fingers extended while he was asleep. Fortunately he abandoned the practice before it damaged his bone structure.

Much of his time was spent improvising, with Zywny carefully noting down tunes and accompaniment, Nicholas lending a hand with copying. Before long the boy was able to note down his improvisations in his own hand, tracing minuscule neat notes on faintly drawn staves. One day in 1817 Zywny walked into the Chopins' drawing-room and from under his grimy cloak triumphantly produced a printed sheet of music. It was a Polish dance, a Polonaise in G minor, which Frederick had recently composed and dedicated in the mandatory French to one of the younger Skarbek countesses. An admiring church dignitary who ran a small publishing business had had it printed.

In a close-knit social and cultural community like Warsaw, the event did not go unnoticed. Not only was it an extraordinary achievement for a little boy, but it was a boost to the national pride smouldering under Russian domination. The *Warsaw Review* made the most of it, writing as follows:

> The composer of this Polish dance, a boy only eight years old, the son of Pan Nicholas Chopin who teaches French language and literature at the Lyceum, is a real musical genius. Not only does he play the most difficult piano pieces with ease and discernment, but he has also composed several Dances and Variations which experts regard as outstanding, particularly in view of the composer's tender years.[4]

The writer of the notice, a true Polish patriot, suggested that had the boy been born in Germany or France, his fame would have spread in no time all over Europe. 'The purpose of this column', the *Warsaw Review* concluded, 'is to point out that geniuses are born in Poland too, and if the fact is not better known, it is only because it has not been given due publicity.'[4]

In Warsaw however Frederick was a celebrity. Once Zywny had spread the word, society hostesses vied with each other to persuade the child-prodigy to play at their at-homes. Escorted by his father and Zywny, Frederick would arrive at the palace of a Czartoryski, a Sapieha, a Potocki, talk politely to beautiful and dazzlingly dressed princesses and countesses, then sit at the piano and play without the least self-consciousness. He was called a second Mozart. Once he was summoned before Grand Duke Constantine, the Russian Commander-in-Chief of the Polish forces, and pleased him enormously by improvising a march in his honour. The duke later had it scored for a military band and played during parades.

Two days after his eighth birthday Frederick had his first public engagement. A committee of ladies chaired by Countess Zamoyska had invited him to take part in a charity concert they had organized at the Radziwill Palace (in its reconstructed form now housing the Presidium of the Council of Ministers) on Cracow Precinct. The items on the programme had been selected by Zywny and included, apart from the piano solo piece, choral and instrumental music performed by local celebrities. The *Warsaw Gazette* gave advance notice of event, venue, price of tickets and names of performers. Frederick's name, last on the list, was spelt 'Schoppin'.[5]

At the concert it became apparent that Schoppin's performance was the success of the evening. He played a piano concerto by the contemporary Czech composer Gyrowetz who was popular at the time. The distinguished gathering was amazed and proud.

Fresh invitations to play kept pouring in and, as was inevitable, attempts were made by well-meaning lady organizers to make him out even younger than he was. His gala dress for such engagements consisted of what was then known as an English Suit, jacket and shorts made of dark velvet, knee-high white stockings and an enormous white collar. The Chopin myth has it that when his mother asked him after the Radziwill concert what the audience had liked best, he said it was the collar.

By that time the Chopins had moved, together with the school, to the vast premises of the restored Casimir Palace on Cracow Precinct, the former premises at the Saxon Palace having been converted into barracks on Duke Constantine's orders. The new residential quarters overlooked a large elegant courtyard and housed, apart from the Chopins, the headmaster and his family, the rector of the Warsaw university, scholars and men of letters. The Casimir Palace community led a cultured and hospitable life. The Chopins were at home to friends and colleagues on Thursdays and Sundays, and many a pleasant evening was spent making music, with Justina singing and Nicholas making up an amateur quartet or quintet as a violinist or flautist. The drawing-room was furnished with polished tables, carved upholstered chairs and, of course, the grand piano.

The household was larger than ever. The number of boarders had increased to six and sometimes eight, and a resident tutor had been engaged to supervise their homework. Justina now had a resident housekeeper and Nicholas, to keep up with growing overheads, accepted yet another part-time teaching post at the Military Cadet School. The family was not uncomfortable; but Nicholas, constantly worried about the irregularity of his salary and obeying a peasant's instinct for thrift, kept exhorting his children to be careful about money and save for a rainy day.

In the autumn of 1818 Warsaw had an imperial visitor, the Tsarina Maria Teodorovna, mother of Tsar Alexander I and Grand Duke Constantine. In the course of her imperial progress she visited the main cultural centres of the capital, of which the Lyceum was one. Frederick, who was being educated at home, was translated for the occasion into one of his father's forms and when the Tsarina was ushered in he recited a poem in French and offered her two polonaises composed in her honour. *The Warsaw and Foreign Gazette* discreetly underlined the Polish character of the offering; it was another boost to national pride.

With all the public acclaim the eight-year-old Frederick accepted his musical talent naturally, as other children might have accepted the colour of their eyes, with neither conceit nor humility. 'Dear Papa,' he wrote on 6 December 1818, the occasion of Nicholas' nameday, 'it would be easier for me to express my feelings in music, but even the best of concerts cannot show the depth of my love for you and therefore, dear Papa, I shall use the words of my heart to place a son's devotion and gratitude at your feet.'[6]

As usual, he signed himself formally F. Chopin, with the solemnity of a little boy performing an adult task. His handwriting had matured, becoming less ornate, yet retaining a prize boy's attention to neatness, margin and even spacing. Although educated at home, he had ample opportunities of associating with boys of his own age. The children of the Casimir Palace community freely called on one another, played hide-and-seek in the large back gardens and as often as not pretended not to hear when anxious parents called them back. Frederick was no exception.

Such games were sometimes interrupted by the arrival at the Casimir Palace of the ducal carriage, with instructions to bring the child prodigy to the belvedere, where Grand Duke Constantine was living with his newly-wedded Polish wife. Morose, unpredictable and often violent, the duke took to the boy pianist as Saul took to David. When the evil spirit was upon him nothing would drive it away but the boy's sensitive playing. Nor was the effect by any means instantaneous. The Chopin myth has it that once, when the boy was improvising with his eyes raised to the ceiling, the duke irritably barked out: 'What do you expect to find up there? The notes?' Nothing daunted, young David played on. After each such session he was allowed to romp in the belvedere gardens with the duke's illegitimate son, a boy of his own age.

Both Zywny and the Chopins neglected no opportunity of giving Frederick the best that musical Warsaw had to offer. He was taken to concerts, introduced to visiting musicians and encouraged to acquaint himself with new forms of music. In November 1819 the Italian soprano Angelica Catalani came to Warsaw to give four recitals. Frederick was taken to hear her and later played in her presence in one of the aristocratic houses of the capital. Catalani was then at the height of her fame and her approval, perhaps the first from the great world outside, was eagerly sought. She gave Frederick the accolade by present-ing him with an adult's gold watch inscribed in French: 'Mme Catalani to Frederick Chopin, aged ten, 3 January 1820'.[7] In fact Frederick was a few weeks short of ten and his tenth birthday, which his family celebrated on 1 March, was the occasion for more greeting cards, more merry-making and, above all, more music.

Adolescence

One spring day a grateful eleven-year-old handed his master a sheet of music inscribed in the mandatory French: 'Polonaise [in A flat major] for the Pianoforte composed and dedicated to Monsieur A. Zywny by Frederick Chopin, 23 April 1821'.[1]

By that time the pupil had long outstripped the master and the weekly sessions were lessons in name only. The young pianist had reached such virtuosity that Zywny confessed himself unable to be of any further use to him. The following year Frederick's formal studying of the piano came to an end. Instead he began taking lessons in counterpoint and composition with Joseph Elsner, director of the newly-founded Conservatoire of music. Zywny gracefully stepped aside and from guide turned into friend, constituting himself a member of the family and following his former pupil's development with affection and pride.

Elsner was a musician of a much higher calibre than Zywny. Having made a name for himself in his native Silesia, he settled in Warsaw at the turn of the century and became one of its leading musicians. As composer, conductor, director of the National Opera and eventually head of the Warsaw Conservatoire, he wielded tremendous influence over the development of Polish music. He composed no less than twenty-seven operas with a Polish libretto and many other works in nearly every form of music. He was a dedicated teacher and his method was imaginative as well as practical.

Although a man of many parts, Elsner had no pretension to being a first-class pianist. From the age of twelve onwards Frederick's pianistic skill therefore developed without formal tuition, and since Zywny and Elsner were the only music teachers he ever had, his achievement was all the more astounding. In February 1823 he was asked to play at a musical evening arranged by the same charitable society which five years earlier had given him his first public performance. This time there were no velvet shorts with a fancy collar. The young lad at the keyboard was dressed with conventional elegance and looked, if anything, slightly older than his age. His performance was dazzling. Analysing the virtuosity of the young pianist, the *Courier of the Fair Sex* concluded with patriotic pride:

The current issue of the *Leipzig Musical Gazette* reports that in Vienna too there is a young musician, List [*sic*] by name, who has performed a piano concerto by Hummel and amazed his audience with his accurate playing, his confident touch and his sure tone. After the 6th Musical Evening we need not envy Vienna her List [*sic*], for our capital can boast his equal and perhaps even his better. The name of the youth who has won such high praise—and we see no reason to conceal it—is Master Chopin. Master Chopin is not yet fifteen.[2]

The music critic of the *Courier of the Fair Sex* would have been even more impressed had he realized that Master Chopin had in fact only just turned thirteen. Under his father's tutelage Frederick spent most of the following months preparing for the entrance examination to the Lyceum. In the autumn he donned the regulation cap and belted tunic buttoned high under the neck and began to attend classes. At thirteen-and-a-half he had been accepted into the Fourth Form, with only three years to go before sitting for the final examination which would allow him, should he so wish, to enrol as a student at the Warsaw university.

The Lyceum was founded during the cultural revival which began under the Grand Duchy, and soon became one of the foremost educational institutions of the country. The pupils were the sons of a culture-conscious gentry while the staff included university professors and well-known scholars. The Polish master was the author of a book on literature; the maths master had written a book on the teaching of logarithms. The classics master had published works on ancient history and taught at the university; the Greek master and science master also taught at the university and the arts master was a recognized authority in his field. Above them towered Headmaster Linde, German-born but a Pole by choice, whose Dictionary became a cornerstone of the Polish language and whose lectures on literature were described by his students as unique. The curriculum of the school was ambitious and at the end of each school year public examinations were held to demonstrate achievements. The text-books were up-to-date, ranging from such works as *On Eloquence and Style* by Stanislaus Potocki, published in 1815, to a *History of the Old Testament* in two volumes, published in 1817.

Frederick took to school like a duck to water. In the mornings he crossed the courtyard which separated the apartment from the main building; in the evenings he did his homework together with his father's boarders. He was keen on Polish history and literature, indifferent to Latin and Greek, positively bored by maths and natural science. He was gifted and willing, and at the end of his first school year was awarded a book prize for diligence and good conduct. But a *Study of Elementary Statics*, however up-to-date, was little calculated to revive his flagging interest in science. At the end of his second school year he had to make do with an Honourable Mention, while at the end of his third and final year he was just Commended. Irrationally, the descending scale hurt his pride; to a trusted schoolfriend he explained that prizes went only to swots and toads.

Nobody could accuse him of being either. During lessons he was known to divide his attention between the work at hand and drawing cartoons of friends and masters. His pencil and chalk drawings had skill as well as wit and pointed to the same coordination between mind and hand which had first been noticed in his piano playing. Headmaster Linde once caught him red-handed during a literature class and confiscated a finished sketch which depicted his august self somewhat unflatteringly. The following morning, having given the offence due thought in the privacy of his study, he returned the sketch without reprimand. On the reverse he had written 'Well done'.

At school Frederick was a boy with the boys. In winter he went skating and snow-balling; in spring he frolicked with friends in the vast school grounds. He soon discarded the uncomfortable regulation belt and walked about with his tunic disdainfully loose. He was full of fun and mischief, tirelessly inventing new pranks to play on friends, boarders, sisters and adults. Sprightly and effervescent, he displayed a great deal of that schoolboy humour of which, happily, even geniuses are not innocent. With his coevals he was popular, for he was affectionate and communicative. Both fellow pranksters and victims remained lifelong friends.

By conventional standards he could not be described as handsome. A dominant nose to which he often called attention in deprecating terms marred any claim to regularity of features. But bright eyes and a vivacious expression redeemed his face from plainness and endowed it with a radiance independent of physical perfection. He was somewhat small for his age and obviously frail, but there was as yet no indication that he might one day be tubercular. Justina however was not taking any risks. She constantly fussed over him, reminded him to wrap up warm, urged him to put on weight. A French-born doctor was in attendance.

After a whole year with his nose to the grindstone and a book-prize to prove it, Frederick was thinner than ever. The boarders were joining their families in the country and the Chopins accepted an invitation for their son to spend part of his summer holiday in the village of Szafarnia, north-west of Warsaw, at the house of a classmate of his. After prize-giving day he submitted to a last examination by the family doctor and was packed off to the country with a bottle of pills and a motherly injunction to keep to a prescribed diet. Much faith was put in the invigorating properties of acorn coffee and linden tea.

For a boy who since his infancy had been living in a big city, a four-week stay in the country was a revelation. Frederick was having his first intimate glimpse of his native province of Mazovia. Together with his classmate Dominic Dziewanowski and the latter's two sisters he took walks in the woods, watched the peasants in the fields, went for rides in the family *bryczka*, attempted to ride a pony. Dominic and his sisters were seasoned riders, but for their city-bred guest every attempt was a test of endurance. 'The pony trots gently in whichever direction he fancies,' Frederick wrote in August 1824, 'while I, like a monkey on top of a bear, cling hard with a sinking heart. So far I have not fallen off because my mount has not wished it, but I shall certainly be thrown off as soon as it feels like it.'[3]

He developed a prodigious appetite, had second and third helpings of the thick country soup served by his hostess, begged to be allowed to eat the local farm bread instead of the specially baked white rolls which Dr Gerardot had prudently prescribed. 'If Gerardot could only taste the local bread,' Frederick pointed out to his mother with infallible logic, 'he would find it better than the rolls and surely allow me to eat it, because doctors like to prescribe for their patients what agrees with their own palates.'[4]

Every day brought fresh experiences which the boy reported back home with exuberance. The turkey took possession of the granary and turned it into a hatchery; the household cat toppled and licked up a bottle of home-made syrup; a hen began to limp and a duck lost a fight, and a foot, to a goose. An indisposed cow was allowed to graze in the garden and a fox stole into the shed and carried off two geese. Last but not least, a swarm of mosquitoes attempted to settle on somebody's prominent nose.

Most of the news items with which Frederick regaled his parents and sisters were written in the form of a newspaper, christened the *Szafarnia Courier* after the *Warsaw Courier* taken at home. M. Pichon, an anagram of Chopin, collected material, edited, copied and despatched, not omitting to submit each edition to a censor—in his case one of Dominic's sisters—as all Polish newspapers were required to do. The flow of farm news and schoolboy humour was inexhaustible. A cat went mad and ran into the fields 'where he stayed mad until he was killed, for when he was killed he stopped being mad'.[5] The cow was grazing contentedly in the garden and 'a general medical concilium pronounced her out of danger'.[5] A young duck was found drowned in the pond. 'The cause of suicide has not been established,' wrote ace reporter Pichon, 'the next-of-kin refusing to comment.'[6]

It was harvest time. Frederick watched the reapers at work, men and women together, mowing wheat and oats with their long scythes and sweeping the fallen rows out of their way. He listened to the traditional Mazovian songs and wondered aloud who had invented such perfect melodies and harmonies. In the middle of August he saw his first harvest festival. The whole village assembled outside the local manor house to present the squire with the traditional wreath of wheat. After the presentation ceremony the squire opened the harvest feast and dance. There was plenty of vodka, the *Szafarnia Courier* observed, and a choir of children sang 'in loud, shrill, off-pitch voices'.[7]

The children's choir excepted, the Mazovian folk music was a constant source of fascination for Frederick. He heard it everywhere; sung in fields and cottages, played at village dances on fiddles and bagpipes. The native Polish melodies fell on his ears like seed on fertile soil. One day he heard a young peasant girl singing a mazurka; but although he absorbed the simple tune of the traditional country dance, he could not make out the words which the girl was singing in the local country dialect. In vain did he strain his ears while strolling backwards and forwards by the low fence on which the girl was sitting. At last he planted himself full square before her and asked her to explain the words. 'The village Catalani'[8] became coy, pursed her lips and refused to utter another sound. Only the offer of three groszy—clearly a very modest reward—eventually cured her of her shyness. The *Szafarnia Courier* triumphantly reported that the words of the mazurka described a wolf who was light of foot but heavy of heart and who even while dancing behind the hills was grieving for a mate. 'This last bit is to be sung twice,'[8] the report added in brackets.

Frederick's hostess was a good pianist and in his first letter home he had asked his father to send, or bring along should he come to visit, a piano work for four hands by Ries, which he wanted to play with her. Some time after the harvest festival the Dziewanowskis arranged a musical at-home for neighbours and their families. Frederick played a concerto by Kalkbrenner and followed it with his own improvisation on a Jewish ritual song he had picked up in the country. 'The concerto was not half so popular as the song',[9] M. Pichon informed his parents. That a Jewish song could yield a pleasant improvisation in no way shook his conviction that Jews were the scum of the earth; by fourteen Frederick had so deeply absorbed the traditional

Polish contempt for Jews that he was never to lose it nor even question it.

The contemporary English clergyman William Coxe wrote in his book of travels that the Jews were 'very numerous in every part of Poland'[10] and that in some parts of the country there were 'swarms'[10] of them about. Contemporary statistics estimated their number as between five and ten per cent of the population, giving it as two million out of twenty before the First Partition, or as half a million out of nine after the Third Partition. In spite of their relatively small number they seemed ubiquitous. 'In some parts of Poland,' Coxe wrote, 'if you ask for an interpreter, they bring you a Jew; if you come to an inn, the landlord is a Jew; if you want post-horses, a Jew procures them, and a Jew drives them; if you wish to purchase, a Jew is your agent.'[10]

The law of the land allowed them freedom of worship but imposed poll tax and residential restrictions. Some towns were permanently out of bounds to Jews, others temporarily lifted restrictions during fairs. Many Jews settled in the villages and became cart-drivers, milkmen and farm hands. 'This is perhaps the only country in Europe where Jews cultivate the ground', Coxe observed, 'and we frequently saw them engaged in sowing, reaping, mowing, and other works of husbandry.'[10]

Among themselves they spoke a brand of medieval German mingled with a few words of prayer-book Hebrew, which became known as the Jewish language, or Yiddish. Socially they were at the bottom of the ladder, despised by both peasants and squires, often taunted and molested. Jewish literature contains many an account of the drunken squire who would summon his local Jew and force him to sing and dance traditional Jewish songs until he dropped half dead at his feet. A favourite number on such occasions was *Ma Yafit*, a ritual song in classical Hebrew in praise of the Holy Sabbath, so called after the opening words which mean *How Beautiful Thou art*.

Whether Frederick heard his first *Ma Yafit* wafting through the open windows of a Jewish household on the Sabbath eve, or played by the village fiddler, M. Pichon did not disclose. He was still working on his own version when Pan Dziewanowski called in his Jewish farm-hand and asked him what he thought of his guest's improvisation. 'Moyshek [every Jew was a Moyshek] came up to the open window,' the *Szafarnia Courier* reported, 'poked his mighty conk into the room, listened and then announced that if M. Pichon felt like playing at Jewish weddings, he could make a mint of money. This encouraged M. Pichon to work harder at this kind of music and one day he may devote himself entirely to such profitable melodies.'[11]

As it happened M. Pichon did not forget his Szafarnia improvisation and ten years later, when already a celebrated composer living in Paris, he revised it and had it published as Mazurka No. 4 Op. 17. By that time he may have forgotten that from the first moment of inspiration he called the tune *Zydek*, the Little Jew, and suggested that he so named it to commemorate a young Jewish boy who had rendered him a service when he was a schoolboy.

Szafarnia gave Frederick his first close look at Jews; he saw them in the fields, on the road, in the village. They became a butt for his wit. 'A whole family was driving in a cart,' the *Szafarnia Courier* reported. 'It consisted of an old sow, three big Jews, two little ones and six very little ones, all squeezed together like Dutch herrings. Suddenly the cart overturned and all the Jews fell into the wayside in the following order. First the brats, in all sorts of postures, mostly with their little feet in the air. Then the sow choking under the weight of the Jews, big and small. In the fall everybody lost their skull-caps.'[12]

In his maturity Chopin sometimes delighted a roomful of friends, in Paris or at Nohant, with his impersonation of an old Polish Jew. His Szafarnia holiday afforded him an opportunity to give a staggering demonstration of his grasp of the Polish–Yiddish idiom. Pan Ramecki, a neighbour of the Dziewanowskis, had just sold a quantity of grain to the local Jewish dealer. Frederick concocted and delivered a letter, allegedly from the buyer, informing the squire that the deal was off. The wording was so characteristic of the Jewish–Polish jargon that it never occurred to anybody to doubt it. The enraged squire had the Jew brought before him and was about to thrash him for breach of contract when Frederick revealed that it was a hoax. Rameckis and Dziewanowskis had a good laugh, Frederick was admired for his clever prank and the story was reported to Warsaw and later retold for the amusement of friends.

In September Frederick returned home to start his second year at school. His mother surveyed him approvingly and agreed that he had put on weight, while his father cautiously hinted that the following summer might again be spent in the country. It had been a profitable year.

The Chopins were a close-knit family who liked taking their pleasures together. The sisters had formed a literary and dramatic club and every member was an enthusiastic contributor. Louisa and Isabel wrote short stories and sketches; young Emily made verse. Joining forces with one or the other, Frederick collaborated in plays written in Polish or French, put on shows, played charades. In a loving family of six, hardly a month went by without a celebration of someone's birthday or nameday. Frederick recited, designed, devised costumes from the purloined parental wardrobe and gave hilarious sessions of mimickry. His *pièce de résistance* in those days was an impersonation of a German protestant clergyman who every Sunday raped the Polish language from the pulpit in his atrocious Teutonic accent. The house was always in a turmoil of creativity in which boarders, schoolfriends, parents and parents' distinguished colleagues took a willing part.

Surrounded by love and admiration as he was, Frederick was perhaps particularly fortunate in his level-headed father. While allowing his son to develop his musical genius, Nicholas saw to it that the boy was not exploited by over-zealous admirers. From the age of thirteen to the age of fifteen 'Liszt's equal' gave no public performances, dividing his time between lessons with Elsner, working at the keyboard on his own, keeping up a creditable school record and trying out new artistic outlets. The year 1825 however brought that useful period of diffusion to an end and pointed the way towards Frederick's future as a professional musician.

In the spring of that year Tsar Alexander I, in his capacity of King of Poland, came to Warsaw to open the session of the Diet. A year earlier a ring of anti-Russian conspirators had been uncovered and its leaders condemned to long prison sentences. The Tsar's visit was intended to encourage the

Polish moderates who had come to terms with the Russian occupation and demonstrate, by a show of good will, the unreasonableness of attempting to overthrow it. For a few weeks the capital wore a festive air. The main squares and public buildings were decorated with imperial and national flags, Duke Constantine held military parades in honour of his brother the Tsar, the theatres put on gala performances and the various musical societies announced ambitious programmes. One was to launch a new keyboard instrument, a hybrid between the pianoforte and the organ, which during its brief life span was known as the aeolomelodicon.

It had been invented by Jacob Frederick Hoffman, an elderly botanist of German origin, who was given to inventions in fields as far apart as music and swimming. The aeolomelodicon was built to his specifications by a reputed instrument-maker and temporarily housed in the Warsaw Protestant church, to which both inventor and maker belonged. There were not many musicians who had had a chance to try their hand at the new instrument and young Frederick, who had recently learnt to play the organ, was one of the first to master the technique.

The guest of honour at the church recital was the Tsar who could hardly decline an invitation to attend a demonstration of a new keyboard instrument invented in Poland and improvised on by a young Polish genius. Whether His Imperial Majesty enjoyed the experience remained a state secret; but the two Poles involved, the musician and the instrument maker, though not the German-born inventor, were each presented with a diamond ring.

That same season Frederick took part in two charity concerts held at the main auditorium of the conservatoire. As usual the programme was a mixed bag. The first concert, held on 27 May, included instrumental and vocal items by Beethoven, Rossini and Elsner. Frederick played the Allegro from the Piano Concerto by Moscheles, a Rondo Brillant by Hummel and finally his own fantasy for the aeolopantaleon, an improved version of the aeolomelodicon. The second concert, on 10 June, had the pianist Kresner and the Italian singer Antonia Bianchi as guest stars, and the programme included works by Kalkbrenner, Spohr and Cramer. Again Frederick improvised on the aeolopantaleon. There were one hundred and seventy people present which, to judge from the tone of the press report a few day later, was a creditable number.

A third concert followed, at a private house, where again Frederick improvised on the aeolomelodicon. By that time he had become the Sunday organist at the Church of the Visitation where the Lyceum boys sang mass. His zeal was more musical than religious and his precocity sometimes led to friction. Once he was so carried away that in the middle of Mass he forgot that he was only meant to accompany and went on improvising. Priest and congregation were bemused and helpless and the choir boys, friends from school, broke rank and crowded round the organ. Only a sharp whisper from the sacristan woke Frederick from his trance and recalled him to holy duty. Worse was to come. One morning when the regular organist was accompanying, Frederick was so intolerant of the hackneyed playing that he pushed the man away and took over. The music improved but relations were strained for a while.

He could not stop improvising. Late at night, when family and servants were asleep, he would lie awake and improvise in his mind, then leap out of bed and rush to the drawing-room to try out his ideas on the piano. In June 1825 he became a published composer. That month the *Warsaw Courier* carried the following advertisement: 'A new rondo for the pianoforte [in C minor Op. 1], composed by Freder. Chopin and dedicated to Mme Linde, published by A. Brzezina. Price: 3 zloty'.[13] Mme Linde, the Headmaster's wife, was a competent musician with whom Frederick sometimes played duets. The reception of his Op. 1 was mixed; musical friends were quick to point out traces of Weber and Hummel. It made little difference. The commercial publication of a Chopin composition by one of Warsaw's leading publishers meant recognition.

There was no question however of the young composer neglecting his schoolwork. 'The end-of-term exams begin on 26 July', Frederick wrote to Jan Bialoblocki, a former boarder who had fractured a leg and was convalescing at his parents' country house. 'Tomorrow I shall have to get up very early and tonight I shall work and work, work and work again, perhaps all night long.'[14] Three weeks later, with the end in sight, he wrote again, gaily alternating between Polish and French in Polish spelling: 'Tomorrow is the last day of our exams. . . . Tomorrow, at this very time, I shall go to bed and not get up before Friday. *Kel boner! Kieplezy!' [Quel bonheur! Quel plaisir!]*[15]

He was in high spirits, looking forward to another holiday in Szafarnia. In his gushing schoolboy style he told Bialoblocki of his holiday preparations, continuing to alternate between Polish and Polish-written French. 'I have a new pair of breeches' he babbled on in this *mélange*. 'Well made too (actually they are not). I also have a new foulard round my neck (a cravat to you), which has cost God knows how many zloty. Honestly I can't remember how much I paid for it out of dear Louisa's purse.'[15]

The stay in Szafarnia introduced him this time to the pleasures of a country gentleman. He joined a hunting party and returned to the manor house with a hare and four young partridges. His riding improved and he was more of a match for Dominic and his dauntless sisters. An ambitious sight-seeing tour took him as far as Gdansk and gave him his first glimpse of the Baltic Sea. It was the first time he visited parts of historical Poland which had been torn away from her by successive international treaties.

He was impressed with the medieval architecture of Torun, the Prussian-held city half-way between Warsaw and the port of Gdansk. He looked at the city fortifications with their renowned leaning tower and trudged round Gothic churches. He marvelled at the ancient town hall which had, he wrote, 'as many windows as the year has days, as many halls as the year has months, as many rooms as the year has weeks'.[16] He inspected an ingenious mechanical construction used for shifting soil and which he knew only by its original German name *Sandmaschine*. He was excited by his visit to Copernicus' birthplace but distressed to see the house occupied by a German family which was totally insensitive to its historic aura. 'In the corner of the room where the future astronomer was born,' he wrote to his schoolfriend Jan Matuszynski, 'there is a bed belonging to some sort of German who, when he has had too many potatoes to eat, no doubt breaks wind there.'[16] But above all, he assured Jan with deadpan earnestness, he was impressed with the local gingerbread which was moulded into shapes of human figures, animals, coats of arms, even a coach-and-horses. The powerful guild of Torun bakers, of which the

gingerbread makers formed a part, would have been gratified
to hear what an acclaimed musician who had the ear of the Tsar
had to say about their ware:

> The gingerbread shops are really long dark alcoves where
> they store dozens of boxes, all well locked. Inside they keep
> their gingerbread, arranged according to size and quality. . . .
> I could tell you more about Torun, but I must say that those
> gingerbread cakes have left the strongest impression on my
> senses. . . . Nothing I have seen surpasses the gingerbread
> cakes. Oh those gingerbread cakes! I have sent some home
> to Warsaw.[16]

In spite of the heavy travelling, Frederick was in rude health,
or so he assured his parents. He also made his first conquest
of the fair sex, in the person of Kamilka, the one-and-a-half-
year-old daughter of his host, who kept clinging to his breeches
and mumbling: 'Kagila love you'.[16] He had written a waltz in
rough and was absorbing the country sounds. 'The air is fresh,'
he wrote to his family, 'the sun is shining gloriously, the birds
are twittering; there is no stream, or it would be babbling, but
there is a pond and the frogs sing beautifully. Most delightful
of all is the blackbird outside my window who tells me all his
adventures.'[17]

In September he was back at home, eager to share his experiences with sisters and parents, play the neglected Hummels,
Rieses and Kalkbrenners piled in disorder over the piano, and
above all recreate the sounds he heard in his mind and heart.
The sojourns in the country had revealed to him the haunting
beauty of folk melodies and forged a feeling of belonging
which neither time nor voluntary exile were ever to efface.

4

Branching out

In the autumn of 1825 the Polish National Opera put on a performance of *The Barber of Seville*. The thirty-three-year-old Rossini was then at the height of his fame and *The Barber of Seville*, first performed in Rome only nine years earlier, was acknowledged all over Europe. 'I liked it very much,'[1] Frederick wrote to Jan Bialoblocki whose fractured leg was keeping him housebound in the country. He was so impressed with his first hearing of the opera that he composed a polonaise based on one of its themes, and had it modestly printed. He was less impressed with the cast and remarked that although they had generally acquitted themselves well, the two leading ladies were uninspired. The fat one kept sneezing, the skinny one kept yawning.

He had no such reservations about the young pianist Alexander Rembielinski who had just given his first Warsaw recital after a six-year stay in Paris. 'He plays the piano better than anyone I have ever heard,' Frederick wrote with excitement. 'You can imagine our joy! We have never heard anything so perfect! He does not call himself a professional but an amateur. I won't go into detail about the agility, the elegance and the ease of his playing. I shall only tell you that his left hand is just as flexible as his right, which is unusual in the same person.'[2]

The bedridden Bialoblocki was a suitable recipient of such comments, for he himself was a pianist. Frederick tried to keep him amused with a detailed account of his social and musical activities. One day he wrote to him from Zelazowa Wola, where he and his eighteen-year-old sister Louisa were spending Christmas with the Skarbeks. It had not been easy to persuade Justina to let the children go away without her, but in the end they won and were fetched in style in a *bryczka*. Frederick and his sister were as close as ever. 'Louisa has composed a Mazur the like of which Warsaw has not heard for a long time,' he informed Bialoblocki one day. 'It is her *non* [*sic*] *plus ultra* as well as the *nonplusultrow* [*sic*] of its kind. It is bouncing, pretty and just right for dancing. Without exaggeration, it is excellent.'[3] His admiration was genuine. He felt that his own Mazurkas, the stylized form of the Mazur, were not for dancing but for playing.

Social and musical activities were inseparable. He became friendly with the pianist Rembielinski whose playing he had so much admired and took to playing some of his compositions. He played works by other contemporary Polish composers, more concertos by Hummel, Ries and Kalkbrenner, melodies by Rossini adapted for the piano, pieces by Field, anything he could lay his hands on. Hardly a day passed by without his dropping in at Brzezina's to see if they had anything new. At home he was given a large cupboard to store the stacks of sheet music he had accumulated.

He was eagerly awaiting the opening night of *Der Freischütz*, which the National Opera had been rehearsing for several months. 'For our opera company to put on Weber's famous work is an achievement in itself,'[4] he wrote in June 1826. Indeed it was a daring undertaking. *Der Freischütz* had had its first performance, in Berlin, only five years earlier. Its romantic music and German folk tale bowled the Berliners over and in the following years it was triumphantly produced in Dresden, Vienna and London. Warsaw however was not so musically sophisticated as Berlin or Vienna, nor was its National Opera so well endowed as the Prussian and Austrian opera houses. Frederick was fully aware of the risk the management was taking in putting such an unusual work before a public reared on Italian opera. To Bialoblocki he wrote:

When I think of Weber's aim in *Der Freischütz*, of the plot which is so German, of the work's strange romanticism, its unusual and abstruse harmonies which are particularly suited to the German taste, I fear that the Warsaw public, used as they are to Rossini's light songs, will praise him at first not from conviction but simply to be able to repeat what the experts say about him and because everybody has been praising him.[5]

When Frederick was thus writing, the news had not yet reached Warsaw of Weber's untimely death in London on 5 June. In the event, the first Polish production of *Der Freischütz*, on 3 July, turned out to be not only a gala performance but also a symbolic memorial service. Frederick was deeply impressed. Two years later, however, when the work had gone into repertoire, it was no longer possible to ignore the imperfections of the production. 'An extremely poor performance last night,' he commented in September 1828. 'The choir kept missing their cues and coming in a quarter of a beat behind each other.'[6] He hoped he would one day be able to hear it somewhere else.

Between going to concerts and playing at home until all hours, coping with schoolwork and taking lessons with Elsner, Frederick attended musical evenings in the drawing-rooms of the Warsaw aristocracy and improvised on the aeolopantaleon and the piano. The strain was beginning to tell. In the winter of 1826 he had to take to his bed with an unremitting headache and swollen glands. A German-born doctor diagnosed catarrh; he made the patient wear a tight-fitting nightcap to shrink the blood vessels in the head and applied leeches to the throat to relieve the swollen glands. Emily too was ill that winter, coughing, spluttering and spitting blood. The spring, if not the leeches, brought a temporary halt to sickness. Frederick resumed his strolls in the untended grounds of the school and was dismayed when a gang of workmen turned up one fine morning to landscape them '*à la manière anglaise*'.[7] There were no more carrots in the gardens, no more cauliflowers, no more dark tunnels and no more clandestine rendezvous with classmates' sisters.

It was his final year at school. As soon as the matriculation examinations were over, Justina took Emily and Frederick, together with the indispensable Louisa, to a rest-cure at Reinertz Spa (Duszniki) in Prussian-held Silesia. The four of them put up at a recommended family hotel called Bürgels Hof and applied themselves in earnest to the business of taking the water.

Frederick found the stolid pace irredeemably boring. He took the water, drank whey and with the uncorrupted eye of youth, observed the vanities and pretensions of his fellow-patients. To William Kolberg, another of his close schoolfriends, he described his daily routine:

> In the morning, at 6 at the very latest, all the patients assemble at the pumproom. A wind-band made up of carica-ture musicians of all sorts, conducted by a bassoon-player, whose hooked snuff-stained nose frightens ladies who are afraid of horses, plays to the visitors as they stroll about. It is like a fashion parade, or a masked ball; it's true they don't actually wear masks, but some of them would do any-thing, even hang themselves, if that happened to be the fashion. This parade takes place in the lovely avenue between the town and the pumproom. It goes on until about eight, according to the number of glassfuls each parader has to take. Then everybody goes in for breakfast. After breakfast I generally go out for a walk until twelve, when we eat our midday meal so as to be able to go back to the pumproom. In the afternoon there is another fashion parade, even grander than the morning one, for everybody has had time to change and dress up. The music blares out again and we stroll about until the evening. Since I take only two glassfuls of water in the afternoon, I have an early supper and then go straight to bed.[8]

As his strength returned he managed to go out for more adventurous walks, climbed some hills and arrived puffed out and panting at a hut where a local hermit was living. The view over the valleys below was rewarding. Back at the Bürgels Hof he sketched a lovely castle overlooking a lake, signed it and dated it in the right-hand corner with the barely visible words: 'In the second week of boredom'.[9]

He made friends with some Polish and German youngsters and paid special attention to an attractive Czech girl who was a waitress at the pumproom. One day he heard that her father had been killed in a factory accident and left her and her brothers and sisters destitute. Immediately the sixteen-and-a-half-year-old Galahad came to the rescue and organized a charity concert in aid of the orphans. According to another version it was not a Czech waitress but a pretty Polish nursemaid who roused his gallantry when her mistress suddenly collapsed in the midst of the cure and left her with two young orphans on her hands. Whatever the good cause, Frederick took part in a charity concert held at the spa auditorium. In fact he played not once but twice, since the first concert was so overbooked that it was necessary to hold a repeat performance.

From the point of view of historical accuracy, these two performances were the first that Chopin gave outside Poland, and the *Warsaw Courier*, the old faithful, duly reported them. Frederick however remembered the occasion mostly for the poor piano he had to play on. 'Would you believe it, sir,' he wrote in French to his music teacher Joseph Elsner. 'This place has not got a single decent piano. All I have seen are pianos which give me more pain than pleasure. Fortunately this martyrdom will not last much longer; we are due to leave Reinertz very shortly and should set off on the 11th of next month.'[10]

September 1826 saw him back in Warsaw, looking noticeably plumper and stronger. A Polish doctor was called in to keep an eye on him and prescribed a diet of oatmeal and laxatives. '*Quasi* a horse,'[11] Frederick snorted. There was some talk of his going back to school for another term so that he could re-sit his examinations and obtain higher grades, but he would have none of it. He argued that he would be bored to death if he had to listen to the same lectures all over again, and further pointed out that poring over textbooks six hours a day would not be good for his health. Ideally he would have liked to go to Paris, as the young pianist Rembielinski had done and as some of his friends were doing. But at seventeen—the age when his father had arrived from Lorraine to try his luck in an unknown country—Frederick was not the independent lad that Nicholas had been. He allowed his parents to make decisions for him as a matter of course and was not rebellious when his movements were sometimes restricted. When he was forbidden to go to a New Year's ball with his schoolfriends, he simply hoped he would be allowed to do so when he was eighteen, escorted by the tutor at his father's boarding house.

Nicholas however was too sensible to insist on his son re-sitting his exams. Without further ado Frederick enrolled at the conservatoire for a three-year course in composition under Joseph Elsner with whom he had been having private lessons since the age of twelve. The conservatoire, established only five years earlier as a college for music and drama, had an ambitious syllabus. There were courses in harmony and counterpoint; classes for strings, keyboard instruments, wind, percussion, singing and deportment; obligatory lectures in Polish literature, lessons in French and Italian. Most of the staff were German, Czech and Hungarian but, like Elsner, they had made Poland their home and contributed to the development of native Polish music.

Frederick's course consisted of six periods a week 'in the theory of music, figured bass and composition from the grammatical, rhetoric and aesthetic aspects',[12] with the occasional Italian lesson thrown in. As before, his pianistic development was left mainly in his own hands, while the craft of composition was learnt from Elsner, an all-round musician who believed in an all-round musical education. 'Playing one single instrument, even if one attains the perfection of a Paganini for the violin or a Kalkbrenner for the piano, should not be an end in itself,' he maintained. 'In musical terms it should only serve as a means for the expression of feeling. . . . Furthermore, no student should be made to dwell too long on one particular method or one particular point of view, nor on one particular style or one particular school. . . . An artist should take advantage of whatever surrounding he happens to live in, remembering at the same time that it is only within his own self and through his own search for self-improvement that he will win the admiration of his contemporaries.'[13]

His most controversial maxim was to tolerate in a student a measure of disregard for conventional rules, so as not to extinguish the creative spark of a tender talent. 'Teaching the art of composition does not consist of dictating rules, particularly when a student has an obvious talent,' he declared. 'It is up to the student to discover them for himself so that he is equipped to surpass himself one day.'[13] Indeed some of his own compositions had been criticized for straying from the straight and narrow path of musical conformity. In Chopin's case he practised his maxim to such an extent that colleagues who heard some of the young student's exercises shuddered with professional indignation. They blamed the master for the technical and theoretical infelicities of the pupil. 'Leave him alone,' was Elsner's much-quoted reply. 'If he chooses to follow an uncommon path, it is because his talent is uncommon. If he does not follow the traditional method it is because he has one of his own, and one day his work will reveal an originality the like of which has never been seen anywhere before.'[14]

In his maturity Chopin would spend long agonizing hours correcting and reshaping compositions which had been easily and painlessly born in a moment of inspiration. 'Not even a genius can write music without being master of all the tributary rules and formulae,'[15] his critics sometimes said, pointing an accusing finger at Elsner for not having been firm enough with his pupil. Whether it was Elsner's indulgence or the young man's own disinclination to explore the labyrinth of the craft which turned Frederick into a less than perfect craftsman, is debatable. Chopin himself retained the highest regard for Elsner's method and when a distinguished Viennese journalist once expressed astonishment that a high degree of musicianship like his could have been acquired in a backwater like Warsaw, he icily replied: 'From such masters as Zywny and Elsner even a perfect ass can learn something'.[16]

At the beginning of 1827 young Emily Chopin was taken seriously ill. The rest-cure at Reinertz which had restored Frederick's health had done little to improve his sister's. She sank fast. Doctors came and went, mother and elder sisters kept a vigil, the household lived in an agony of fear and futile ministrations. In March Frederick wrote to Bialoblocki in the country:

> We have illness in the house. Emily has been in bed these last four weeks. She started to cough and spat blood and Mamma was frightened. Dr Malcz ordered bloodletting. They bled her once, twice, they applied countless leeches, vesicators, mustard baths, herbs. What a to do, what a to do! All that time she has had nothing to eat, she has grown so thin you would hardly know her, now she is beginning to look a little more like herself. Imagine it for yourself if you can, for I cannot describe what has been going on here.[17]

Emily died on 10 April 1827, aged just over fourteen. The

death certificate gave the cause of death as consumption.
Shortly afterwards news reached Warsaw that young Bialoblocki had also died of consumption. The effect of the two
deaths, identical in cause and so close in time, was shattering.

It was a welcome distraction when the Department of Public
Works served notice on the Chopins to vacate their quarters
in the Lyceum building to make way for the extension of the
Warsaw university. There began a search for alternative
accommodation, the hustle and bustle of packing and unpacking,
the excitement of settling into new premises. As it happened
the family only moved across the road, to an apartment in the
converted Krasinski Palace facing the Lyceum. After the
ravages of the Second World War the palace was rebuilt to
house the Academy of Arts, with one room reconstructed and
furnished as the Chopins' drawing-room used to be.

The household remained as gregarious as ever, with boarders
coming and going, tutors dividing their attention between
boarders and the young ladies of the house, friends calling at
all times. The family drawing-room, in spite of its excellent
piano, was no longer a suitable working-place for a serious
musician. In due course a box-room on the top floor was converted into a study and a second-hand piano and desk were
moved in. Frederick acquired privacy and a splendid view over
the Vistula and the meadows beyond.

He was constantly trying out new musical patterns. His
1827 compositions included an Ecossaise, since lost; a Mazurka
(in A minor Op. 68, No. 2); a Waltz (in A flat major); his
first Nocturne (in E minor, Op. 72, No. 1), a form of music
until then mainly associated with the Irish composer John
Field; a Funeral March (in C minor, Op. 72, No. 2). That year
also saw his first foray into the realm of orchestration. The
Warsaw Opera had just put on Mozart's *Don Giovanni* and
Frederick conceived the idea of using one of its themes for
Variations for piano and orchestra. He chose one from the duet
sung by Don Giovanni and Zerlina in the first act (No. 7), and
the work came to be known as *La ci darem la mano* variations, listed
as Variations in B flat major Op. 2 for Pianoforte and Orchestra.
The orchestration presented a challenge, and when the academic
year came to an end, Frederick packed the unfinished score
into a suitcase and left for his annual holiday in the country.

He spent it at the house of his godmother née Anna Skarbek, who was living with her husband in the province of Poznan. Again there were trips and drives in the country, and again he absorbed the sounds and melodies of the native peasants. He stood up well to the hardships of travel by stage-coach and carriage, and paid a second visit to Gdansk. As usual he was handed from one host to another with the utmost solicitude and at Gdansk found himself staying with Herr Linde, the German-speaking brother of his former headmaster.

His godmother and her husband introduced him to Prince Radziwill, the Polish governor of Prussian-held Poznan, who was staying at his nearby summer residence. This was high society indeed, for the prince, a scion of one of the most distinguished families in Poland, was also related by marriage to the royal house of Prussia. He had expressed a wish to meet young Chopin because he himself was a musician who played the cello and composed. Each year the Berlin Academy of Singing performed a new work by him. His wife and two daughters were equally musical and the first meeting soon ripened into friendship.

Between trips and social visits Frederick continued to work on his Variations. On his return to Warsaw he showed the draft to Elsner, who praised it, and to his friend Jan Matuszynski, who kept it. Weeks later, when he wanted to make a fair copy of the piano part, he had to send an urgent note to Matuszynski asking him if he might borrow the manuscript for a day or two. The finished work confirmed Elsner in his view that young Szopen, as he invariably spelt his pupil's name, had an uncommon talent transcending age and experience. He was equally pleased with a Sonata (in C minor Op. 4) which Frederick dedicated to him at the beginning of 1828. He sent both to Vienna, to be considered for publication by his friend the music publisher Tobias Haslinger.

The network of friends was expanding. One day Frederick received a letter from a Polish pianist in Paris associated with the *Revue musicale*, asking him to contribute a series of articles on Polish music and musicians. The writer of the letter had heard of Chopin from Joseph Jedrzejewicz, a visiting compatriot, who was an habitué of the Chopin household in Warsaw and an aspirant to Louisa's hand. Frederick had no hesitation in turning the offer down. 'I have no intention of getting mixed up in that sort of thing,' he wrote to his friend Titus Woyciechowski. 'I am not yet possessed of a judgment worthy of Parisian journals where only truth should prevail.'[18] But his reasons for refusing the flattering offer were not entirely due to modesty and naïveté. He did not want to antagonize Karol Kurpinski, an eminent composer and director of the Warsaw opera who wrote regularly for foreign music journals, nor did he want to offend any of the local musicians with a less than enthusiastic appraisal. 'If I accepted I would have a lot of people after my blood,'[18] he told Titus. The plain fact of the matter was that he wanted to write music, not to write about music.

What he wanted above all at this stage was to go abroad, throw himself into the mainstream of European music, listen, learn, absorb and expand. Paris, Berlin, Vienna, it was all the same to him. There was no question of allowing him to travel on his own, but his father had promised to take him to Vienna during the summer holidays of 1828. Preparations were actually being made when a venerable matron of the Chopins' acquaintance asked if she might join the party. Unfortunately she kept putting off the date of departure and by the time she decided she would not be going away after all, Nicholas too had had second thoughts about venturing out of Poland. Frederick was despondent. He spent most of the summer in the country house of friends at Sanniki, some fifty miles south-west of Warsaw, and amused himself as best he could. He revised a Rondo for two pianos (in C major Op. 73) which he had started during the winter, and took long walks in the garden with the resident young governess who had a free heart and a vacant bed. He was not attracted to either. In September he returned to Warsaw resigned never to see the exciting musical world outside.

Then the miracle happened. Dr Felix Jarocki, a professor of zoology at Warsaw university and a friend of the Chopins, had accepted an invitation to attend an international congress of scientists in Berlin. As he was showing Nicholas the invitation-card printed on vellum and admiring the efficiency of the German organizers who had reserved two hundred hotel bedrooms and arranged to serve the participants with communal dinners, it suddenly occurred to him that Frederick could come with him. The rest followed with head-spinning speed. Seats were booked on the stage-coach to Berlin, a new leather suitcase was bought and packed, parental advice was solemnly given and taken. On the eve of departure, 9 September 1828, Frederick dashed off a long excited letter to Titus. 'I think I am going mad,' he wrote feverishly while his luggage was being sent ahead to the coach-station. 'I do not know whether I am coming or going. Today I am leaving for Berlin.'[19]

Enter Chopin

'Berlin is too sparse. Twice as many people could fit into it just as comfortably,'[1] Frederick wrote home on 16 September 1828, after two days' strenuous sightseeing. But he was impressed with the tidiness of the city and admired the attention to detail which had gone into its planning.

Five days' travelling in an unsprung Prussian stage-coach had left no mark on him. As soon as they put up at their allotted hotel, Professor Jarocki took his charge on a round of calls and introduced him to the congress organiser who, apart from being a professor of zoology and keeper of the zoological gardens, was a member of the Academy of Singing and father of a talented daughter who had just given a performance of a concerto for piano and orchestra. Not all participants in the congress were musically inclined. At dinner Frederick found himself seated next to a biologist from Hamburg who ill-concealed his annoyance at being forced to talk to a youngster who had no business at a meeting of scientists. Fascinated, Frederick watched him dissect beef steak, pull out the entrails of hard rolls, mop up gravy. Back in his hotel he drew one cartoon after another of famous scientists at work.

But he had come to Berlin to hear music, not to poke fun. After his first experience of a communal dinner he obtained Professor Jarocki's permission to dine early on his own so as not to miss whatever concert was on in the evening. He considered himself fortunate in having so much music to choose from. 'Every day there is something different on, as if specially laid on to suit me,'[2] he told his parents. He could not have enough. He saw Spontini's *Ferdinand Cortez*, Cimarosa's *The Secret Marriage*, *Le Colporteur* by George Onslow, Winter's

Das unterbrochene Opferfest and, at long last, a German production of Weber's well-remembered opera. 'Tomorrow *Der
Freischütz*,' he wrote to his parents on 20 September. 'Just
what I wanted. Now I shall be able to make comparisons
with our singers back home.'[2] He heard also Handel's *Ode
for St Cecilia's Day* and assured his family that it came nearest
to his ideal of great music. About individual performances
he was more reserved; even the most celebrated singers of
the Berlin opera, like the contralto Tibaldi or the seventeen-
year-old Pauline Schätzel, seemed to him less than perfect.
'There is always a *but*,' he mused, then added without suspecting the chilling effect on his father: 'Paris is probably the only
place where there won't be any buts.'[2]

Mindful of his father's exhortation to make the most of
his visit to Berlin, Frederick attended a session of the congress
and flitted through the thirteen halls of the zoological exhibi-
tion mounted for the occasion. He spent a much more profitable
morning browsing at one of Berlin's leading music stores. He
also visited two well-known piano workshops in order to try
out a German piano, but found none in a state of completion.
To his delight the hotel piano proved of high quality. One
morning he was taken to the Berlin University Library and
was thrilled and proud when he came across an original letter
in the hand of Kosciuszko.

The evenings were all music, the glitter of the audience
outshining the glitter of the stage. At the Academy of Singing,
just before curtain rise, Frederick noticed a man splendidly
arrayed in what looked like a royal livery. Carefully choosing
his German words, he asked his neighbour whether the liveried
gentleman was by any chance King Frederick William's
personal valet. It was Professor Alexander von Humboldt,
the eminent naturalist, explorer, geographer and chairman of
the congress. Frederick looked at the women in their opulent
outfits and dazzling jewellery. Not one could hold a candle to
the beautiful Warsaw ladies with their peach complexions and
lovely hair. What had possessed his fellow-student Marylski
to praise Prussian womanhood? 'Tell Marylski he does not
know what he is talking about if he thinks Berlin women are
beautiful,' he wrote to his mother and sisters. 'They have
sagging cheeks and toothless mouths. They dress well enough,

but what a waste of lovely muslins, they look like painted puppets.'[3]

Promises to introduce him to the leading musicians of the day had come to nothing and for the first time in his life he found himself attending musical events from the fringe. Any other young man on a first visit to Berlin might well have spurred himself to present himself to the celebrities of his choice without waiting for a formal introduction, but Frederick's inherent lack of push made it impossible for him to do so. He had had high hopes of meeting the fifty-four-year-old Italian composer Gasparo Spontini whose operas were the delight of Berlin; now he only eyed him from a distant corner of the foyer. The seventy-year-old composer and conductor Karl Zelter was another celebrity Frederick had hoped to meet; now he watched the venerable musician talk to his former pupil Felix Mendelssohn and shrank further into his corner. Even Mendelssohn daunted him because at nineteen, only a year older than himself, he was already the acclaimed composer of several operas, a symphony and the overture to *A Midsummer Night's Dream*. 'I did not have the courage to introduce myself,'[4] he confessed to his family. Then as in later life, he needed a protective hand to take charge of him and remove obstacles from his way, real or imaginary.

Two weeks in Berlin passed like a flash. The first lap of the return journey by stage-coach was shared with two unsociable Germans who kept smoking foul tobacco. At the post station of Sulechow, just beyond Frankfurt-an-der-Oder, no fresh horses were readily available and the passengers resigned themselves to a long wait. Frederick walked into the station inn, sat himself at the piano and started improvising. Innkeeper, innkeeper's wife, daughters, fellow travellers and one or two locals were all entranced. When the postilion finally came in to announce that fresh horses had been procured, he was told to shut up and listen. The small circle was bewitched, sensing in the young man's improvisations a breath of Poland's genius. Two hours later, utterly exhausted, Frederick was carried into the coach, loaded with cakes, sweets, wine and the blessings of simple folk who for a charmed moment had felt transported into another world. In years to come Chopin would say that the homage paid to him by those chance listeners had moved him more than many a later triumph in the most sophisticated drawing-rooms of Europe.

The five-day endurance test on the stage-coach was eased by a stop in Poznan where musician and zoologist had been invited to dine with a bishop who was related to Pan Wiesiolowski, who was married to the former Countess Anna Skarbek, who was Frederick's godmother. There was also another call on Prince Radziwill with more piano and cello playing. On 6 October Frederick was back home, bursting to tell his family and friends of all the exciting experiences he had not had time to describe in his letters.

He now entered on his third and final year at the conservatoire. Emotionally he was an adolescent who had much to learn, but musically there was little his master could teach him. He was trying his hand at various forms of music. He started a Trio in G minor (Op. 8) for Piano, Violin and Cello, dedicating it on completion to Prince Radziwill. He composed a Grand Fantasy on Polish Airs for Piano and Orchestra in A major (Op. 13), which may well have had its moment of inception at the old piano at Sulechow coach station. Before the year was out he had also composed a Concert Rondo for piano and orchestra (Krakowiak, in F major Op. 14). The following year there were songs, more mazurkas, waltzes, polonaises. In the early summer of 1829 Paganini arrived in Warsaw and gave ten recitals in two months. None of Frederick's letters of those months are extant, but his Variations in A major, which he sub-titled *Souvenir de Paganini*, suggest that the recitals made an impact. They may well have indicated on whose side he was during that extraordinary competition between Paganini and the Polish violinist Lipinski who claimed to be the Italian's superior and left Warsaw in a huff having played to half-empty houses during his rival's season.

In the midst of the growing unrest against the Russian regime, Warsaw continued to pursue its cultural activities. Frederick saw operas and plays, took part in amateur theatricals in Polish and French, read the *Warsaw Courier* and talked to fellow students about the cause of Polish liberation. He was hoping to go abroad again.

His visit to Berlin had convinced him, and more pertinently his father, that his musical career required a prolonged stay in the main European centres of music. Nicholas began to think in terms of a three-year study tour and, encouraged by the example of the young composer Nidecki who a few years earlier had won a government grant for the same purpose, applied to the Minister of Cults and Education for help. On 13 April 1829 he sent the following letter:

Your Excellency,

Having exerted myself for twenty years in the teaching profession at the Warsaw Lyceum and convinced that I have acquitted myself of my duties to the best of my abilities, I take the liberty of submitting my humble petition for a government grant, which would be my highest reward.

I have a son whose inherent talent destines him to the study of music. His Imperial Majesty the late Tsar Alexander, King of Poland, had condescended to present him with a precious ring in token of his pleasure when my son had the honour of playing before the sovereign. His Imperial Highness the Grand Duke, Commander-in-Chief, has kindly allowed my son to give in his presence many a proof of his progress. Illustrious persons and musical connoisseurs would confirm that my son could be useful to the country in his chosen profession if he were given an opportunity to carry on with the necessary studies. He has already completed all such studies as are available here, as will be confirmed by M. Elsner, Principal of the College of Music and Professor at the University. All my son needs at this stage is to visit foreign countries, mainly Germany, Italy and France, in order to model himself on good examples.

To carry out such a tour of study, which may last up to three years, funds are required which my modest salary as a teacher cannot provide. I therefore address my most humble request to Your Excellency, begging you to secure for my son's studies such help as is available to the Administration from official funds.

I am Your Excellency's most humble and obedient servant,
Nicholas Chopin
Teacher at the Warsaw Lyceum[5]

The minister passed on the application with a recommenda-

Justina Chopin
(1782–1869),
Frederick's mother,
by A. Miroszewski,
1829

Nicholas Chopin
(1771–1844),
Frederick's father,
by A. Miroszewski,
1829

Cracow Precinct, Warsaw. Aquatint by F. Dietrich, 1817

tion for a two-year grant of five thousand zloty a year; but
the Commission for Internal Affairs and Police, under whose
jurisdiction the petition came, turned it down. The application
was returned to the minister with a covering note to the effect
that Pan Choppin's [*sic*] son was not eligible for a grant and
that no public funds were to be wasted on artists of his kind.
The word 'wasted' had been thinly crossed out and 'assigned'
substituted.[6]

While this exchange was taking place, Frederick went about
his studies as before. In July 1829 he was pronounced a graduate. In the conservatoire log-book, where names of students
were entered with an assessment of their achievement and
potential, Professor Elsner recorded with his usual brevity:
'Third year, No. 9: Szopen Friderick [*sic*], outstanding ability,
a musical genius etc.'[7]

The graduation ceremony was hardly over when Frederick
was already having his bags packed for another foray abroad.
Since the idea of a long study tour had had to be abandoned,
a short visit to Vienna was projected instead. Nicholas
provided the funds, Professor Elsner the indispensable letters
of recommendation, mother and sisters the equally indispensable
velvet jackets, pressed trousers, silk foulards, kid gloves and
travelling rugs. As on the previous occasion, Frederick was
trusted to the care of a family friend, one Professor Hube, a
lecturer in law, who was going to Italy via Vienna. There were
seven other fellow-students in Hube's party, all ready to set
out the moment the last exam was over. The academic year of
1829 ended on 20 July. On 31 July, having already spent a
few days sightseeing in Cracow, the professor and his eight
young men descended on Vienna.

'Vienna overwhelmed me,' Frederick told his friend Titus
Woyciechowski after his hectic fortnight in that international
centre of music was over. 'It intoxicated me, got hold of me
to such an extent that I was not homesick once, although I
have had no letters from the family all that fortnight.'[8] To his
parents he candidly admitted why he felt so much at home in
the Austrian metropolis. 'There are so many Poles about,'[9]
he wrote.

Armed with his letters of recommendation, he lost no time

3

in calling on Tobias Haslinger, the well-connected music publisher to whom Elsner had sent the manuscript of *La ci darem* Variations more than a year earlier. Haslinger could hardly believe his own good luck. The Variations were scheduled to be published in his elegant *Odéon* series, and there was the young Polish composer on his doorstep, just in time to give the work a boost by a personal appearance. He immediately suggested a concert to introduce the new composition, with the composer at the piano. 'Out of the question,'[10] Frederick said with a sinking heart.

Not to seem ungracious, he hastened to explain that he had not touched a piano since his departure from Warsaw some two weeks earlier. It was only an excuse. The truth of the matter was that he had a phobia of large audiences, which age and experience were to increase rather than cure. Ideally he liked to play before a small gathering in an aristocratic music-room. Appearing in a larger but familiar setting, where most of the audience consisted of friends and acquaintances, was still tolerable; but exposing himself to a crowd of strangers in a vast theatre was a proposition which had only little to do with his self-estimation as a musician. His reaction to Haslinger's suggestion was the first clear manifestation of what was to become a recurrent pattern: the instinctive need to make music, the instant recoiling before the chance to do so in front of a large audience, the weakening resistance and the final capitulation.

For the next few days Frederick concentrated on going to concerts and meeting people. Elsner's letters and Haslinger's patronage opened all doors before him. There was no question of eyeing celebrities from a distant corner of the foyer; celebrities asked him to their homes and introduced him round as Chopin, the Polish pianist and composer. At nineteen he was a most presentable young man, slim, his brown hair worn short, his clothes elegant according to the dictates of fashion. His new acquaintances and hosts were captivated by his caressing Polish courtesy, eager to hear him play.

For his part he was exhilarated by his meetings with the musical eminences of the day. He met the violinist and conductor Schuppanzigh, a former friend of Beethoven's, whose embonpoint had earned him the nickname of Lord Falstaff. He was presented to the composer and piano teacher Czerny, whose manner he found more engaging than his piano studies, and the journalist Blahetka, whose daughter Leopoldine was a noted professional pianist. He exchanged civilities with the violinist Mayseder, the composer Seyfried, the theatre director Count Gallenberg. He talked technicalities with the piano makers Graff and Stein. He paid his respects to the composer Lachner who had known Schubert and the composer Kreutzer who had known Beethoven. He shook hands with Gyrowetz whose piano concerto he had played at his first public appearance at the age of eight, renewed his acquaintance with Wilhelm Würfel, the Czech pianist who had taught at the Warsaw conservatoire before moving to Vienna, fell into the arms of Thomas Nidecki, a graduate of the Warsaw conservatoire and the only musician in that venerable galaxy who was still under thirty.

As in Berlin the summer before, Frederick attended every possible performance. 'Some concerts were quite mediocre,'[10] he informed his family. He also saw four contemporary operas: Boieldieu's *La Dame blanche* which had been proclaimed a masterpiece, Rossini's *La Cenerentola*, Meyerbeer's *Il Crociato* and Méhul's *Joseph*. 'Orchestra and choirs are excellent,'[10] he wrote.

He was asked to a dinner party to meet Vienna's musical élite and later played some of his compositions. All those who heard him play in private urged him to play in public. He was subjected to a constant barrage, tirelessly led by the old well-wisher Wilhelm Würfel. 'He assures me', Frederick told his family, 'that the moment is opportune and that the Viennese are keen on new music. He says it won't do for a young musician like me to neglect such an opportunity. If I was only a performer, he says, my début would not create much interest, but as I am to play my own compositions, he says I must accept the challenge etc.'[10] Frederick was still torn by indecision when Würfel whispered in Count Gallenberg's ear that the young Polish virtuoso, of the calibre of Kalkbrenner and Moscheles, was prepared to play at his theatre without a fee. On the evening of Saturday 8 August, as the young virtuoso was standing outside the Kärntnerthortheater talking to some of his new friends, the Count came out and asked point blank whether M. Chopin would play for him on Tuesday 11 August. Suddenly M. Chopin gave in.

The three days between Saturday and Tuesday were a whirlwind of activity. A programme was arranged, scrapped, re-arranged; participants were brought in, programmes printed, bills posted. Würfel organized, cajoled and soothed frayed tempers. Frederick had to decide what piano he would play on. He was recommended a Stein, for its sonority; he chose a Graff, for its delicacy. Sandwiched between a Beethoven overture, arias by Rossini and Vaccai, and a short ballet, were his own two works for piano and orchestra, *La ci darem* Variations and the Krakowiak. An orchestral rehearsal was called for the morning of the day of the concert.

At the conservatoire Frederick had little if any experience of playing with an orchestra; he was certainly not familiar with the requirements and expectations of a professional one. No sooner had he arrived for the rehearsal, flanked on either side by Würfel and Nidecki, than a wave of hostility surged towards him. 'Probably because I was a newcomer,' he later observed without rancour, 'someone hardly arrived in Vienna who was already having his works performed God knows why.'[11] It was hard going. The players kept a stony expression which altered only when they wanted to show irritation with the unfamiliar, and to their mind occasionally erratic, score. Würfel conducted. The Variations were steered through to the end, but the Krakowiak presented unexpected difficulties. Frederick, whose writing was neat and beautiful where the piano part was concerned, had not been as meticulous as he might have been when it came to noting down the orchestral score. The players stared with exasperation at what looked like two conflicting sets of rests, one above the stave one below, and downed instruments. All hell broke loose. Würfel, Nidecki, the elderly titled stage manager, all rushed in with conciliatory suggestions. Frederick attempted to explain which set of rests he had in mind, then threw in his hand and called out that he wanted the whole thing cancelled. Eventually a truce was arranged. Frederick agreed to have the Krakowiak scrapped—though it was too late to alter the printed programme—and improvise solo instead; and Nidecki carried off the score of the Variations, with which the players were not altogether happy, promising to put in some modifications in time for the evening performance. Orchestra and composer parted coolly.

The concert at Vienna's Kärntnerthortheater, on 11 August 1829, was Chopin's real professional début. By seven, the time scheduled for the start, the hall was not full, although the sympathetic stage manager assured Frederick that those who mattered, musicians, counts, ladies of society, were all present. As the orchestra struck up the first notes of Beethoven's Prometheus overture, Frederick was being buoyed backstage by an optimistic Würfel, a tense Nidecki and a drink of sugared water brought in by a male Polish member of the *corps de ballet*. Four of his Warsaw friends posted themselves at strategic points about the hall so as to be able to overhear and report back any comments on the performance. On no account were they to lead the applause.

The overture duly dispatched, the main business of the evening was about to begin. The orchestra sat in the pit as if for an opera, Chopin and his grand Graff occupied the centre of the stage. A rouged young man who was to turn the pages managed to whisper, over the polite welcoming applause, that he was highly thought of by eminent pianists, he had rendered the same service to Hummel, Moscheles and others. Chopin was pale but not frightened, goaded by rage at the morning's proceedings. 'Who knows,' he later reflected, 'but what my bad temper and the risk I was taking did not spur me on that evening to a better performance. . . . I was desperate.'[11]

He was an instant success. The audience applauded after every single variation and so fervently that the orchestral *tuttis* were entirely drowned. At the end of the work he was made to return to the stage for a second bow, an unusual honour to judge by the way he described it to his family the day after.

But the best was yet to come. After the set of arias sung by a lady from the Saxon Court Opera, the dignified stage manager in his gala dress informed the astonished audience that instead of the advertised programme the Polish virtuoso would improvise on a theme suggested by them, a common concert practice of the time. Chopin was offered a theme from Boieldieu's *La Dame blanche* which he had seen only a few days earlier and which his audience knew well. Then, when the stage manager suggested that he should weave in a Polish theme, he began improvising on *Chmiel*, a catchy drinking song, or hops-song. The audience was carried away. They swayed to the rhythm, danced up and down in their seats, applauded madly, recalled him for yet another bow. Even the orchestra, from behind their music-stands in the pit, clapped unstintingly. Backstage there was much shaking of hands, slapping of backs and, woe, some talk of a repeat performance. The four scouts burst in and reported that the audience had adored Chopin, particularly the ladies. There was only one adverse remark made by a patronizing matron: 'What a pity the young man carries himself so awkwardly.'[12]

A second concert was arranged for the following Tuesday. It was a point of honour, Frederick wrote home, to show the world that he was not running away from the battlefield after only one assault. He had good cause to react that way, for when the first wave of enthusiasm had died down, some critical voices were raised. The *Wiener Theaterzeitung*, among others, while commending the absence of flashiness in his playing and music, missed the customary fireworks. 'His touch', the paper wrote, 'is neat and sure, but it lacks the virtuoso's brilliance'.[13] Chopin stood his ground. 'Concert-goers who are used to the thumping technique of the Viennese pianists', he wrote the day after his début, 'are mostly of the opinion that my playing is too soft, or rather too delicate. I rather expected this sort of criticism because one of my critics is a journalist whose daughter bashes the piano as hard as anything. It does not matter. There will always be a *but*, I would much rather have this sort of criticism levelled against me than have it said that I am a thumper.'[14] The influential Count Lichnowsky, who had given his patronage to Beethoven and now wanted to see Chopin silence his critics, offered to put his own magnificent piano at the young man's disposal. Frederick tactfully explained that there was nothing wrong with the quality of his chosen Graff, it was his manner of playing which was responsible for the small volume.

The programme on 18 August included an Overture by Lindpainter, a Polonaise for Violin by Mayseder, and again a ballet. Chopin was to play his Variations as well as the Krakowiak, which the devoted Nidecki had corrected during the previous week to meet the orchestra's criticisms. The attendance was better and the takings pleasingly higher. 'This is surely not on account of the ballet, which most people have already seen,'[15] the theatre business manager said beamingly to Chopin, who was again playing without a fee.

It was another tumultuous success. Musicians, music patrons, society ladies, all thronged backstage to offer their congratulations and express admiration for the very delicacy which the thumping-school champions had regarded as a fault. Since Chopin had already booked a seat on the stage-coach of the following evening, his well-wishers urged him to pay a return visit as soon as possible and were astonished to hear him say that he was hoping to come back to Vienna to study. Nobody regarded him as a student. He himself felt that in one week he had matured by four years. All the same he had not shaken off the student's way of thinking and was apprehensive of his former music teacher's judgment. 'I wonder what M. Elsner would say to all this,' he wrote home. 'Perhaps he will be displeased that I gave a public performance. But they pestered me so much I could no longer refuse.'[16]

He would have liked to stay a little longer in order to relish his success more leisurely, but travel arrangements and Nicholas' purse were inflexible. On the morning of departure he paid a round of farewell calls, bid a sentimental adieu to pretty Leopoldine Blahetka whom he had temporarily persuaded to bash the piano less hard and collected six new letters of recommendation to musicians he was hoping to meet on his return journey through Prague and Dresden. Of the original party of eight five had made alternative travel arrangements. Frederick and the remaining two met at the stage-coach station in time for the nine p.m. chaise for Prague.

Reflecting on the past fortnight, with its incredible developments, tensions, triumphs and pin-pricks, Frederick recalled an incident which had had a sobering effect on him. He was having a late supper in his hotel after his second concert when another guest joined the communal dining table. The guest was wearing an opera cloak and a fellow-diner conversationally enquired what he had seen and whether he had liked it. The gentleman replied that he had seen and enjoyed a ballet, then changed the subject; he had obviously recognized Chopin and did not wish to criticize him to his face. 'You cannot win them all,' Frederick observed in retrospect. 'The man has not yet been born who has nothing but praise lavished upon him.'[17]

Before leaving Vienna he had arranged for press notices to be sent on to him to Warsaw. He was sensitive to criticism and was distressed when the Warsaw journals, quoting some of his Viennese critics, had mistranslated or misunderstood remarks which to him seemed laudatory in the original German. Several months after his return he at long last saw a copy of the *Allgemeine musikalische Zeitung* of 18 November, which gave him the final accolade. The paper wrote:

Herr Chopin, a pianist from Warsaw, is a master of the first rank, who has an exquisitely delicate touch, an indescribable finger dexterity, and a deep feeling which is expressed in his shading. Both his interpretation and compositions bear the stamp of genius. He is a virtuoso generously endowed by nature, a light flashing across our musical horizon like a brilliant meteor.[18]

Emotional gropings

From early childhood Chopin felt at home in female company. Women, more than men, held out to him that promise of solicitude and strength which his nature craved.

There was no segregation of the sexes in the genteel society into which his musical precocity had brought him. Grand Duke Constantine habitually rewarded the child prodigy for his playing with permission to romp in the Belvedere gardens with young Paul, his own natural son, and little Alexandrine, the daughter of the resident French tutor. The Lyceum, although a boys' school, brought no change in the established pattern. Tradition has it that Frederick once hid with someone's sister behind a bush on the school grounds while a trusted schoolmate assured Nicholas, who had come out in search of his truant son, that Frycek had gone straight home. Nor was it an isolated instance. 'In 1824 [he was fourteen] I was in love with a young girl from the convent school,' Chopin recalled in his maturity, 'and her father was annoyed with me for trying to arrange secret rendezvous with his daughter. Our go-between was a Jewish boy called Leibush, son of the shopkeeper who supplied us with pens and writing paper. Leibush had a good ear, he would not accept payment for his services, he only wanted to have lessons with me and would listen for hours under my window when I was playing. That messenger of love was a very important person in my life at that time.'[1]

To achieve a hold over him, even a mild one, a girl needed to be attractive, talented, sensitive to his music and, as circumstances were to show time and again, emotionally prepared to take the initiative; a combination which might well have had its origins in his early association with beautiful matrons whose adulation was matched by their organizational zeal at charity concerts. Several young ladies of his acquaintance possessed some of the ingredients of the mysterious chemistry; none, as yet, the perfect solution. One was Countess Alexandrine de Moriolles, who had retained a weakness for her childhood playmate; another was Emily Elsner, the professor's gifted daughter. To Alexandrine he dedicated, on its publication in Warsaw in 1828, his early Rondo à la mazur (in F major Op. 5); to Emily he played many of his latest compositions and copied some with his own hand into her album.

The tentative gallantries at the keyboard were innocent enough but beneath their apparent decorum boys and girls knew perfectly well that love was not made in heaven but in bed. When Countess Pruszak, at whose country house Frederick had spent part of his 1828 holiday, found out that her resident governess was pregnant, she immediately assumed that her eighteen-year-old house guest was the seducer. From her town house in Warsaw she charged into the Chopins' drawing-room and faced them with the accusation. Fortunately the real seducer owned up, the governess was laid off and Frederick, wholly exonerated, was invited to give the Pruszak youngsters private lessons until alternative arrangements could be made.

Far from being offended, Frederick had taken the accusation as an implied compliment. Amorous adventures, and the bragging thereof, were not uncommon among the young sparks of his set. To his intimate friend Titus Woyciechowski he described the non-adventure in basic Italian: 'We had taken some walks in the garden, nothing else. She wasn't attractive and I, fool that I was, had no appetite for her. Just as well as it turns out.'[2]

Obviously he had not yet met the woman who would overwhelm him and initiate him. He was still at the stage when an undefined craving would find an easier outlet in a sentimental friendship with someone of his own sex. After the untimely death of his childhood friend Jan Bialoblocki, Frederick became attached to his classmate Titus Woyciechowski and focused on him that tense dependence which is often indistinguishable from love. Indeed it would not be wrong to say that Titus was Frederick's first love, in the confused and non-physical sense which is often characteristic of a first awakening.

Like most of his classmates, Titus was a year or two older

than Frederick and a good few inches taller. Since his home was at Poturzyn near Tomaszow (now in the district of Zamocz), he boarded with the Chopins during term time. He was gifted as well as practical and when he had passed his matriculation examinations, with better grades than Frederick's, he went on to university to study law. On the face of it he and Frederick were opposites. Frederick delicate, wiry, tense, indecisive; Titus athletic, with large hands, placid, emanating calm strength. Yet Titus, like all Frederick's chosen schoolfriends, was musical and a competent pianist. In his students' lodgings he kept an excellent piano on which Frederick improvised whenever he dropped in. The virile Woyciechowski had an empathy with Chopin's delicate music and in his presence inspiration would come more readily than in the musical gatherings at Warsaw's genteel drawing-rooms.

When his student days were over Titus returned to Poturzyn to lead the life of a country gentleman. He farmed, hunted, practised the ancient crossbow. From time to time, though never frequently enough for Frederick's liking, he came up to the capital to see to business and pay court to the young ladies of their acquaintance. In between visits the friends wrote to each other. Frederick wrote about anything which came into his head, his summer holidays, his fortnight in Berlin, his experiences in Vienna. He informed Titus which of their friends had gone abroad, who had died, who was getting married. He gave his opinion on concerts and plays he had been to, discussed his latest compositions and his plans to try them out. Titus was his diary. Sometimes Frederick would turn to him impulsively and write three long letters in a row; sometimes he would neglect him for weeks. Titus was less erratic; he was consistent in writing seldom. Unfortunately none of his letters has survived.

Frederick loved him. He clung to the strong, undemonstrative young man with all the sensitivity of an adolescent. 'Dearest Titus,' he began on 9 September 1828, 'you won't believe how much I have longed to hear from you and your mother and how pleased I was to receive your letter.'[3] He urged him to write again. 'Take pity on me', he said at the end of a long chatty letter, 'and write sometimes. A word, half a word, a syllable, a single letter, it will mean such a lot to me.'[3] He signed off with 'Give a kiss to your faithful friend'.[4] On 27 December he wished Titus a Happy New Year and congratulated him on his nameday on 4 January. 'You do not like to be kissed,' Frederick wrote. 'Allow me to do so today.'[5] On 12 September 1829 he ended his detailed account of his concerts and triumph in Vienna with 'I kiss you heartily, right on the lips if I may.'[6] He addressed Titus as an anxious woman might a reluctant lover. 'Don't kiss me now for I haven't washed yet,' he wrote one morning. 'How silly of me! You wouldn't kiss me even if I were to bathe in all the perfumes of Byzantium, unless I forced you to by some supernatural power. I believe in such powers. Tonight you shall dream you are kissing me.'[7]

There were always kisses in Frederick's letters. His schoolboyish notes to Jan Bialoblocki ended with 'Give me a kiss'; his letters home included 'kisses, kisses, kisses' for his sisters; his missives to Titus deposited kisses 'on the hands and feet' of the latter's ailing mother. Such expressions formed part of the Polish epistolary courtesy of the age and were in no way as literal as they sounded. Indeed some had become hackneyed; but such was Frederick's love for Titus that he wanted to re-infuse the spirit of the gesture. 'I kiss you lovingly,' he ended once, then added thoughtfully, 'This is how people usually sign themselves off, but they don't really understand what they are writing. I for one mean what I write, for I love you dearly.'[8] Even after such protestations he would sign himself formally as F. Chopin, occasionally varying his signature to Fr. Ch. or F. Chop.

He dedicated to Titus the Variations, the first-fruits of his orchestral labours, because he felt that Titus was the only one who understood the innermost meaning of his music; then, since he had done so without the courtesy of asking, he had misgivings. 'I have put your name on the Variations,' he informed Titus on 9 September 1829, long after the manuscript had gone off to Haslinger's in Vienna. 'Perhaps it was presumptuous of me to do so, but my heart dictated it, our friendship seemed to allow it, please do not take it amiss.'[9] Titus accepted with pleasure. When *La ci darem* Variations were eventually published by the procrastinating Haslinger in January 1830, the elegant *Odéon* edition carried the name of Titus Woyciechowski in thick bold type, commanding the centre of the title page.

After his return from Vienna Frederick was becoming moody. Warsaw with its mere 214 streets and 150,000 inhabitants made him feel constrained; he was hardly back when he began talking of going abroad again. His father suggested Berlin, where there was a chance of free board and lodging at Prince Radziwill's; Frederick toyed with the idea of returning to Vienna, visiting Italy, exploring Paris. The more he discussed his plans the more he realized that his next trip abroad would not be in the nature of a fortnight's holiday but a matter of months, perhaps years. Even a more enterprising young man would have felt apprehensive at the prospect; Frederick became a bundle of nerves. He announced the day of his departure, found a thousand and one excuses to put it off. He became unpredictable, one moment bouncy and excited, the next listless and apathetic. He tried to ward off the moodiness by playing chamber music on Friday nights, returned home to nurse a new fit of depression. The weeks turned into months without his being able to make up his mind. He was losing his grip, unable to halt the ebbing away of will power and physical strength.

The havoc in his soul was due however to a deeper cause than the ostensible inability to follow up a heady triumph abroad. Frederick was at a difficult age, no longer a boy yet not quite an adult. At nineteen the process of emerging from the chrysalis of adolescence was all the more harrowing because of the imbalance between his musical and emotional development. Musically he was mature and had a fairly clear idea of what he wanted; emotionally he was as indecisive as a child. That quality of indecision, which he was never wholly to outgrow and which by the end of the following year nearly drove him to the verge of a nervous collapse, was manifest not only in his inconclusive travel projects but, more pointedly, in his approach to his first courting.

He had noticed Constance Gladkowska some months before his trip to Vienna, a pretty student in the opera class of the conservatoire, with fair hair, blue eyes, a fresh complexion and a good mezzo-soprano voice. The moment he heard her sing he felt the awakening of love. He had not been formally introduced to her, but within a short while he managed to learn all there was to know about her. She was nineteen like him, daughter of the superintendent of the royal castle, holder of a state scholarship and a boarder at the conservatoire students' hostel. She was a gifted singer and even as a student was already assured of a chance to appear in leading parts at the National Opera. Watching her at students' concerts he noticed that every now and then she would be wearing an eye-patch; he thought her all the more perfect. To Titus he described her, namelessly, as his 'ideal'.[10]

It would have been the easiest and most natural thing in the world for a fellow musician to have himself introduced to her, but everything in Frederick's nature recoiled from such a resolute step. For a whole year, from the spring of 1829 to the spring of 1830, he watched her from afar, languishing and pining, longing for an introduction and doing nothing to bring it about. His heart swelled when he heard her sing at students' concerts, sank when he noticed enterprising Russian officers leap backstage to offer their compliments.

It was no lack of confidence in his ability to please which kept him at bay. His musical genius, combined with his natural charm and vitality, were qualities much appreciated by women; nor was he unaware of the interest he was rousing. In Vienna, when the twenty-year-old Leopoldine Blahetka presented him with the signed manuscripts of her own piano compositions, he realized full well that she must have been very fond of him to have done that. Excited, he decided that she was an excellent pianist—he forgot that only a few days earlier he had called her a thumper—and pronounced her intelligent as well as pretty. But no sooner was he back in Warsaw than her memory faded and the image of his 'ideal' returned to haunt him. Still he made no move to speak to her.

There was obviously something in his nature which made him prefer fantasy to reality. He needed the exquisite ache of undeclared love to fire his inspiration and his longing for Constance found an outlet in many of his compositions in 1829 and 1830, notably in the slow movement of his Concerto in F minor (Op. 21). On the morning of 3 October 1829 the thought of her moved him to write a Waltz (in D flat major Op. 70, No. 3), which he immediately sent off to Titus at Poturzyn; no one else could be trusted to play with feeling a composition inspired by Constance.

He was desperate for a word of comfort from Titus. 'How awful not to have anyone to go to in the morning, to share my joys and my sorrows,' he wrote on the same day. 'It is dreadful when something weighs on your mind, not to have a soul to unburden yourself to. You know what I mean. I tell my piano the things I used to tell you.'[11] The more he day-dreamed about Constance, the more he needed Titus' infrequent reassurances of affection. 'I love you to distraction,'[11] he wrote in one of his black moods. He had tied a pretty ribbon round Titus' earlier letters and carried the latest one about his person so as to be able to re-read it at any time.

A firm invitation from Prince Radziwill to spend a few days in his country house at Antonin offered a temporary release from limbo. For eight days Frederick gave himself up to the pleasure of making music in a gracious and sympathetic household. The prince sought his opinion of his opera *Faust*; the princess treated him without condescension; and the two young princesses could hardly leave him alone. The eldest, Princess Eliza, had him pose for her while she sketched him in her album, as she had already done on a previous visit; the younger, Princess Wanda, did not let a day go by without practising his Alla Polacca (Op. 3) for Piano and Cello which he wrote for the family while he was there. He was as keen a teacher as she was a pupil and enjoyed the sensation of guiding her hands over the keyboard. He liked both sisters equally well and imagined himself in the Garden of Eden with a beautiful Eve on either side. His strength was returning. On his way back he stopped at nearby Kalisz and attended a dance at a friend's house, where an attractive young lady made him partner her in a mazur.

He had already started on another Concerto (in E minor Op. 11) and immediately on his return settled down to work on the third movement. His Viennese experience had taught him how important it was to work closely with an orchestra and he was wondering if he could have an informal try-out in his parents' drawing-room. It was fairly spacious and five newly-painted family portraits lent a touch of opulence to its modest elegance. Nicholas had commissioned them earlier that autumn from the artist Miroszewski, one of each member of the family. Old Zywny liked them so much that he too had himself painted; he still came and went like a member of the household.

Frederick was hard at work when an invitation came for him
to take part in a motley musical evening on 19 December at
the Merchants' Hall. The account given the following day in
the *Polish Courier* makes good reading:

Pan Bielawski [violin teacher at the conservatoire] began
the evening with a concerto for violin and orchestra; then
Pan Capello sang and Pan Chopin accompanied. Pan Soliva
[the Italian head of the singing department at the conserva-
toire] accompanied the French singer Pan Dorville, then Pan
Bielawski played a solo. Finally Pan Chopin entertained the
audience with improvisations on well-known melodies.[12]

His modest contribution drew an unexpected laudation from
the *Warsaw Courier* which had withheld praise in its account
of Chopin's début in Vienna. Four days after the Merchants' Hall
concert the paper authoritatively informed its readers that the
works of the young composer bore 'the stamp of genius' and
called for a public concert which would prove to the whole
of Europe that 'Poland too can produce great talents'.[13]

This time however Frederick was not going to be bullied
into a public performance with an orchestra without careful
preparation; he began to sound seriously the chances of a try-
out at home. Much string-pulling, negotiating and harping on
patriotic feelings was required to persuade the National Opera
Orchestra to accept an invitation to appear at a private function
not held at the palace of a Czartoryski, a Sapieha, a Krasinski.
There were reservations and petty jealousies but in the end it
was agreed with Kurpinski, the opera director, that the try-out
would count as a rehearsal for a public concert, the date of which
was to be left open. On Sunday 7 February 1830 the Chopins'
drawing-room seated a small orchestra as well as friends and
music critics. Chopin played his Concerto in F minor and a few
days later saw both work and execution acclaimed in the press,
with another exhortation to play in public. He still did not feel
ready. On Wednesday 3 March another so-called rehearsal
was held at his home, this time with all the paraphernalia of a
real concert.

The drawing-room was full to capacity with an overspill
into the adjacent rooms, confirmed admirers mingling with as

yet unconverted newcomers. The programme began with a repeat performance of the Concerto in F minor, conducted by Kurpinski himself, and ended with the Grand Fantasy on Polish Airs. It was a resounding success. Distinguished guests vied with each other in their quest of superlatives, Elsner walked from one group to another with a beaming face, old Zywny cried unashamedly. There was no possible excuse to put off a public performance any longer. Within days the press carried notices of Pan Chopin's forthcoming concert in Warsaw's National Theatre on 17 March.

Until then Chopin had played, his performance in Vienna excepted, only before small audiences in semi-private functions. Appearing on the stage of Poland's National Theatre, which had housed such ambitious productions like *Der Freischütz* or *Don Giovanni*, was a fearsome undertaking; and he knew only too well that for a native artist appearing in his own land it was more difficult to conquer than for a visiting musician with the aura of Germany or Italy around him. But there was no going back; public curiosity had been whetted and concert-goers flocked to buy tickets for the first public appearance of someone acclaimed by the inner circle as the Paganini of the pianoforte and the glory of Poland. Three days before the 17th all nine hundred seats were sold, stalls, pits and boxes.

Present day concert-goers would be amused to hear how their 1830 counterparts were given their first taste of Chopin's Piano Concerto in F minor. The programme opened with an overture by Elsner; then Chopin and the orchestra, conducted by Kurpinski, played the first movement of the Concerto, acknowledged the polite applause and put the music away. The next item was a Divertissement for French horn composed and played by Pan Görner. Only after the audience had been thoroughly diverted by the horn did pianist and orchestra resume the Concerto, playing the second and third movements with no more than the obligatory pause in-between.

The second half was less bizarre. It opened with yet another Overture, this one by Kurpinski, included Paër's Variations for Voice sung by Pani Mayer, and concluded with Chopin and orchestra playing his Grand Fantasy on Polish Airs. This work, more easily understood than the somewhat recondite Concerto, brought the house down.

The press gave Chopin rave reviews, the *Warsaw Courier,* the *Polish Courier,* the *Correspondent's Gazette,* the *General and National Journal,* the *Courier of the Fair Sex,* the *Official Bulletin.* What few reservations were made about the first movement of the Concerto and the over-delicacy of the playing were swept away in the flood of praise for the Grand Fantasy on Polish Airs. A patriotic chord had been struck in the hearts of musicians and laymen alike, and the *Courier of the Fair Sex* expressed a generally-held view when it wrote:

> The audience was particularly charmed with the works based on folk tunes, for Pan Chopin knew how to fuse the lovely simplicity of our native melodies with his sublime composition and exquisite playing. Every note he played not only pleased the ear but touched the heart and spoke to the very soul.[14]

The reviews fired the public imagination. At a time when Polish patriotism was strained to the limit by the Russian occupation, a young native composer was weaving Polish folk tunes into his music and making them sound as great as the greatest compositions in the European repertoire. There was no question but that he was a through and through Pole; his semi-French parentage was only fleetingly referred to. There was a public demand for a repeat performance and five days later, on 22 March, a second concert was held at the National Theatre. Chopin however had had to give way on one fundamental point. He had agreed to put aside his own pantaleon, which he used for opening the concert, and play instead on an instrument with a higher potential volume. Even his most ardent admirers, Elsner amongst them, insisted that the delicate tone of the pantaleon had not done justice to his compositions and failed to make them sound as masterly as they could be. Accordingly a sonorous Viennese piano was hastily borrowed for the occasion from a music-loving Russian general.

The National Theatre was again full to capacity. Again the Concerto in F minor was split in two, the first movement being severed from the second and third by Beriot's Variations for Violin and Orchestra played by old friend Bielawski. In the second half Chopin and orchestra played the Krakowiak, Pani

Mayer sang an aria by Soliva and finally Chopin improvised solo on the theme from the aria just sung. The audience went berserk, clapping, shouting, clamouring for yet another concert. The press surpassed itself. The *General and National Journal* went as far as to say that Providence, which had given Mozart to the Germans, had done right to give Chopin to the Poles. 'It's all such nonsense,'[15] Frederick told Titus.

There were other pleasing reactions. Alexandrine de Moriolles sent round a hero's crown of laurels, an anonymous admirer dropped in a sonnet, Brzezina sent word that they would like to issue posters with his portrait on. He withheld permission. 'I won't have people wrapping butter in me,'[16] he said soberly, recalling the fate of a well-known personage who had succumbed to the offer only to see his posters used for just that.

He was disappointed to hear that with two full houses he had cleared only five thousand zloty. He turned down an offer to play at the very large City Hall, explaining that the expected takings would hardly justify the change of venue. To Titus he confessed that he could not face the nervous strain which was inseparable from his public appearances. Each concert, he said, had been preceded by three days of near hell.

He was feeling deflated, even let down. Unaccountably Titus, his Beloved and Dearest, had stayed entrenched on his farm and not come up to Warsaw to attend his friend's début at Poland's foremost theatre. Frederick could not hold back a mild rebuke. 'My own sweet heart,' he began a letter a few days after his second concert. 'Never have I missed you so badly as I do now. You are not here and I have no one to talk to. One look from you after either of my concerts would have meant more to me than all the praises of the press, the Elsners, the Kurpinskis and the Solivas put together.'[17] His depression was upon him again. He no longer sought a rational reason for it, he already sensed that it was partly brought on by his own self-indulgence. 'I wish I could shake off the thoughts which mar my happiness,' he wrote with a flash of self-awareness, 'yet I seem to enjoy wallowing in them. I wish I knew what is wrong with me.'[18]

His family was alarmed, encouraged him to go out with friends. He allowed himself to be led like a sleepwalker. 'I often take night for day and day for night,' he wrote to Titus. 'I am awake when I dream and asleep during the day, but it is not real sleep and instead of being refreshed by this daytime torpor, as one should by real sleep, I get weaker and more tired than ever. Please love me.'[19] He had reached his lowest ebb.

In the spring of 1830 the unavoidable happened; after a whole year of silent worship Pan Chopin was formally introduced to Panna Gladkowska and her friend Panna Wolkowa. How the hurdle was surmounted is not certain; the likelihood is that the introduction took place at one of the conservatoire students' concerts. There was no dramatic transition from depression to happiness, but a certain equilibrium gradually resulted. Reality drove away the day dreams and with them the listlessness and the torment.

From then on Frederick became an assiduous visitor to the conservatoire practice rooms. He, who had not given much thought to vocal composition, now composed one song after another and practised them with Gladkowska and her apparently inseparable companion Wolkowa. Constance could hardly fail to guess his feelings and may well have been inclined to reciprocate them; but since Frederick could not bring himself to speak his love and she was not a girl to be forward, nothing was said.

At this time Warsaw was getting ready for the formal opening of the Diet by Tsar Nicholas, Tsar Alexander's successor as King of Poland. Again the capital exerted itself to mark the occasion with a rich fare of cultural events, inviting celebrities from abroad and putting forward native talents. Gladkowska and Wolkowa were selected to sing the leading parts in two new productions scheduled to coincide with the Tsar's visit. It was a great honour and both girls rehearsed hard, Chopin accompanying either the one or the other as they practised. He had recovered from his torpor and was rushing around from one concert to another. He heard every visiting celebrity and gave Titus news and views of whatever performance he had heard. He was particularly impressed with the German soprano Henrietta Sontag and had he not already found his 'ideal', may well have offered his silent devotions at her feet.

Henrietta Sontag was twenty-four at the time, famed for

her singing as well as her charm, the idol of Vienna, Prague, Paris and London. Chopin attended every one of her eight concerts at the National Theatre. He adored the quality of her voice and her perfect musicianship. When he was introduced to her he fell completely under her spell. He appraised her slender figure, delicate features, large eyes and auburn hair and decided that she was incomparable. He became a frequent caller, sat beside her on the sofa, could not take his eyes off her. His letters to Titus were full of her. He told him what a hit she was with the Polish and Russian aristocracy, how her ante-chamber was crowded from early morning with chamberlains, senators, district-governors, generals and adjutants. He could not help bragging about the informality of his own calls. 'In a morning outfit she is a million times prettier and more attractive than in a grand evening toilette,' he wrote, 'although those who do not see her in the morning still find her irresistible in the evening.'[20]

One morning he found Constance, Wolkowa and their music master Soliva in her rooms. The girls had just sung to her and were awaiting her verdict. She said quite frankly that although they seemed to have had good training, they would do well to learn how to produce their voices differently, or else they would not be able to sing at all in a year or two. She offered to coach them during the rest of her stay. Soliva was offended and the girls confused, but Frederick could only see Sontag's generosity.

The double début at the National Theatre was approaching. Gladkowska was to sing the title role in *Agnese*, by the contemporary Italian composer Paër, while her friend and rival Wolkowa was to sing the lead in Rossini's *Il Turco in Italia*. After the two-nights run in July, Frederick gave Titus an enthusiastic account:

Gladkowska leaves nothing to be desired. The raised stage shows her off to better advantage than the school platform. I am not speaking of her acting, it is marvellous and I have nothing to say about it. As for her singing, if it were not for an occasional F sharp and top G [she was a mezzo-soprano] we could wish for nothing better. You would have loved her phrasing. Her shading is first class and although her voice was somewhat shaky at first, she later sang with much confidence.[21]

He was annoyed to see the audience cheer Wolkowa more appreciatively than Gladkowska and hastened to assure Titus that it had nothing to do with the quality of the singing. Wolkowa, he wrote, sometimes sang decidedly off pitch but conquered with her curves while Gladkowska, a perfect musician, was second to none in the matter of delivery and tonal purity. He was firmly biased in Constance's favour, as indeed a lover should be; but his romance had not progressed beyond the gift of a ribbon which he wore next to his heart. He waited to be taken in hand; the hand that was stretched did not pull hard enough. The attraction began to pall. At times he no longer knew whether he was still in love. To Titus he wrote with yet another flash of self-awareness: 'Even if I were in love I would probably conceal my ineffectual and incommunicable fervor for several years more'.[22]

He was still talking of going to Vienna, but deep down he already knew that he would never go anywhere unless he had someone to go with. The ideal travel companion would have been Titus, practical, musical and dearly loved. Titus had in fact been toying with the idea of going abroad but life on the farm suited him and the pull of foreign parts was not strong enough. Perhaps he did not want to be saddled with an emotionally clinging friend who was also a genius. Having made a half-hearted promise to come along, he found endless pretexts to put the date off. There was too much to see to on the farm, he kept telling Frederick; there was the mill to be put up, the distillery to be planned, the lambs to be shorn, the wood to be gathered, the fields to be sown. Frederick swallowed the excuses and found reasons of his own to stay put. His family was puzzled, suspected an illicit love affair, tried to interest him in an eligible but totally unattractive young lady. 'You are the only one I love,'[23] he assured Titus, who needed no such reassurance.

In June Titus invited Frederick to spend a fortnight on the farm, which was about 185 miles south-east of Warsaw. Frederick thought nothing of the distance. The holiday in the

country was a great success. The two young men played the
piano and practised the crossbow, Frederick showing more
skill and taking more pleasure in the sport than his delicate
physique may have warranted. Titus tried to put some heart
into his friend and repeatedly told him how important a year
or two abroad could be for his career. Frederick promised he
would go away soon, very soon, as soon as he had his passport
endorsed. The word went round that he was really leaving.
At the end of August Titus came to Warsaw to be present at
a farewell dinner given by some former fellow-students, with
Nicholas Chopin the only elderly guest among them. A young
doctor who had recently qualified in Paris proposed the toast,
enjoining Chopin never to forget, even when he had conquered
the musical world, as he was bound to do and as all those
present dearly wished him to do, that he was a son of Poland.
Drink flowed like water, and music flowed like drink. Everybody improvised at the piano on Polish folk tunes.

Still Chopin hung on. On the last day of August he wrote
sheepishly to Titus who had returned to the country convinced
that he had given his friend the last farewell embrace: 'This
letter will probably rouse anger in your lion heart, I'm lucky
to be forty [*sic*] miles away from you or else the whole weight
of your wrath would descend on me. . . . Yes, I am still in
Warsaw, and since I love you there is nothing to tempt me
to go away. But next week, I promise, I shall really leave
here.'[24] The following week he wrote: 'I am still here, I
haven't got the strength to fix a date.'[25]

He fell back on the usual excuses. He was putting the finishing
touches to the score of the Concerto in E minor, he was going
to try it out with a group of chamber players, he was planning
a full-scale orchestral rehearsal at home. Titus apparently
replied that if Frederick cared to hold on until late autumn, he
might be free to go with him after all. Frederick nobly refused.
How much more delicious, he wrote back, to go away on his
own and await the arrival of his dearest Titus in his own
lodgings somewhere in Dresden, or Vienna, or wherever; how
exquisite the moment of reunion, how much more rewarding
than a dreary journey undertaken together. He dutifully went
through the motions and at the beginning of October informed
Titus: 'My trunk is bought, my outfits ready, my scores

bound, my handkerchiefs hemmed, my trousers pressed.'[26] He booked a seat on the stage coach to Vienna, cancelled it. He was worried about what Titus would say. 'I know you love me,' he wrote nervously, 'but I'm afraid of you as if you were some sort of tyrant. I don't know why I'm afraid of you, God knows you are the only one who has power over me, you and . . . well no one else.'[27] He held another orchestral try-out at home and was persuaded to give another concert at the National Theatre on 11 October with Soliva conducting.

According to the custom of the day, the Concerto in E minor which was having its first public performance, was heard in two sections. The Allegro was followed by Panna Wolkowa and choir. When she had dazzled the audience with her beauty and taken her bow, Chopin returned to the stage to play the Adagio and Rondo with the orchestra. Then everybody had refreshments.

The second half opened with Constance Gladkowska singing; both girls had been included in the programme at Chopin's own request. Constance appeared clad in white with fresh roses in her hair and sang so movingly that Frederick forgot his stage-fright. He was perfectly at ease throughout the Grand Fantasy on Polish Airs and for the first time since he had begun to perform the work in public, he felt at one with the orchestra. 'If Soliva had not taken the score home to look over and if he had not conducted in a way which made it impossible for me to run on at breakneck speed, I don't know how it would have gone last night,' Frederick admitted with much candour. 'He succeeded so well in keeping us together that it was the first time I played so well with an orchestra.'[28] The audience sensed it. They clapped and clapped until they brought him back four times. He acknowledged the applause like a seasoned performer; having remembered what a Viennese matron had once said about his clumsy bearing, he had taken some instruction in stage deportment. His most abiding memory of the evening was however of Constance, a vision of beauty clad in white, singing the cavatina and recitative from Rossini's *The Lady of the Lake*. Shortly afterwards he plucked up enough courage to ask her for a walk in the Saxon Gardens and offered her a thin wire ring with a shiny stone which tradition later described as a diamond; she too gave him a ring. Still nothing was said.

Titus had again failed to attend the concert; instead, after Frederick had re-booked and cancelled his trip to Vienna twice more, he sent word that he was free to join him in the first week of November and suggested that they should meet in Kalisz, near the Polish-Austrian border of the time. Suddenly everything became clear and simple. Frederick had his passport endorsed for Austria, Nicholas made arrangements with the bank to transfer money to his son abroad, the big new trunk was packed. There was a last round of farewells, a last visit to the theatre, a last call to an artists' café; he was off.

Just outside Warsaw the coach was brought to a halt. The loyal Elsner and a group of students had gone ahead to the next post-station and when Chopin's coach approached they signalled for it to stop and sang a farewell cantata which Elsner had specially composed for the occasion. 'Even while you are away,' they sang to the accompaniment of a guitar, 'let your heart forever be with us.'[29]

And Constance?

The parting must have been as muted as the courting. A few days before his departure she wrote two verses into his album in which she did not exhort him, like everybody else, to love Poland, but to remember those back at home who loved him. She may well have been describing her own feelings when she wrote:

> The time for change has come
> And follow your destiny you must
> But wherever you are
> In Poland you will be loved
>
> To keep your laurels green
> You renounce family and friends
> Strangers may honour you more
> None could love you better than those here.[30]

Less than fifteen months after his departure Constance married a well-to-do gentleman who began to court her, resolutely, as soon as Frederick had gone away. Perhaps she was hurt to see Frederick so happy to go away from Warsaw; perhaps she was peeved that he had never made his feelings clear. An indignant Isabel Chopin informed her brother that Constance had married 'for the sake of a palace'.[31] Perhaps she had. She gave up her musical career, settled down in the country and bore her husband five children. At the age of thirty-five she lost her eyesight though apparently not her general good health, for she lived to be seventy-nine, surviving Chopin by forty years. They never met again but some eight years after their parting, when he was already an experienced man in the ways of the world, he happened to re-read the two verses and added thoughtfully at the bottom of the second one: 'You could.'[30]

On his own

When Chopin left Warsaw in November 1830, aged twenty years and eight months, he had already written a number of works which were to become part of Europe's musical heritage. Maurice Brown lists some fifty-nine compositions written by that date including six works for piano and orchestra—the only orchestral ones Chopin ever wrote—as well as several Studies from Op. 10 and Nocturnes from Op. 9 and 15. With Chopin, as with Mozart to whom he was sometimes compared by Warsaw admirers, the mysterious fountain of creativity burst forth at a remarkably early age.

He was never in doubt about his vocation although once, in a moment of depression, it had pleased him to say that he would be better employed as a clerk on the Woyciechowski farm. It was only his way of admitting that he was totally incapable of embarking on a daunting journey abroad without someone to take him in hand. Once he met Titus at Kalisz as arranged he shed the morbidity of the past thirteen months and regained a sense of purpose. He felt fit and was eager to explore. He sought music wherever he went. In Breslau (Wroclaw) he presented his letters of recommendation and rushed to hear a German opera. He accepted an invitation to play at a semi-private function and instructed Titus, who had never witnessed any of his past triumphs, to sit with the audience and cock his ears for any comment. Disappointingly Titus reported back that while the Germans admired the pianist's light touch on the keyboard, they did not think much of his compositions. The *Kapellmeister* however made up for his compatriots' lack of discernment by stroking the young composer under the chin and telling him how good he was.

The next port of call was Dresden, where Chopin renewed

contacts made during his return journey from Vienna the year before. The two young men were indefatigable. They left their hotel first thing in the morning to return only late at night, having roamed the city, presented letters of recommendation, attended an evening performance. The Italian opera still reigned supreme in Dresden, despite the late Weber's attempts to oust it in favour of a native German opera; Frederick saw no less than three performances. He made the most of his time—how Nicholas must have approved—and paid a visit to the city's famous art gallery.

He was inundated with social invitations. Dresden was full of Poles, followers of the late King Frederick Augustus I of Saxony and the one-time Grand Duke of Warsaw. Some still held office at court and were on visiting terms with members of the royal family. One evening Chopin, to whom all Polish doors were thrown open, found himself improvising in the presence of royalty. He was promised letters of recommendation from the heir-apparent and two princesses who were all related to the reigning houses of Sicily, Rome and Milan. Of far greater moment, though he could not have guessed it at the time, was his meeting at the house of the Polish Countess Komar with her married daughter Countess Delphina Potocka. The beautiful and exciting Delphina, already estranged from her husband, was to become one of the most enduring, though the least publicized, of Chopin's loves.

After a hectic week in Dresden and a short stop in Prague, Frederick and Titus arrived hale and hearty in Vienna. They put up at one hotel, found the prices too steep, moved to another, hurried to a bank to cash their respective money drafts. Chopin was flattered when the banker recognized his name and said he was honoured to meet such a *Künstler*; piqued when the banker gratuitously added that *Herr Künstler* would find it difficult to give a concert in Vienna since only the most celebrated of artists could hope to do so. 'You wait and see, you dog-flaying Jew,'[1] Chopin wrote home angrily. He little imagined how true the banker's well-meant warning was going to prove.

With money in their pockets the two young men now began looking for a place of their own where they would be able to entertain and hold musical evenings. Their choice fell on an elegantly-furnished apartment in a house owned by a baroness in reduced circumstances who professed to have heard of Chopin and to be fond of Poles. The out-going tenant was an English admiral, and while waiting for that 'bewhiskered, gaunt, seedy-looking greenish-purplish-yellowish sailor'[1] to weigh anchor, the friends stayed on at their hotel. Chopin took to practising in the afternoons at the store of the piano maker Graff who had not forgotten the preference shown for his instruments by the young composer during his début at the Kärntnerthortheater. He promised to lend him one free as soon as Chopin was settled in his apartment.

Chopin was confident. He was not deterred when he heard that Leopoldine Blahetka and her influential journalist father had left Vienna; that the manager of the Kärntnerthortheater had been dismissed and replaced by a former ballet dancer noted for his stinginess; and that old Würfel, the moving spirit behind his Vienna début, was spitting blood and unable to be of any assistance. He was not discouraged even by his call on Haslinger who, without shedding his charm, kept talking about hard times and made no mention of paying for the Variations for Piano and Orchestra which he had recently published. With a sonata and some piano variations safely tucked in his drawer he shuffled and hedged until the composer —he was learning fast—realized that the purpose of the exercise was to get him to agree to another publication without fee. He was not going to let anybody exploit him, he wrote home indignantly. 'It's all over, this business of working without pay. From now on *bezahl*, you cur.'[1]

He had caught a cold and put off presenting his letters of recommendation to the Viennese musical aristocracy until he was in better shape. Instead he dragged Titus to the opera every night, gorged himself on *strudel*, looked appreciatively at the pretty Viennese girls and wrote home that he was living very economically. The only person of consequence he called on was Dr Malfatti, the court physician and Beethoven's one-time doctor, who was married to a Polish countess who received her compatriot with open arms.

Judging by his previous experience, Chopin was certain that arranging a concert would be a matter of days. When a week had gone by and nothing was yet in the offing, he felt he had to defend himself to his family. 'I simply don't know how the time has flown,' he wrote home on 1 December, 'We haven't had a moment to turn round and nothing has been arranged so far about my concert.'[1] He was in no doubt that it would soon be held and the only thing which worried him was the choice of work. 'What concerto should I play? In F or in E?' he asked himself rather than his parents and concluded: 'All goes well. With God's help and Malfatti's, that excellent Malfatti, I hope it will go even better.'[1]

The following day, 2 December, he and Titus moved into the three-roomed apartment which the seedy admiral had at long last vacated. They unpacked their trunks, hung up their clothes, stacked the sheets of music over the Graff which had been promptly delivered, and made exciting plans for the future. Then, on 5 December, they heard the first reports about the Polish insurrection which had broken out a few days earlier, and all their plans fell to pieces.

When in 1815 the Congress of Vienna confirmed the partitioning of Poland and allowed no return to independence, it had reckoned without the fiery spirit of Polish patriotism.

Of what used to be Poland, only Cracow with its immediate surrounding retained the status of a free city republic. The rest was distributed roughly as before. Great Poland, with Poznan for its centre, was left to Prussia. Austria remained in possession of Galicia. The eastern borderlands, from Lithuania and White Russia to Volhynia and the Ukraine, continued to be incorporated in Russia. What was left of central Poland, about three-quarters of the former Duchy of Warsaw including Warsaw itself, was constituted the so-called Congress Kingdom of Poland under the Russian Tsar. With a measure of autonomy, an army and its own national flag, this small kingdom kept the flame of patriotism burning more daringly than the territories under direct foreign rule.

During the reign of Tsar Alexander I, first king of Congress Poland, the Diet sat three times, in 1818, 1820 and 1825. Each session was ceremoniously opened by the Tsar and was the occasion for a display of official goodwill on both sides; it was during the imperial visit of 1825 that Frederick had been presented with a diamond ring for personal merit and his contribution to Polish musical life. The pomp and circumstance could not however silence the Polish nationalists for whom nothing would do but the overthrow of the Russian regime and a return to independence. Students and young army officers aspired and conspired, were caught and punished, remained unrepentant and became martyrs. The country was seething with secret patriotic societies.

When shortly after the opening of the 1825 Diet Alexander I died, he was succeeded as Tsar and King of Poland by his brother Nicholas I. Grand Duke Constantine, brother to both Tsars, stayed on in Warsaw as Commander-in-Chief of the Polish army with his authority extended. He became the symbol of Russian oppression. By the time Nicholas I came to Warsaw to open the 1830 Diet, anti-Russian feelings were running high. On the face of it Warsaw was putting itself out to mark the occasion with the usual wealth of cultural activities, yet underneath there were rumblings of discontent which the authorities recorded and duly acted upon. At a concert given at the royal castle in honour of the Tsar, Chopin was conspicuous by his absence. The omission of a notable Polish musician from the list of performers may well have been a silent warning to a young man who, though not politically active, was known to associate with suspected patriots.

A few months after the Tsar's visit the insurrection broke out. On the night of 29 November 1830 eighteen young army officers hid in the Belvedere gardens waiting to kill or kidnap the Grand Duke. Simultaneously a unit of cadets was detailed to storm the Russian town barracks. At a given signal—an old brewery by the river bursting into flames—both groups attacked. Several senior officers loyal to the Russian administration were killed, but Grand Duke Constantine slipped through the net. There followed a night of chaotic fighting with the leaders of the uprising marching through the streets and calling their compatriots to arms. It took a week before the insurrection became general. In the meantime Constantine had withdrawn his own troops and Warsaw was clear of Russians. Ironically, it was thanks to the Grand Duke's own military fanaticism that the Poles now had a well-drilled and well-equipped army of thirty thousand men. It was clear however that it would not be sufficient to meet the new contingency and thousands of volunteers hastened to swell the ranks of the fighting force.

When the first reports from Warsaw trickled into Vienna, the two young patriots' immediate reaction was to return home and join up. Titus was clear about his own course; he was physically fit, the owner of lands which because of their nearness to the Russian border might be among the first to be swept by the enemy, and in any case in Vienna only on holiday. Frederick's course was less obvious; he wanted to go back with Titus but after an all-night discussion had to admit that he could better serve Poland with his music than his blood. He helped Titus pack the trunk which had barely been unpacked, saw him off to the coach station and returned to the house. The comfortable apartment which only a day earlier looked like home was now desolate and cold. He walked from one room to another, looked at the empty cupboards, the half-open drawers, the strewn papers, could not bear the loneliness. Frantically he flung his own things into a trunk, had it rushed to the coach station and left with the first available express in the hope of catching up with Titus. It was too late. When the express pulled up for the first change of horses, Chopin was told that the early mail coach was hours ahead, the chase was hopeless. Stunned, he allowed the postilions to remove his trunk and put it on the return coach to Vienna. When he got back to the apartment he flung himself on his bed. He was on his own.

The next few weeks were harrowing. Poland was at war, his nearest and dearest were in danger, and the Austrians were clearly unsympathetic. One day, in an Italian restaurant, he overheard a conversation from the next table. 'The good Lord made a mistake when he created the Poles,' said one diner. 'Poland is not worth bothering about,'[2] agreed the other. Chopin realized that among his numerous Viennese acquaintances there was not one he could call a friend. He could not bear to be on his own. He sought out Poles and clung to whomever he could. To live more economically he ceded his overlarge apartment to an English family and moved up to the fourth floor, where he still had comfort and elegance at a reasonable rent. The Graff went up with him.

His thoughts were with Poland. Most of his Warsaw friends had joined up, his sisters were making bandages for the wounded. He felt guilty about not going home, not in the least relieved when his parents, particularly his mother, urged him to stay away. He was wondering about Constance. He began to see her as his own sweetheart trapped in an enemy-ridden homeland and wrote emotional letters to his former school-friend Jan Matuszynski asking him to call on her and tell her of his love. He could not bring himself to write to her directly. 'What if my letter should fall into the wrong hands?' he defended himself to Jan. 'It would surely cast a stain on her reputation.'[3] There was no reason why he should not have written to her openly and respectfully with her parents' consent, but that was too definite a step for him to take. He wanted someone else to find the right words and speak them for him. 'I'll agree to whatever you say in my name,'[3] he pleaded with Jan. But Jan soon joined the army as a surgeon and the fantasy of love remained locked in Chopin's mind.

In the meantime the prospects of a concert were receding. Theatre managers who had seemed keen enough when they thought that Chopin would be playing without a fee, became distinctly cool as soon as he mentioned that he expected to be paid. His name was not a box-office draw. What impact he may have made eighteen months earlier had been forgotten and promoters were not inclined to put their money on anyone but a celebrity. There were other reasons as well. Poland was not popular in a country which under the terms of the Congress of Vienna was occupying large slices of it and which therefore could not but condemn an uprising against a partner in the spoils. Promoting a newly-arrived Polish musician, and a relatively unknown one at that, was inviting failure. Besides, musical fashion was changing, serious concertos were being ousted by light music. Chopin described the new trend in a letter to his parents:

A most popular form of entertainment in Vienna consists of musical evenings held in fashionable restaurants where Strauss [the elder] and Lanner, who are something like the Swieszewski dance-band leaders back home, play waltzes while the audience are served with a meal. After each waltz there is a thunderous burst of applause; and if the musicians go on to play a jumble of light operatic tunes, songs and dances, the audience go into a frenzy of delight. It just goes

4

to show how debased the taste of the Viennese public has become.[4]

He might still have been able to give a concert on his own terms had he been temperamentally more aggressive; but chasing slippery promoters, cornering evasive patrons, practising the art of self-advertisement from which even less sensitive a nature would shrink, was anathema to him. He virtually gave up trying, allowing himself to drift, using up his father's savings and guiltily wondering whether he should not push off to Italy or Paris. Unfortunately there was no one to make up his mind for him. 'Shall I go to Paris?' he wrote to Jan Matuszynski. 'Shall I return home? Shall I stay here? Kill myself? Stop writing? Do tell me what to do.'[5]

He fared no better with publishers to whom he offered some of his compositions. Haslinger was playing safe and publishing works—Chopin flinched at the use of the word *works* to denote ballroom waltzes—only by Johann Strauss [the elder] and Joseph Franz Lanner. Other respectable publishers like Diabelli, Mechetti and Joseph Czerny seemed no less cautious and unimaginative. The music some of them were publishing, he wrote home, was fit only for a cabaret. It was no comfort to hear some of his acquaintances say that Vienna was not what it used to be only two or three years earlier, when both Beethoven and Schubert were still alive.

He was leading a busy social life, accepting invitations to lunches, dinners, receptions, dances, anything that might drive away loneliness and professional frustration. He became a young man about town; but for the unnatural circumstances he would have enjoyed the new style of life which agreed with his love of luxury and elegant society. He admitted as much to Jan Matuszynski to whom he described his daily routine:

In the morning an extremely stupid servant wakes me up, serves coffee. I sit down to play, let the coffee get cold. At about nine my German teacher comes in. After that I usually play, or Hummel [the composer's ten-year-old son] paints my portrait and Nidecki practises my concerto. All this with me in my dressing gown until noon. Then a pleasant young German calls for me, Leidenfrost his name is, he practises at the law-courts. If it's fine we take a walk on the ramparts round the town. Then it is time for lunch, either I have an invitation or we go together to the Bohemian Cook, where the students eat. After lunch we take black coffee at the finest café, that's the fashion here. . . . Then I pay my calls, return to my place just before dark, curl my hair, change, off to a party. I get back about ten or eleven, never later than twelve. I play, cry, read, stare, laugh, get into bed, blow the candle out and dream about home.[6]

He also frequented operas and concerts and made the acquaintance of most of the musical élite of the day, the singers Binder and Fonti, the composers Hummel and Stadler, the pianist Bocklet, the violinist Lafont. He was particularly impressed with the cellist Merk with whom he played once or twice at a musical at-home, and the Czech violinist Slavik with whom he struck up a warm friendship. 'Except for Paganini, I have never heard anyone like him,' he wrote of the twenty-four-year-old Slavik. 'He plays ninety-six staccato notes with one stroke of the bow.'[7] The more he heard him the more he was impressed. 'The other evening Slavik played like a second Paganini,' he wrote on another occasion. 'Like a second *young* Paganini. I am sure that in time the second will surpass the first.'[8] Whether Slavik would have lived up to Chopin's expectations will never be known, for he died two years later.

Chopin's letters home were full of random comments on performances and musicians. As usual his first preference was for the opera; but with the exception of the veteran tenor Wild and the young soprano Sabine Heinefetter, he felt that the Vienna Opera was not living up to its name. He even had some reservations about Heinefetter, of whom he wrote: 'She has a voice such as one rarely hears, she is always in tune, her notes and *portamenti* pure and supple, everything perfect. But she is cold. The other night I thought my nose was about to freeze when I was listening to her in the stalls.'[9]

Of young Adolphe Hesse from Breslau who was to become a famous church organist and give demonstrations of his art in London, he wrote: 'He has talent, this boy. He knows how to handle an organ.'[10] He was less generous towards fellow pianists —it rankled to see them perform in public while he was being

pushed from pillar to post—and dismissed them as 'an uninter-
rupted succession of mediocre players'.[11] Of young Sigismund
Thalberg, the future formidable rival of Liszt and the protégé
and reputed natural son of the influential Count Dietrichstein,
he wrote:

> Thalberg plays splendidly but he is not my man. He is
> younger than me, popular with the ladies, improvises on
> themes from *La muette de Portici* [by Auber], achieves his
> *piano* with the pedal instead of the hand, takes tens as easily
> as I do octaves and wears diamond shirt-studs. He does
> not much like Moscheles and so it's not surprising that only
> the *tuttis* of my concerto please him.[12]

And he was at his deadliest about the violinist Herz about
whom he had made up his mind even before he heard him play:

> I am going to a concert to hear Herz, that Jewish violinist
> who only just missed being booed at Mlle Sontag's concert
> in Warsaw. . . . At the end of the concert Herz is going to
> play his own Variations on Polish Airs. Poor Polish Airs!
> How he is going to pep them up with Jewish *Ma Yafits*,
> calling them Polish to attract the public. How can anyone
> defend Polish music after a thing like that? Just try to point
> out that his tunes are phoney, and they think you are mad;
> all the more so since Czerny, Vienna's musical authority and
> great fabricator of musical tit-bits, has never used a Polish
> theme in any of his compositions.[13]

Chopin's twenty-first birthday came and went. A Polish lady
who had seen him in Warsaw shortly before his departure and
now met him again in Vienna, was amazed at the change in him.
His face had lost the bloom of youth, his hair was long and
neatly curled, he was growing side whiskers. He had become a
man.

It was spring. The Viennese flocked to the Prater to breathe
the fresh air and Chopin, mingling with the crowds, thought
achingly of the Polish countryside. His cellist friend Merk was
going to take part in a celebrity charity concert organized by
the singer Mme Garcia Vestris, and it may well have been
thanks to him that Chopin agreed to be included in the pro-

gramme. It was obviously his only chance of being heard outside the drawing-rooms circle. Other volunteers were Sabina Heinefetter with one of her five popular sisters, the tenor Wild, the violinists Böhm and Helmsberger and the two horn-playing brothers Levy. In the *Allgemeine Theaterzeitung* of 2 April, where the celebrities were listed, Chopin was the only participant who needed a gloss; the word 'pianist' appeared in brackets after his name. Small wonder he was not looking forward to the occasion. In his notebook he wrote:

> The papers and posters have announced my concert, it is taking place in two days' time, but I don't really care, it is as if nothing is going to happen. I take no notice of the congratulations, they seem more fatuous than ever. I wish I were dead, I wish I could see my parents.[14]

The concert was held on the morning of 4 April 1831—it was a matinée in the original sense of the word—and left no more trace than any other charitable event. Chopin drifted on, playing from time to time at the homes of Polish families, amusing them with his carping imitations of Austrian generals. He had not taken to the Austrian people or their language; both lacked the niceties of courtesy which to a well-bred Pole were second nature. He missed Titus. Once he imagined he saw him in the street and followed him only to come face to face with a surprised Viennese. He returned to his piano.

He had been composing; even at its lowest and driest, the mysterious fountain of creativity still spurted forth, turning longing and melancholy into sounds of beauty. Among the compositions written during the sad eight months in Vienna Maurice Brown lists nine mazurkas (Op. 6 and 7), Scherzo No. 1 in B minor (Op. 20), three songs (Op. 74), a Waltz in E flat major (Op. 18) and another in A minor (Op. 34, No. 2), and the rough sketch of the Ballad No. 1 in G minor (Op. 23). He also completed the sixth and last of his orchestral works, the Grand Polonaise in E flat major for Piano and Orchestra (Op. 22) which he had started in Warsaw. He could still find no publisher for his works, but in May he had the first intimation that Vienna, in spite of its neglect of him, was not altogether insensitive to his merit. To his parents he wrote:

Yesterday I went with Kandler [the musicologist] to the Imperial Library. I have been meaning to see this rich collection of ancient musical MSS for some time, but somehow have not had a chance so far. I do not know whether the Bologna library is larger or more systematically arranged; anyhow, imagine my surprise when among the recent acquisitions I noticed a volume in a case bearing the name Chopin. Quite thick and well-bound too. I have never heard of another Chopin, I thought to myself. I knew there was a Champein [1753–1830, French composer of some twenty odd operas], so I thought his name had got distorted or something like that. Kandler took the volume out of the casing, looked, it was my handwriting. Haslinger had presented the MS of my Variations to the Imperial Library. Silly fools, I thought to myself, haven't you got anything better to keep?[15]

The implied compliment was a balsam to his hurt pride. Another pleasant surprise awaited him when among the four hundred music MSS belonging to the collector Aloys Fuchs, he noticed the MS of his own Rondo for Two Pianos in C major (Op. 73). But while a private collector and a national library were quick to appraise the future value of a Chopin MS, theatre managers remained intractable about fee-paying concerts. All he got was another offer to take part in yet another charity performance.

That concert, the last he was to give in Vienna, was held on 11 June at the Kärntnerthor, scene of his long-forgotten triumph. Chopin chose to play his Concerto in E minor, apparently because the score for the one in F minor had been mislaid. As in Warsaw, the Concerto was heard in two sections, the first movement being separated from the second and third by an all-male vocal quartet. The last item on the programme was a ballet danced by Fanny Elsler. There were one or two notices and Kandler, who among other things was also the Vienna correspondent of the Leipzig *Allgemeine musikalische Zeitung*, promised to review the Concerto in his next round-up of musical events in Vienna. He was obviously not smitten with it for when he did, on 21 September, he only said that it was 'a serious composition which gave no cause to revise one's earlier impression of the composer'.[16] Five days after publica-

tion he was carried off by the cholera epidemic; by that time
Chopin had left Vienna never to return.

His departure was eventually brought about by a happy meeting
with a fellow Pole who had completed his studies in Vienna and
was planning to move on. Kumelski, a few years older than his
compatriot and a future biologist of some repute, became for a
while the prop that Chopin so much needed. Ironically, once
Chopin had a mind to leave, every conceivable petty bureau-
cratic obstacle seemed to come his way. The Russian embassy,
whose permission was required to extend his stay abroad, held
on to his passport longer than was strictly necessary; the
Austrian authorities took their time over issuing a health
certificate confirming that the bearer was free from cholera,
without which nobody was allowed to cross into Bavaria; at
some stage his passport mysteriously vanished from the Vienna
police station. To allay suspicions that he might be planning
to join a hard core of exile Poles who were prejudicing France
against Russia, Chopin had been advised to apply to the
Russian embassy for a permit to go to London rather than
Paris; accordingly his passport was stamped with the words
'Passing through Paris on the way to London'. After that the
French embassy could only issue him with a transit visa. To
the end of his life Chopin would say to his Parisian friends
with a twinkle in his eye: 'I am only passing through.'[17]

On 20 July the two young Poles started on their leisurely
journey towards Munich, where Chopin was expecting a
money draft from his father. 'Please economise as much as you
can', Nicholas had written a few weeks earlier. 'My heart
bleeds for not being able to send you more than I do.'[18] While
waiting Chopin made the acquaintance of Munich's leading
musicians and a few weeks later played, without fee or orchestra,
his Concerto in E minor and the Grand Fantasy on Polish Airs
at a matinée arranged by the Munich Philharmonic Society. In
the first week of September, having at long last received the
expected sum of money, he went on to Stuttgart while Kumelski
took himself off to Berlin.

As soon as he was on his own Chopin was beset by dark
thoughts. The news from Poland had been bad for months, the
army had suffered severe defeats and the Russians were

advancing on Warsaw. He could think of nothing but corpses, corpses everywhere. He was also worried on his own account, for his Russian passport, issued nearly a year earlier in Warsaw, was about to expire and not likely to be renewed while he was abroad. He felt uprooted, drifting like a leaf in the wind. While still waiting in a Stuttgart hotel for his connection to Paris, he heard that on 8 September Warsaw had fallen to the Russians. It was the end, the end of Poland, the end of his world. Stunned, deaf to the town clocks striking the small hours of the night in perfect unison, he scribbled in his notebook like one demented:

The enemy is within. They have ravaged our homes, burnt them down. Oh Jan! Oh Willie! He must have died on the ramparts. I can see Marcel a prisoner, Sowinski, that brave man, in the hands of the scoundrels! Oh God, do you exist? You do exist and yet you don't avenge us. Have you not seen enough of the Russian atrocities or are you too a Russian? Poor father, poor kind father, perhaps you are starving, perhaps you have no money to buy bread for mother. My sisters, perhaps in the hands of rampaging Russian soldiers. Paszkiewicz, that cur from Mohilev, occupying the palace of the first monarchs in Europe! The Russians masters of the world! Oh father, are these the rewards of your old age? Poor suffering gentle Mama, did you survive a daughter [Emily] only to see the Russians trample on her bones? Oh Powonski, [the cemetery where Emily was buried] have they respected her grave? They have trampled on it, thousands of corpses are over it, they have burnt down the town. Oh why couldn't I kill at least one Russian! Oh Titus Titus! And what has happened to her? [Constance] Where is she? Poor girl, perhaps seized by a Russian. A Russian is struggling with her, strangling her, murdering, killing. Oh my sweet I am here on my own, come to me, I'll soothe the pain by speaking of the past, the days when there were no Russians about, only one or two Russians courting you and you spurned them because of me, not because of Grabowski [Constance's future husband]. Have you a mother? Is she unkind to you? Mine is so sweet, but perhaps I no longer have a mother. Perhaps a Russian has killed her, murdered her. My stricken sisters will not yield to the soldiers—no—my father desperate, helpless, no one to help him lift Mama up—and here I am —doing nothing, groaning, pouring my grief on the piano, going mad—being of no use. God oh God, let the earth tremble and swallow up this generation, let your wrath fall upon the French for not coming to our aid.[19]

Tradition has it that during those demented night hours in Stuttgart Chopin composed his famous Study in C minor (Op. 10, No. 12) popularly known as the March of the Revolution, although Maurice Brown maintains that 'there is no particle of evidence for this most firmly entrenched legend in the Chopin literature'.[20] Whatever the time and place of composition, the Study, with its tremendous emotional ferocity, was a fit monument to a Poland unvanquished even in defeat, which Chopin was never to see again.

A Pole in Paris

When he arrived in Paris in September 1831 Chopin had few letters of recommendation and hardly any money. Heavy of heart and light of purse he took a room with a view of Montmartre on the top floor—he variously referred to it as fourth or fifth—of a house in boulevard Poissonière and began to look around.

His immediate reaction was one of delight. Brought up as he had been in a close-knit community where fear of public opinion discouraged flagrant violation of social conventions, he was amazed and charmed to discover what degree of freedom a metropolis could confer upon its citizens by virtue of their anonymity. 'Paris is whatever you care to make of it,' he wrote to Titus who had come through the fighting with only a superficial wound. 'In Paris you can enjoy yourself, yawn, laugh, cry, do anything you like. No one takes the slightest notice of you because there are thousands of people around who are doing exactly the same thing, each in his own way.'[1]

He was agog with wonderment at what he saw. Well-groomed gentlemen sported green, red or blue waistcoats not in obedience to trends of fashion but to demonstrate political affiliation; pretty girls accosted passers-by with beguiling smiles; brazen pedlars proclaimed for a sou apiece such literary works as *The Art of Making Lovers and Keeping Them*, *The Secret Love Life of Priests*, and *The Archbishop of Paris and the Duchess of Berry*. There were frequent demonstrations against Louis Philippe who only a year earlier had become King of the French by the Will of the People; popular manifestations of sympathy for defeated Poland; clashes with the police. He was discovering the many contradictory facets of a big city. It did not take him long to make the following observation:

Here you have the greatest splendour and the greatest
filth, the greatest virtue and the greatest vice, at every
street corner you see posters offering cures for ven [ereal]
diseases. There is more shouting, clamour, clatter and mud
than you can possibly imagine. You get swamped in this
paradise, but actually it is rather convenient that nobody
is bothered about the way you live. You can walk about in
rags and still call on the best people. One day you buy a
splendid meal for thirty-two sous at a restaurant with gas
lighting and mirrors in gilt frames; the next you lunch at a
place where they hardly serve enough to feed a sparrow
and charge you three times as much.[2]

A facet of the Parisian scene much to his liking was the
presence of an aristocratic Polish community. He was not
surprised by the size of it; in the generally sympathetic political
climate of France the capital was a natural haven for those
who had had to flee from Poland in the wake of the insurrection.
What did surprise him was the fact that some of the exiles no
longer sought the company of their compatriots. He himself
felt at home only with fellow Poles. 'If I ever manage to look
happy, outwardly at least,' he wrote to Titus, 'it is mostly
when I am amongst my own people, and by that I mean
Polish people.'[3] For their part his compatriots welcomed him
most warmly into their homes and gracious hostesses showed
him off to each other with proprietory admiration. He became
a familiar figure at Count Louis Plater's, Count Albert
Grzymala's, Countess Komar's, Countess Delphina Potocka's.
By the end of a month or so he knew that he wanted to stay
in Paris indefinitely and wondered how to go about obtaining
a residence permit.

One of his few letters of recommendation was from the
Italian-born Dr Malfatti, physician-in-ordinary at the Imperial
Court in Vienna, to his compatriot Ferdinand Paër, master
of music at the court of Louis Philippe. Sixty-year-old Paër,
reputedly unfriendly and crotchety, listened with pleasure to
the young Pole's account of the Warsaw production of his
Agnese, in which a certain Constance Gladkowska had made
her début, and promised to be of service. He was as good as
his word. In December, when told that Chopin was in Paris

on a transit visa and that his Russian passport had expired, he asked a friend at the passport office to help out. The friend passed Paër's request to the appropriate *Préfet*, judiciously adding that M. Chopin was born of a French father and enjoyed the patronage of His Majesty's Master of Music. Back came the note with a marginal scribble in the *Préfet*'s own hand, granting M. Chopin permission to stay in France indefinitely and practise his art, reserving however 'the right of withdrawal'.[4]

Paër also introduced Chopin to Cherubini, then the high priest of Paris musical life. One introduction led to another and in the briefest of time Chopin met such celebrities as Rossini, Meyerbeer, Hummel, Auber and many others. His natural inclination however was to seek out pianists and of all the pianists he had met none impressed him as much as Friedrich Wilhelm Kalkbrenner.

At forty-six Kalkbrenner was acknowledged one of the foremost pianists in Europe. Born in Germany, he lived in various centres of music and in 1824, after nine years in London, settled down permanently in Paris where he played, composed and taught. Contemporary high opinion of him was only matched by his own; he was reputed to be conceited beyond endurance and an insufferable prig. A prolific composer, he was at his best as an interpreter. His technique was impeccable, his tone full, his style elegant if somewhat lacking in emotion. He was much in demand as a teacher, for he had evolved a remarkable new method of developing fingers, wrists and left hand, octave handling and pedal management. His *Méthode pour apprendre le pianoforte à l'aide du guide-mains*, published shortly before Chopin's arrival in Paris, became a standard text-book.

Chopin had no mean opinion of his own technical prowess and in his heart of hearts dismissed most of the pianists he had met as mere show-offs; but when he heard Kalkbrenner he felt he was in the presence of an Olympian. 'I am not fit to tie his shoelaces,'[5] he said with humility. He was conscious of the fact that since his early lessons with old Zywny who was primarily a violinist, he had had no formal piano instruction and felt the need to study with a master. Accordingly he asked Kalkbrenner whether he would accept him as a student and was none deterred when the master, having auditioned him, pronounced that he needed three years' training to become really perfect. He immediately wrote home for advice and funds.

Nicholas was dumbfounded. He could not understand why his son, whose playing had been considered superb in several European centres of music, required a further three-year course of instruction; but being a devoted father he was prepared to dig further into his meagre savings provided he was assured that the sacrifice was really necessary. He took Frederick's letter to Professor Elsner and was indeed reassured when the venerable musician snorted contemptuously and accused Kalkbrenner of all manner of mischief and petty jealousy. When he had recovered his composure Elsner settled down to warn his former pupil against Kalkbrenner's narrow concept of music. 'How can the man decide on the strength of one hearing,' Elsner argued, 'that your musical genius should be limited to piano playing and piano compositions? I believe that when he comes to know you a little better he will change his initial opinion of you.'[6]

Indeed Kalkbrenner, having heard his prospective pupil once again, graciously conceded that perhaps the course need not be as long as he had stipulated and even offered to waive his fee. Chopin saw it as proof, if proof were needed, that the original offer of tuition had not been motivated by a desire to keep him down but by genuine good will. He put his dilemma before his closest colleagues of the time, Hungarian-born Franz Liszt who had been living in Paris since 1823, German-born Ferdinand Hiller who had been appearing in the capital for the past three years, and German-born Felix Mendelssohn who had arrived in December with his reputation preceding him. All three, Chopin knew, had studied at one time or another with some of the most celebrated teachers of the age: Hiller with veteran pianist and composer Hummel, Liszt with Czerny, Paër and Reicha, and Mendelssohn with Zelter. Without being over-impressed with his new friends' technique, he felt that perhaps there was something to be gained from formal tuition. He had a vague notion that to make his way as a composer he should first win recognition as a concert artist and it was disconcerting to hear some critics suggest that while he was unrivalled when playing his own compositions, he was less than perfect when rendering other people's. He

had also taken to heart Kalkbrenner's remark that his performance was uneven; good when he was inspired, not quite so
good when he was not.

To his surprise he found that his young friends took the
same view as old Elsner whom they had never met. Twenty-
year-old Hiller, twenty-year-old Liszt and twenty-two-year-old
Mendelssohn were all appalled at the thought that Chopin,
whose individual style of playing they genuinely admired, should
subject himself to the Kalkbrenner straitjacket. But for once
Chopin knew what he wanted and would not be dissuaded.
He insisted that far from losing his individuality by absorbing
the best of the Kalkbrenner method, he would be gaining in
strength and confidence.

Since most of his Paris letters to his family were destroyed
in 1863 during a Russian punitive action in Warsaw, there
is no knowing what he thought of the classes once he began
attending them. All that is known is that after a very short
while, perhaps a matter of weeks, he gave them up without
in any way antagonizing the illustrious master. They remained
on cordial terms, Chopin dedicating to Kalkbrenner his Concerto
in E minor which was published in 1833 in Paris and Leipzig,
Kalkbrenner acknowledging his own debt to his pupil in his
Variations Brillantes Op. 120 'based on a mazurka by Chopin'
(Op. 7, No. 1). There was no further talk of studying.

Paris in the nineteenth century was the Mecca of Europe,
writes Alfred Cortot, where virtuosos of all nationalities and
grades came to seek their confirmation. This was never truer
than in the 1830s, when Chopin first came to know it. There
was a galaxy of native and resident foreign composers, a
constant flow of first-rate performers and three of the best
orchestras in Europe: that of the Conservatoire, that of the
Académie royale and that of the Théâtre des Italiens under
Rossini.

On the personal level Chopin took to musicians of his own
age: pianists like Liszt, Hiller, Osborne or Mendelssohn, and
Franchomme the cellist. The pianists, every one of them a
foreigner, often dined out together, talked music late into the
night, carrying their animated discussions into the cold dark
streets. Sometimes they assembled at a fashionable *salon* and

illustrated their respective points of view on the piano. On one such occasion, at Countess Plater's, Chopin claimed that only a Pole could do justice to a Polish melody. To prove him wrong Liszt sat down there and then and played a tune which was very much in vogue at the time, a march by Dombrowski entitled *Poland Shall not Perish*. Hiller played it next and finally Chopin. Not only the Platers' guests, who were mostly Poles, but even the two contestants freely conceded that Chopin's rendering was the most poignant.

On a wider musical plane his main interest remained the opera, which in Paris he found to be more sophisticated, imaginative and exhilarating than any he had seen in Berlin, Dresden or Vienna, let alone Warsaw. On 12 December 1831, having re-established his disrupted correspondence with Titus at Poturzyn, he told him of his latest impressions:

> Never before have I heard the *Barber of Seville* so superbly performed as I did last week with Lablache, Rubini and Malibran-Garcia, nor *Otello* with Rubini, Pasta and Lablache, or again *The Italian Girl in Algiers* with Rubini, Lablache and Mme Raimbeaux. In Paris they have everything just right. You cannot imagine what Lablache is like. They say Pasta is not as good as she used to be, but I have never heard anything more sublime. Malibran conquers with her marvellous voice, she dazzles, she is a marvel. Rubini is an excellent tenor, his notes are true, never *falsetto*. Sometimes he lets his ornamental runs go on for hours and he also uses a *tremolo* effect, but he brings the house down. His *mezzo voce* is incomparable. I've also heard Schröder-Devrient though she is not such a rage here as she is in Germany. She sang Desdemona to La Malibran's Otello. Malibran is slight while the German lady is huge, it looked as if Desdemona was strangling Otello. It was an expensive performance, twenty-four francs a seat to see La Malibran with her face blackened and not very good at that. . . .[7]

He had recently attended Meyerbeer's new opera *Robert le diable* and was stunned by both quality and production. To Titus he wrote:

> It is a masterpiece of the modern school in which devils,

forming the huge chorus, sing through speaking trumpets
and spirits arise from the grave, not like Kurpinski's *The
Charlatan*, but in groups of fifty or sixty. On stage there is
a set which towards the end is transformed into the interior
of a church brightly lit up as for Christmas or Easter,
monks and congregation seated, with censers and the like,
and most remarkable of all, with a grand organ whose sound,
from the back of the stage, is stunning and virtually drowns
the orchestra. Meyerbeer has made himself immortal. But
then he had to wait three whole years to have it staged and
they say he had to lay out 20 thousand francs on the cast. . . .
At the Opéra comique they are now showing *La Marquise
de Brinvilliers*, you know, the story of the poison plot during
the time of Louis XIV or XV. Eight composers collaborated
on the music: Cherubini, Paër, Berton, Hérold, Auber,
Batton, Blangini and Carafa. I think it should be impossible
to bring together a finer team.[8]

He himself had no ambition to write an opera or compose
anything on a grand scale. As a student in Warsaw he had
allowed himself to be guided, and goaded, into writing for
piano and orchestra; but he was the first to realize that the
orchestra was not his medium and had little hesitation in aban-
doning it. Liszt later commended him for having had the good
sense to realize his limitations early and confine his creative
genius to the small calibre of the piano. But that evaluation
was written after Chopin's death, while in 1831, on the threshold
of his career, the young composer still had to defend his
apparently narrow scope. When Elsner urged him all the way
from Warsaw to try his hand at an opera, Frederick did not
have the heart to tell him that he did not feel he had it in him.
Instead he went into a long rigmarole about the financial
advantages of composing for a single instrument, which
allowed the fortunate composer to bring his work to the notice
of the public without a crippling outlay of money. His reasoning
went thus:

> To be a great composer one needs to have a tremendous
> amount of experience, and one gains it, as you yourself
> have taught me, not only by hearing other people's work

but by listening very attentively to one's own. Now many talented young students of the Paris Conservatoire have been waiting with their hands in their pockets for a chance to hear their works performed, either operas, symphonies or cantatas, which nobody knows about except Cherubini and Paër, who had seen them on paper. . . . Even Meyerbeer, who has been a celebrated opera writer for ten years, has had to kick his heels in Paris for three whole years, and spend a lot of money, before he managed to have his *Robert le diable* put on, which is now the rage. He had had to wait for the public to grow weary of Auber. That is why I feel that happy is the composer who needs no other interpreter than himself.[9]

Elsner could have pointed out a dozen flaws in his former student's reasoning; as it happened it did not take Chopin long to discover for himself that even when a composer was able to interpret his work single-handed, he was still dependent on a supporting cast to fill a hall. Wherever he turned he encountered fresh difficulties. At first he could not get permission for the opera stars of his choice to sing at his projected concert; then Kalkbrenner, who had volunteered to appear in a piano concerto of his own composition, was taken ill. There were a thousand and one hitches. Conditioned as he was by the speed and ease with which concerts had been arranged for him in Warsaw and on his first visit to Vienna, Chopin could not get used to the long preliminaries that a Paris performance seemed to necessitate. 'It takes at least two months to get up a concert in Paris,'[10] he wrote to the anxious folk at home.

In the event he had to wait five months for his Paris début. It took place on 26 February 1832 at the Salle Pleyel, put at his disposal free of charge through the good offices of Kalkbrenner, who was a partner in the firm. He played the F minor Concerto and the Variations on *La ci darem la mano*, both without orchestra. Supporting items included a Beethoven quintet, an oboe solo, some vocal numbers and a Kalkbrenner circus act entitled Grand Polonaise with Introduction and March for Six Pianos, played by the composer, Chopin, Hiller, Osborne, Stamary and Sowinski.

The Salle Pleyel of the time held only three hundred seats, but even then the hall was not full. What audience there was consisted mainly of Poles who had come to support their compatriot and the gentlemen of the press, who had been given complimentary tickets. Liszt and Mendelssohn, in the front row, led the applause though their lead was hardly necessary. The Polish community applauded for all it was worth and even the galaxy of concert pianists could find no fault with their rival's technique. A week later, on 3 March, Fétis, the founder of the *Revue musicale*, gave his considered opinion:

In Chopin we have a young man who abandons himself to his natural bent and follows no set model. Even if he has not brought about a total transformation of piano music, he has given shape, at least in part, to an abundance of original ideas the like of which are nowhere to be found and which until now have been vainly sought. This is not to say that M. Chopin has the power of a Beethoven or that his music has the great composer's masterful conception. Beethoven wrote music for the piano; Chopin writes music for pianists. His inspiration paves the way for a fundamental change of form which in the future may well exercise a considerable influence on works written for this instrument.[11]

Fétis was appreciably less enthusiastic about Chopin as a concert pianist. Like so many of his predecessors he too missed the mandatory sonority and volume. 'The tone M. Chopin produces from the piano is rather small,' he complained, adding somewhat unexpectedly: 'In that he seems to take after the German school of playing.'[11]

As Chopin had half expected, the concert failed to bring in the cash. 'Even the King hasn't got any money to throw away,' he mourned. 'Most artists are having a lean time, only the English can pay.'[12] He tried to fall back on giving piano lessons, but Paris was full of celebrated pianists who already had a firm stake on the teaching profession. Eking out his allowance with the help of one or two lessons within the Polish community, he described himself afflicted with that widespread ailment known as 'consumption of the purse'.[13]

He had to wait three more months for his next chance to

play in public, by which time he knew better than to baulk at being asked to give his services free. In point of fact he had high hopes of the occasion for the charity concert on 20 May was a splendid affair held at the Conservatoire auditorium and attended by the wealthy and noble. Furthermore, although his own contribution to the evening consisted only of the first movement of the F minor Concerto, he had an orchestra to accompany him and counted on the work making an even greater impact than it did unaccompanied. The opposite was the truth. Fétis, in his subsequent review, remarked that Chopin's orchestration was awkward and reiterated the view that his piano tone was weak. The rider that Chopin was all the same a composer to reckon with fell on deaf ears. No offers for further concerts ensued and no inroads into the music-rooms of the rich were made. After eight months in Paris, in spite of his popularity with fellow-pianists and the discerning few, Chopin felt he had made no headway. Paris looked like becoming a second Vienna. He began toying with the idea of emigrating to America, as many of his compatriots were doing.

Suddenly, unexpectedly, his luck changed and from an impecunious Polish musician he turned into the darling of fashionable Paris. Chance gave him his lucky break.

The Chopin myth has it that on the very day he made up his mind to emigrate he ran into young Prince Valentine Radziwill, with whom he had once or twice attended the Paris opera, and told him of his decision. The meeting, goes the story, took place on a street corner. That same evening the prince introduced his compatriot into the Rothschilds' *salon*, where Chopin played so exquisitely that before he left he had several society ladies clamouring to become his pupils, Mme de Rothschild herself heading the queue.

Whether the timing was indeed as dramatic as legend would have it has never been proved, but the outcome of the introduction was certainly magical. Overnight Chopin became the idol of the French moneyed aristocracy. Requests for piano lessons poured in, his high fee of twenty francs an hour was met without a murmur, he became the most popular teacher on the social circuit. Would-be professionals were also knocking at his door. 'Conservatoire students, pupils of Moscheles,

Herz, Kalkbrenner, all accomplished musicians in their own right, come to me for lessons and place my name next to Field's,' he wrote to his childhood friend Dominic of Szafarnia. 'Today I have five lessons on schedule. But don't run away with the idea that I am making a fortune. All I make, and more, has to go on a cabriolet and white gloves, for without them I would not be considered *bon ton*.'[14]

All the fashionable *salons* were thrown open to him; to Dominic he gave this account of his new station in life:

> I find myself introduced to high society, ambassadors, princes, ministers—I don't know by what miracle for I have done nothing to put myself forward. People say this sort of thing is a must, for this is the society which decrees what good taste is. If you have been heard at the English embassy or the Austrian embassy you are immediately taken to possess higher talent; and you must be a better pianist if you are known to have been patronised by Princess Vauldemont.[14]

Soon *le tout Paris* claimed to have heard of him. His name became a draw and fellow artists were asking him to participate in their own concerts. In December he accepted such a request from Hiller and together with Liszt, another guest artist, they played the *allegro* of Bach's Concerto for Three Pianos. Some time later he and Liszt played during the entr'acte of a theatrical performance in aid of Harriet Smithson, the Irish actress to whom young Hector Berlioz had lost his heart and who was soon to become his wife. The following April Chopin and Liszt—they were inseparable—were the guest artists at a concert given by the Austrian brothers Jacques and Henri Herz; the four of them performed a concerto for eight hands on two pianos, playing in formation being the fashion of the day. Although such guest appearances were proof of his growing popularity, they did not cure him of his phobia of large audiences. For the next year or two the *salons* became his main outlet and were to remain for ever his chosen habitat.

Private recitals at Countess So-and-so's or the British Embassy were not reviewed in the press; but contemporary accounts suggest that on such occasions Chopin's genius shone at its best. The pianist Marmontel, the future teacher of Bizet, d'Indy and Debussy, recollected in his old age how at sixteen, having just won the Conservatoire first prize for piano playing, he first heard the twenty-two-year-old Chopin. Marmontel recalled:

> In 1832 . . . I had the honour of being introduced to Chopin and Liszt at the same musical *soirée* and of playing before these two great masters with all the audacity of youth. It was then I saw, for the first time in my life, the manifestation of their own wonderful talent. Under Chopin's nervous and flexible fingers the most arduous phrases and the most subtle contours were shaded and moulded with exquisite delicacy. His hands, agitated and skilful, formed elegant, expressive, luminous and colourful phrases. He knew how to communicate his feelings which stemmed from his sensitive nature and the ailing and impressionable character of his person; he was a truly sensitive artist.[15]

The 'ailing character' of Chopin's person and its effect on his music was something that a sixteen-year-old student, hearing him for the first time, could have hardly observed; that judgment, written in retrospect, was probably based on further study of Chopin's music and no doubt reflected John Field's harsh dictum against his younger contemporary.

Chopin had not yet heard John Field play his own compositions, although he had heard them performed by others and played some himself. Even in his early Warsaw days people were remarking on the similarity between his own piano compositions and those of the legendary Irishman who since 1802 had been living and performing only in Russia. Warsaw critics wrote that Chopin's music had a touch of Field about it; a Prague musician said the same, and so did the Olympian Kalkbrenner. 'He said I had Field's touch with Cramer's technique,' Chopin wrote home shortly after his arrival in Paris. 'I was delighted.'[16]

To what extent Chopin's early familiarity with Field's style influenced his own is a question which musicologists have not been able to agree upon. He was certainly flattered when he was compared to a well-known composer who, long before him, had had the courage and sensitivity to write mainly for the piano. When news reached Paris that Field was sallying forth from Russia on his one and only European tour, he was looking forward to hearing him. Field's short Paris season began at the end of 1832 and was an occasion for mutual disenchantment. Chopin thought he lacked elegance, subtlety and elementary technique; Field, for his part, coined the phrase which was to dog Chopin for many years: 'His is a sickroom talent,'[17] he said disgustedly. Fashionable Paris however took little notice of what an ageing and coarsening Irishman was saying about their young idol.

The year 1832 was Chopin's *annus mirabilis*. In December his Four Mazurkas (Op. 6) and Five Mazurkas (Op. 7), all composed during the dark days in Vienna, were published in Leipzig; the following summer they appeared in Paris and London. True to his vow never again to allow his work to be published without pay—*bezahl*, you cur—he haggled with his new publishers like a Mazovian Jew over a corn deal and called them all manner of names behind their backs when they failed to pay up promptly. His gratitude and graciousness went to people of another social order. His Four Mazurkas were dedicated to young Countess Pauline Plater, his first Paris pupil and daughter of Count and Countess Plater who were among the first Polish aristocrats to open their homes to him.

With the name and income came the luxuries. The garret with the view of Montmartre was abandoned and a better accommodation taken and relinquished in turn when a large elegant apartment fell vacant at rue de la Chaussée d'Antin. He moved in with a Pleyel and a childhood friend called Alexander Hoffman, son of the Warsaw inventor of the aeolomelodicon. It was exciting, having had to account to his father for his general outgoings, to be suddenly able to lavish freely on anything he fancied, his own equipage, a hired coachman, knick-knacks, masses of flowers, dozens of pairs of white gloves, clothes. With the compulsion characteristic of someone not to the manner born, he groomed himself with extra care, shunning any tendency to flamboyance, ordering his outfits from the best tailors, taking pride in conforming to the strictest standards of *bon ton*. His studied elegance did not fail to impress and his compatriot Orlowski wrote home that soon Paris would be wearing gloves *à la Chopin.*

Success made him think all the more of his family who had always encouraged him in any way they could. He wrote home regularly and at length and waited eagerly for their replies. He heard with pleasure that his twenty-five-year-old sister Louisa was about to marry Joseph Kalasanty Jedrzejewicz, a former pupil of Nicholas Chopin's at the Lyceum and by now a professor of law at the Institute of Agronomy outside Warsaw. The marriage was solemnized at the church of Brochow, where the old Chopins had been married and Frederick baptized, and a reception held at the Skarbek's place at Zelazowa Wola. Frederick's wedding-present to the young couple was a mazurka.

His father kept him informed of any changes in the family fortunes. After the 1831 insurrection the Lyceum closed down and Nicholas applied for a state pension. There was no more teaching of French at the Military Cadet School either. Only the boarders remained, but with the school closed and Nicholas having to provide his own teaching staff, there was not much profit in the business. It was a relief to have one daughter off his hands, another soon to follow suit, and a son who was at long last self-supporting. Diminishing parental obligations could not however change the mentality of a lifetime. When Nicholas heard of his son's new style of life, he chided him for his extravagance and counselled saving for a rainy day. As usual, he wrote in French. *'Il faut garder une poire pour la soif,'*[18] he warned, his peasant heritage dictating his choice of idiom. As for the two French sisters who were still growing pears or vegetables in Lorraine, it was inconceivable that Nicholas should re-establish contact and acquaint them with his son's presence in Paris. It would have shattered Chopin —and quite likely wrecked his career—to have found two strange peasant women installed in his drawing-room with their baskets full of cabbages, eggs and chickens, waiting to tell him that they had come to spend a few weeks with their newly-found nephew. There could be no reversal of a policy of silence based on an acceptance of class distinctions.

Delphina

Chopin's inconclusive courting of Constance Gladkowska in Warsaw had left him at a loose end. It was inevitable that sooner or later he would take the plunge or, more in keeping with his nature, allow himself to be seduced. A first assault was apparently made in Vienna by one Theresa. Who she was nobody knows for certain; a tantalizing reference in a letter to his travelling companion Kumelski did not reveal much. There was a budding romance, possibly an attempted consummation, certainly an unexpected twist which made him, at least for a while, wary of feminine blandishments. When accosted in Paris by ladies of easy virtue who patrolled the pavement outside his garret, he turned his back on them; and when a well-meaning compatriot advised him to forget Theresa—obviously the mis-adventure was no secret—and find consolation somewhere else, he mumbled something about 'forbidden fruit'.[1]

But at twenty-two he was not a young man to be left alone; his delicate and sensuous music, his melancholy air, his obvious need to be comforted, all offered a challenge few women could resist. The virtuous were motherly and solicitous; the not-so-virtuous solicitous and inviting. He was clearly ripe for plucking. Nobody was more aware of that than Countess Delphina Potocka, one of the most seductive and experienced women of Parisian society.

She was born in 1807 at Kurylowice in the district of Podole, and at eighteen was married off to Count Mieczyslas Potocki, seven years her senior and an inveterate rake. The bridegroom was considered a catch, for the Potockis were one of the noblest families in Poland while Count Komar, Delphina's father, was said to have collected his title along with his newly-acquired wealth. In six years Delphina bore her husband five children, all of whom were to die young; rumour had it that the count was spent, possibly an epileptic. The marriage was unhappy from the start, Delphina being high-spirited, avid for pleasure and demanding admiration, her husband selfish, brutal and not in love with his wife. After several years of friction Delphina packed her bags and returned to her parents who took her to Dresden. At her mother's she made the acquaintance of young Frederick Chopin and Titus Woyciechowski, who in November 1830 passed through Dresden en route for Vienna.

The following year the Komars and two other daughters of marriageable age moved to Paris. Delphina had come to an understanding with her husband and set up house in Paris on her own, having demanded and obtained from him an annual allowance of one hundred thousand francs. That same year another estranged wife, one Baroness Dudevant, shortly to become known as George Sand, also arrived in Paris in order to live her own life, although on a more modest allowance of three thousand francs a year.

Once in Paris Delphina put marital frustration behind her and hurled herself into the merry-go-round of amorous adventures. Gossips of the time gave her for lovers the *crème de la crème* of French society, the middle-aged Count Flahaut, the young Duke of Orléans who was Louis Philippe's son and France's Dauphin, the very young Duke of Monfort. The list was inexhaustible, new lovers overlapping with old, vying with each other for her favours, pandering to her every whim, resigned to whatever she was pleased to bestow. She wore her new aura as disdainfully as she did her very select jewellery; once, when a lady friend boasted about her own numerous conquests, Delphina dismissed her condescendingly as a mere débutante. Mickiewicz called her 'the greatest sinner of them all';[2] only her intimates were allowed a glimpse of the emotional disenchantment behind the brazen façade.

At twenty-five she was statuesque, with dazzling white shoulders and generous breasts, dark blue eyes and golden hair worn in ringlets or piled into a bun. She was well read and had an ear for poetry, but above all she was a musician. She played the piano, composed and from time to time entranced a private audience with her beautiful singing. Paris pronounced

her one of its most alluring hostesses and her *salon* became a
meeting place for people of talent and position.

Chopin had not been long in Paris when he was invited to
dine at Countess Komar's and shortly afterwards at her
daughter's. Countess Potocka asked him to give her piano
lessons and he became a regular caller, often outstaying the
hour-long sessions in order to accompany her singing. The
music, the physical proximity, the opulent and gracious atmosphere, all had an intoxicating effect. Delphina had no difficulty
in guessing that the young genius at the keyboard was inexperienced in love and, as the romantic biographer Pourtalès
so felicitously put it, she offered him what he wanted long
before he thought of asking for it. By the end of 1832 they were
lovers.

The news of the affair spread in the Polish community like
wildfire, with intrigued speculations as to its possible duration.
When the excitement died down friends and acquaintances
registered the liaison with equanimity. What more natural
for the worldly Countess Potocka, who had a surfeit of unin-
spiring French aristocrats for lovers, than to take a young Pole
for a change? And what better *éducation sentimentale* for young
Frycek than to be the lover of one of the most sophisticated
women in Paris? Since both parties behaved in public with the
utmost decorum, friends too remained discreet. When the news
of Chopin's attachment reached Warsaw—as it was bound to
do sooner or later—it was so innocuously presented that his
family gained the impression that their Frycek was honourably
courting an eligible young woman. 'I do not yet know the name
of the young person to whom, if I am to go by what your dear
sister Louisa tells me, you are about to unite your destiny,'[3] old
Elsner wrote to Frederick on 13 November 1832, prematurely
rejoicing in the good news.

It is difficult to gauge what Delphina's feelings were for her
young lover; some of her contemporaries claimed that she
never allowed her affairs to go to her heart and remained
hard-headed to the last. In Chopin's case however her love was
of that rare kind which, when all passion had been spent,
would quietly survive as a tender friendship. That was yet to
come. In the meantime Chopin was maturing. Under Delphina's
guidance he was being transformed from a shy adolescent into

an uninhibited lover. Loving and confident of being loved, he shed his reticence, took a young man's pride in his prowess and made up daring code-words to denote the ardour of his desire.

One such code-word in his new vocabulary of love owed its derivation to Robert Schumann. One day in 1831, when Chopin had only just arrived in Paris, his mail included a thick envelope with a German postmark, from which a ten-page letter dropped out; it was a draft copy of a yet unpublished article by young Schumann, whose name Chopin had not yet heard. The writer expressed his admiration for Herr Chopin's *La ci darem* Variations and proceeded to analyse them one by one, bar by bar. In the third variation the German fancied he saw Don Giovanni pressing Zerlina to his heart and 'kissing her on *des-dur'* [E flat]. 'On which part of her anatomy is *des Dur* situated?'[4] Count Plater asked when shown the letter. *Des dur*, or *des durka* as said in the Polish way, became a source of endless jokes among Chopin's intimates.

When he became Delphina's lover he felt it witty to revive the joke and, when writing to her, deposit a kiss on her *des durka*, whichever part of her anatomy she would allow it to be. Later he specified where he wanted it to be, falling back on a pun. There was a well-known artists' café in Warsaw which he used to frequent before he went abroad. Its name, a household one in Polish circles, was *Dziurka*, the Little Hole. What more subtle than to sign off a letter to a mistress with a kiss on *des durka*, rhyming with *dziurka*, indicating the location of a lover's ardent longing? 'I kiss your *des dur* [and sometimes *des durka*] very very hard,'[5] he would write.

Delphina's love for him did not however change her style of life. During the season she went to London where, if gossips of the time are to be credited, she added more names to her list of conquests. In the summer she went to her lakeside villa at Enghien, near Paris, amusing herself in the company of aristocratic holiday makers. Chopin was jealous. He had never realized, as no man would in the first flush of love, that Delphina was not going to give up her other lovers for his sake. He did not understand that she was too restless, too much in need of a challenge, too much of a seductress to be satisfied with one conquest, however precious. There were quarrels, reproaches and fresh assurances of love. Comforted, he would sit down at the piano and improvise a little something as a peace offering, later to be incorporated into whatever he was working on at the time, a study, a waltz, a mazurka.

In between storms he found in Delphina not only an exciting mistress, but a perfect recipient of his musical confidences. He talked to her about music and musicians as easily and chattily as he used to talk to Titus Woyciechowski; even more so, for Delphina was a practising singer who took a professional interest in his views. He talked to her of Bach, the only composer whose music he found so absolutely perfect that he could not conceive it written in any other way; Mozart, whose easy inspiration he admired; Beethoven, whose orchestral genius he revered but whose piano works, he said, betrayed impatience with the exigencies of the instrument.

When she was away he wrote to her. 'Last night I dreamed I heard you sing,' he began one of his undated letters written while she was spending the summer months at her lakeside villa. He was missing her badly—it was probably their first long separation—and he spent the rest of the morning mooning about in his apartment. He was no great hand at putting his feelings on paper; he could write long chatty letters to his family or close Polish friends about things he did or saw, but when it came to expressing emotions his only outlet was music. Even at the age of eight he candidly informed his father, on the occasion of the latter's name-day, that 'it would be easier for me to express my feelings for you in music rather than words'.[6] To Delphina he wrote in the same vein:

You yourself told me I could say it with music rather than in writing. I wish I could write you beautiful and poetic letters because I know you like such things, but as much as I love you, you must not expect such an accomplishment from a mere piano player. Please accept my letters for what they are and when you come back I'll play you my love, my longing and all the other things I am not able to express in writing.[7]

He wove his love into the instruction he continued to give her even when she was away. It was a happy lover who wrote to his pupil on the use of the pedal, an art in which Chopin surpassed most of his contemporaries:

Be careful with the pedal, little Phindela [he was as given to anagrams as ever], it is a rascal, sensitive and noisy at the same time. Treat it politely and tactfully, for as a friend it may be useful, but it is not easy to win its intimacy and love. Like a society lady anxious about her reputation, it won't yield just like that. But when it does yield it can perform miracles, like an experienced mistress.[8]

Sometimes Delphina wrote back; he chided her for writing in French. 'We may know other languages,' he told her severely, 'but why should the two of us speak or write to each other in a foreign tongue?'[9] French never ceased to be a 'foreign tongue' for him, even when he had been living in France for many years. His spoken French was near-perfect, with only a trace of a Polish accent; but after the conscious effort of babbling French all day, he longed for the fluency and comfort of his mother tongue. As for his written French, he insisted that he could not write it without mistakes, kept a dictionary handy for checking his spelling, or used only such words he thought he could spell without checking. Delphina must have taken his chiding to heart for her only extant letter to him, written some fifteen years later, was in Polish.

During her absences from Paris he channelled his pent-up longing into composition. He was discovering in himself what was to become a fundamental element in his creative process. His head would be brimming over with musical ideas but as soon as he sat down at the piano—he always composed at the piano—he would be beset by doubts. He would try this phrase and that, be dissatisfied with both, try again, think out an alternative solution, go back to his original phrase; all would seem good, all would seem unsatisfactory. 'Creating a work of art is like giving birth to a child,' he told Delphina, who had had five. 'Some of you women die in childbirth, others spit a baby out like a pip. As for me, I have labour pains. I feel I have in my head a beautiful idea all ready to come out, but when I write it down I realise I have left gaps and it is not what I had in mind. On paper everything looks different and it drives me to despair.'[10]

He was working on his Studies, sometimes putting them aside to work on a mazurka or a ballad, which seemed to come to him more easily, then returning to the grind. It was probably in the summer of 1833 that he wrote to Delphina:

> I spend nights on end with my beloved singing women—aren't my Studies like women? You won't be jealous of them, will you? Well no, the Studies are more like daughters, and the two I like best are the one in A minor and the one in C minor, for parents usually love best those born to them last. If I had a child by you I would wish it to become a musician, with two such parents as us he is bound to have a good ear.[11]

He was so engrossed in the Studies he could hardly think of anything else. He took no notice when addressed by friends, did not look where he was going, barely heard Paris coach drivers hurl obscenities after him for his distracted way of crossing roads. Once the last Study of the current series was finished to his satisfaction, he took a look at himself in the mirror and was dismayed at what he saw. His nose loomed larger than ever in an emaciated face, his eyes were deeply sunk in their sockets. For a moment he was tormented by the fear that Delphina would no longer find him attractive and hurried to inform her that he too had admirers and should not be left too long to his own devices. 'In the *salons* people tell me how handsome and interesting I look,' he wrote in the hope of awakening her jealousy. 'Women buzz round me like flies round a pot of honey, you know I'm not exaggerating and I only wish you were as faithful to me as I am to you, although sometimes I am subjected to the most cruel temptations.'[12]

Delphina had asked to be sent a copy of the finished Studies so that she could try them out at the villa. He told her it would be better if they tried them out together on her return to Paris. He had already shown some to Liszt and was overwhelmed by his performance of them. 'I wish I could steal from him his manner of playing my Studies,'[13] he wrote to his fellow pianist Ferdinand Hiller on 20 June 1833.

Looking back at the year's crop, which included not only several Studies from his Op. 25 but also the Nocturne in G minor (Op. 15, No. 3), the Mazurka in C minor and the first sketches for some of his preludes, he could not but admit to himself that while Delphina was away he was working better. There was no temptation to drop everything and rush to be with her, no claims made on his virility. He decided that enforced abstinence had a beneficial effect on him. To Delphina he expounded his thoughts on the subject at great length, expressing himself in those short inelegant sentences, somewhat repetitive, somewhat incoherent, which were characteristic of his Polish correspondence:

[Summer 1833?]

My beloved Phindela, my one and only,

Once again I am going to bore you with matters of inspiration and musical creativity, but you will soon see that it concerns you closely. I have been thinking a great deal about inspiration and creativity and I have very slowly made an important discovery. Inspiration and ideas only come to me when I have not had a woman for a long time. When I spend myself dry inspiration shuns me and not one new musical idea comes into my head. Think how strange and marvellous it is, that energy which is spent on fertilising a woman, on creating life inside her, is the same which creates a work of art. It is the same precious life-giving fluid, and the male squanders it away for the sake of a moment's pleasure.

The same force operates and guides scientific works, and scientists who devote themselves to research and scientific discovery keep away from women. The prescription seems simple enough. A creative person must keep women out of his life, the energy collecting in his system will not go from his cock and balls into the woman's womb but into his brain in the form of inspiration and will perhaps give birth to a great work of art. Think of it, the temptation which drives us men into a woman's arms can be transformed into inspiration! But this only holds for those who have talent, for if a mere nobody decides to do without women he will only go mad with frustration and still won't be able to produce a work of art before God or man.

Longing for a woman, desiring her passionately, there's a way towards creativity. When I long for you musical ideas come rushing into my head. Love and unrequited passion excite us men when we see the object of our dreams, they burn us alive, they can also give us inspiration. Norwid is a good example.[14] I don't know about Mozart, I think perhaps his wife was for him like his daily bread, his love and passion for her must have cooled off so he was able to create many works. I have never heard talk of mistresses in Mozart's life.

Think of it, my sweetest Phindela, how much of that precious fluid and energy I have wasted on you, ramming you to no purpose, since I have not given you a baby and God only knows how many of my finest inspirations and musical ideas have been lost inside you. *Operam et oleum perdidi.* Ballads, polonaises, even a whole concerto may have been lost forever up your *des durka,* I can't tell how many. I have been so deeply engulfed in my love for you I have hardly created anything, everything creative went straight from my cock into your *des durka*, you are now carrying my music in your womb. It's a crazy idea, but you must admit it's striking. Think how many works of art I have thus sacrificed, perhaps the best. Time runs out, life is short and a lost moment will never come back. The saints are right when they say that woman is the gate of hell. No no, I take back this last sentence, I disclaim it. I won't cross it out because I know you won't leave me alone until you worm out of me what I have crossed out and I haven't got the time to start all over again. You are for me the gate of heaven, for you I will give up fame, work, everything.

> Loving you is my favourite occupation
> Bed is better than inspiration
> I long for your lovely tits
> So says your faithful Fritz

I know you like my cock and balls and after this dissertation you ought to respect them all the more because they are not only a source of pleasure but the source of my artistic achievement. Supreme pleasure, creation of life, science, art —everything stems from them, the all powerful, so long may they live.

Oh Phindela, my own little Phindela, how I long to be with you. I am trembling and shivering, it's as if ants are

Delphina Potocka (1807–1877), miniature by M. M. Daffinger

Marie Wodzinska (1819–1896) in Marienbad, 1836. Self-portrait

crawling all over me from my brain down to my cock. When the *diligence* will at long last bring you back I'll cling so hard that for a whole week you won't be able to get me out of you. Bother all inspiration, ideas and works of art.

I have invented a new musical term instead of *des durka*. From now on we shall call it a rest. Let me explain. In music a rest is a hole in a melody, so a hole is a musical term, most suitable to describe *des durka*. Hoffman [Chopin's flat mate until early 1834] has just come in and put an end to my epistolary inspiration, soon my pupils will arrive, so I had better stop and try to catch today's post. I kiss you all over your dear little body and inside.

> Your faithful Frycek, your most talented pupil who has mastered the art of love.

P.S.
Yesterday I frittered my time away and did not post the letter, so here are a few more lines. I have just finished a new prelude in which I have immortalised our eleventh frolic. There are eleven notes to indicate our favourite game. When I play it to you I shall explain so that you may appreciate the subtlety of it, I am sure the music will become our favourite, as the game has.

P.S.
Yesterday I was made very angry on your account. Can you imagine it, evil tongues say you cannot have a baby because you have had too many lovers, grass won't grow on a well-trodden path and more such nonsense. I nearly burst into tears when I heard them. Forgive me for telling you all this. My own beloved, when you come back please stop refusing to become pregnant, let me give you a baby and silence those liars. Society ladies who have natural children are not ashamed of them. Natural children are often very gifted, it is well known. I think and dream that our child will become a great, a very great musician and his work will surpass ours. You'll see. I must finish now, finish and run for the post. Answer quickly, your letters are my only joy and pleasure.

> F.F.C.[15]

Paris in August was deserted. After his hard summer's work on the Studies Chopin was exhausted and his cough, that creeping companion which from now on would never leave him, was getting worse. He was pleased when the cellist Franchomme invited him to go down with him to his family near Tours. Liszt winked and spread the word round that Chopin was having a good time turning the head of some gaping provincial beauty. Indeed the liaison with Delphina had in no way diminished Chopin's instinctive urge to cast a spell over a pretty audience and his compatriot Orlowski admiringly described him as 'turning the head of every woman he meets and making every husband jealous'.[16] True to pattern, the womenfolk of the Franchomme household fell under the spell but, more sensibly than their Parisian rivals, showed their adoration by trying to fatten him up.

By the end of a week he had put on weight and was playing a local country game with his hosts. A bagful of flour was carefully poured on a plate in the shape of a pyramid, on top of which a thin wedding ring was placed. Each player had a go at lifting the ring off the pyramid with the tip of his nose. Franchomme, with his short thick snout, always had his face covered with flour; Chopin, his beak-like conk for once being put to good use, often succeeded in removing the ring without making the pyramid collapse. After several riotous rounds, when everybody's face was white with flour, cellist and pianist would make music together.

The autumn saw Chopin back in Paris busy with lessons, calls, musical gatherings and compositions. His works—new as well as those early ones he had brought over from Poland— were being published simultaneously by Breitkopf and Härtel in Leipzig, Maurice Schlesinger in Paris and Wessel in London. Critics were no longer discovering him; they were discussing him. Every new publication was reviewed, though not all reviews were favourable. A German called Rellstab was particularly acid, writing in his own magazine *Iris* that Chopin was composing only for effect and that his piano pieces were finger-twisters without merit. Some Parisian reviewers also had their reservations. Chopin was discovering, and not for the first time, that critics were asses.

'The critic', he wrote to Delphina, 'cannot look at a work in the same way its creator does. He tries to see in it things never intended by the artist. But of course a critic has to say such things or else he won't have anything to write about.'[17] On another occasion he uttered what must surely be the *cri de coeur* of all artists since art criticism first began. 'A critic of scientific works needs a well-equipped and well-ordered mind, that's enough,' he wrote. 'But a critic who reviews works of art should have not only a good head on his shoulders but a warm heart, feeling and sensitivity.'[18]

Heart was a key-word in his musical vocabulary. He, who in his social intercourse was reserved and careful not to reveal his feelings, cried unashamedly after he had seen Bellini's *Norma* which had its first Paris performance in 1834. 'I can only admire works which move me deeply and make me shed tears,' he explained to Delphina. 'I cannot go into raptures over a piece of music which leaves me cheerful. Only a work of art which has been distilled through my tears will remain forever in my heart, and what has not been through my tears will not. This is how it has been with me ever since I was a child.'[19]

In the spring of that year he and Hiller went together to the Lower Rhine Music Festival at Aachen, meeting Mendelssohn who was then the conductor of the Düsseldorf Orchestra. The three of them spent their time listening to concerts and playing their own works to one another. Mendelssohn, who had not heard Chopin since their early Paris days, was more impressed than ever and compared him with Paganini for versatility and mastery of instrument. 'Unfortunately,' he added in a letter to his family, 'both Hiller and Chopin affect that Parisian mania for melancholy. They overdo the feeling, and as a result both rhythm and shape are affected.'[20]

At the end of the year Chopin took part in two public concerts. The first, with a full orchestra, consisted mainly of works by Berlioz conducted by Berlioz, Chopin playing only the Andante from the F minor Concerto. The juxtaposition with the rich orchestration of such works as *Harold in Italy* was hardly in his favour. In the second concert he appeared as a pianist, playing with Liszt a work for four hands by Moscheles, then Liszt's improvisation for four hands on a theme by Mendelssohn. That part of the programme must have been particularly

irksome; if there was one thing Chopin thoroughly disliked
about Liszt, it was his aspiration to become a composer instead
of restricting himself to performing other people's works. He
poured out his heart to Delphina:

> A strange fellow Liszt. He has not got in his head one
> worthwhile idea before God or man, he covets other people's
> ideas as a cat covets cream. Instead of using a telescope he
> gets hold of a piece of enema tube and peers through it at
> the stars. Then he selects one, pulls it down, dresses it up
> in ill-fitting clothes, with ribbons and tinsel, claps an enor-
> mous wig over it and launches this scarecrow into the world.
> Some people admire this sort of thing, but I think that even
> if it is cleverly done it hasn't got a trace of talent.[21]

In the years 1833–35 Liszt had not yet embarked on those
works which were to establish his reputation as a composer.
Chopin thought of him only as another of those brilliant
pianists like Thalberg or Kalkbrenner who aspired to a composer's laurels and who, by improvising on somebody else's
themes, claimed the right to be called original. The practice of
embroidering on other people's themes was common enough;
he himself had followed it time and again, borrowing from
Mozart for his *La ci darem* Variations, from Meyerbeer's
Robert le diable for his Grand Duo in E major for piano and cello,
and more besides. But when it came to other people borrowing
his own themes he felt differently. Once, in Warsaw, he had
nearly fallen out with his fellow-student Orlowski for having
published a waltz based on 'a theme by Chopin'; in his early
Paris days he allowed Kalkbrenner to use one of his themes
because he was a new boy and needed to win friends; but once
he had come into his own he made no more exceptions. Liszt
became noticeably cool when Chopin refused him permission
to improvise on a theme of his. One evening, at Count Perthuis',
they were joined by Fétis. 'Fétis', Chopin informed Delphina,
'praised my playing and said that between my *piano* and
pianissimo there were a hundred graded shades. Liszt only
gave us a wry smile.'[22]

There were other points of antipathy. Chopin was first
and last a musician, with no intellectual pretensions and no

manifest interest in any other form of art. Liszt was a thinker, a searcher for moral truth, a delver into social questions. Chopin resented Liszt's way of monopolizing the conversation and above all Liszt's insistence on being creative. To Delphina he wrote with increasing venom:

> When I think of Liszt as a creative artist I imagine him heavily made up, raising himself on stilts, blowing hard into the trumpets of Jericho. *Fortissimo* and *prestissimo.* Or I see him holding forth on art, the art of creating, how to be creative. Yet when it comes to creative imagination he is an ass. He knows everything best. He bores everybody stiff with his endless talk of literature, religion, philosophy, astronomy. I sneak out of any *salon* as soon as he gets going. He wants to reach the summit of Parnassus on somebody else's Pegasus. *Entre nous,* he is an excellent bookbinder who puts other people's ideas between his own covers. You know what he does? He applies an enema to himself and then, with much effort and groaning he relieves himself of a composition.[23]

Whatever his private thoughts, he kept a perfectly amicable façade. In late 1833, when the Paris edition of his Study in E flat major (Op. 10, No. 11) was published, it carried the dedication 'To his friend J. [*sic*] Liszt'.[24] They continued to play at the same *soirées,* called on each other and professed admiration for each other's virtuosity. An acid remark about Liszt's pianistic acrobatics was only for the ears of Chopin's intimates.

The Paris ambience suited Chopin. He no more thought of going on to Italy than of returning to Warsaw, however much he missed his homeland. He felt at home; and he was very much in love. To Delphina, again on one of her jaunts, he wrote in the romantic vein of the day: 'I wish I could die listening to your singing'.[25] Fifteen years later, when called to his deathbed, a still attractive Countess Potocka fought back her tears and complied with his wish.

The rise and fall
of a matrimonial project

In April 1835 Chopin gave two public concerts which were to set the seal on his phobia of public concerts and keep him away from the concert hall, with few exceptions, for the next six years.

The first was held on the 5th at the Théâtre des Italiens, with the Conservatoire Orchestra under its resident conductor Habeneck. It was a charity performance in aid of Polish refugees and the programme was arranged with an eye to box office appeal rather than musical homogeny. Opera stars sang popular arias, a flautist displayed his virtuosity, Chopin and Liszt played a sparkling work for two pianos. Into that undemanding framework was fitted the first Paris performance of the Piano Concerto in E minor.

Habeneck conducted with his usual skill and both orchestra and pianist responded with their customary brilliance. Alas when the last chord died down it became obvious that the delicate music and the pianist's light touch had failed to impress the far corners of the auditorium. There was a polite round of applause and a few cheers, but no real enthusiasm. Even the *Gazette musicale*, which had a vested interest in Chopin's Paris publishers, was unusually restrained in its praise. It merely remarked that while piano concertos sometimes tended to be monotonous, Chopin's was free of that fault. For a sensitive, and by now a celebrated artist, both experience and faint praise were humiliating.

Later that month he appeared again with the Conservatoire Orchestra at the invitation of the distinguished *Société des concerts* whose patronage he had in vain sought when he first arrived in Paris. However hurt he was at the mixed reception of his earlier appearance with that orchestra, he could hardly back out of an arrangement which had been made long before. He decided to play the work which was later published as Grand Polonaise in E flat major for piano and orchestra (Op. 22) with its Andante Spianato for piano solo. Again Habeneck conducted.

It is pleasing to record that the concert on 26 April was a success. The Conservatoire auditorium, more intimate than the Théâtre des Italiens and with better acoustics, was kinder to the delicate music. The audience was enraptured, the press was appreciative. Characteristically, Chopin decided it was an opportune moment to turn his back on public performances. Had he been a novice he might well have felt honour-bound to fight more battles, as he had done after his first public concert in Vienna on 11 August 1829; but in 1835 he felt sufficiently sure of himself to step aside and follow a course more congenial to his nature: 'I am not cut out to play in public,' he told Liszt quite frankly. 'Crowds intimidate me, their breath stifles me, their stares petrify me, their strange faces throw me into confusion. With you it is different. When you cannot win them, you stun them.'[1]

He was retiring from the concert platform at the very moment when those crowds whom he could not abide were clamouring for him to go on. Nobody suspected the hurt and bitterness which had led to his withdrawal; and his consistent refusal to appear in public was interpreted by and large as sheer selfishness. 'Under his apparent air of contentment', Liszt wrote with hindsight, 'Chopin concealed the wound to his legitimate pride with such good grace that nobody ever sensed it.'[2] Chopin already knew, ahead of his contemporaries, that his was an intimate form of art. He had considered and shunned operas, choral works, complex instrumentation, anything that meant vastness of scope and sound, turning his inspiration to a percussion instrument which under his unique genius yielded the most captivating sounds. Recitals as such were still unknown; he chose the nearest contemporary equivalent and for the next few years reserved the manifestation of his talent for the chosen few, playing his new compositions only in the intimate setting of the elegant Paris *salons*. Some of his contemporaries said that he was a snob who would not play unless he had a countess or two close by; he probably was, but his preference for a drawing-room recital was guided, at least in part, by the knowledge that it created the right *ambiance* for his kind of music.

Once the April concerts were over Chopin's thoughts turned to a project which had been much on his mind. It was nearly five years since he had left home and he longed to see the father he loved and respected, the mother he idolized, the sisters he was attached to. A return visit to Warsaw had been considered and rejected. For one thing he did not wish to renew the hated 'Muscovite' passport without which he could not return to Poland; for another he feared that once back in Warsaw he would be dependent on the whims of a petty Russian official every time he wanted to go abroad. His family could of course visit him in Paris; many Poles were granted exit permits for limited periods and those who reached Paris always made a point of calling on Chopin whose hospitality towards visiting compatriots was becoming proverbial. But Nicholas, even after a lapse of forty-seven years, was not going to risk a return visit to France. Frederick never questioned his father's disinclination to re-visit his country of origin and Isabel came up with the alternative suggestion of a family reunion half-way between Warsaw and Paris. Nicholas turned it over in his mind and circumspectly informed his son that his health was not what it used to be and that he had been ordered to go to Carlsbad to take the waters. He indicated that if travel permits were granted, he and Justina would get there some time in the summer. While waiting for further news, Chopin learnt that Count Thun, whose sons and daughters had been having lessons with him, was also going to Carlsbad and tentatively arranged to meet him there.

The spring had long turned into summer without any firm date coming from Warsaw. The seasonal exodus from Paris had started and the capital was losing its counts and countesses to fashionable resorts. That summer there was no staying behind in a sultry apartment to work on new 'singing women'; Chopin rented a charming villa at Enghien, right by the lake, and joined in the ritual of taking the waters.

Or perhaps it was just a convenient excuse to be near Delphina who was already at her lakeside villa. There were walks on the promenade, drives to nearby St Gratien to visit his new admirer the Marquis de Custine, meals out at select restaurants. Above all there was love, unclouded, uninhibited and unobtrusive. When a long time later Chopin was showing a newly-arrived compatriot round Enghien, he pointed out the villa by the lake and said with a glow that his stay there had been the happiest in his life.

He was still at Enghien when word reached him that his parents had left Warsaw and were on their way to Carlsbad. He dashed back to Paris, had a French passport issued on 1 August 1835—his French parentage standing him in good stead—and jumped into the first mail coach. He travelled for nine days without a break, reaching Carlsbad in mid-August. Count Thun and one of his sons were already there, as well as some Polish friends who had been forewarned of his arrival. He registered at the first available hotel and together with his friends went to check the official Visitors List to see if his parents had arrived. Their name was not on it. Exhausted, he went to bed.

All his life Chopin was blessed with friends who would put themselves out for him and do their utmost to give him what he wanted without waiting to be asked. One of his Polish friends, having left him to his bed, continued the search and walked from one hotel to another asking whether Herr Chopin from Warsaw was by any chance staying there. It was already four o'clock in the morning when he put the question to the porter of the Golden Rose, one of the most fashionable hotels in town, right opposite the pumproom. The porter replied that there was a Herr Chopin in the hotel, together with his *gnädige Frau* and a manservant. Up ran the friend, knocked hard at Nicholas' door and woke him up with the news that his son was only a stone's throw away. With Justina's help Nicholas got dressed as quickly as possible, not omitting hat and stick, followed the good friend to Frederick's hotel and woke him up in turn. When the transports were over Frederick moved to the Golden Rose to be near his parents. Later the same day he wrote to his sisters in Warsaw:

Carlsbad, 16 August 1835

Dear children,

This is the first letter written by Papa and me. I cannot begin to tell you how happy we are. We kiss and kiss, what better? What a pity we are not all of us here. The baby [the grandparents had brought a picture of Louisa's baby boy] is adorable. God has been kind to us. I'm writing without order, better not think of anything today and just enjoy the happiness which has been granted to us. What we have now is something unique. The parents haven't changed, they are still the same, aged a little, that's all. We take walks and offer our arms to little Mama, we speak of you, we imitate the little nephew when he throws a tantrum, we keep telling one another how many times we had been thinking of one another. We take the waters together, eat together, spoil one another, tease one another. *Je suis au comble de mon bonheur* [*sic*]. The same old habits, the same ways I have been brought up on, the same hand I haven't kissed for such a long time. . . . A dream has come true, oh what bliss what bliss.[3]

The next three weeks were idyllic. Frederick had long forgotten his boyhood mockery of the ways of the fashionable set at a watering place and threw himself whole-heartedly into the daily routine. Morning promenades, bows to the left, bows to the right, offering his arm to Mama, introducing his parents to his Paris friends. Count Thun had taken an elegant apartment and had a piano moved in for his son to practise on during the holiday; Chopin was a frequent visitor, played and improvised. A fourth week was spent at Teplice and then the entire party, Chopins and Thuns, went on to the Thun castle at Tetschen, conveniently situated on the return route to Poland. After an overnight stop Nicholas and Justina bade farewell to their son and continued their journey to Warsaw. They were never to meet again.

At the insistence of the Thuns Chopin stayed on for a few more days. The eldest of the daughters later wrote in her diary: 'On the first day after his parents' departure for Warsaw it was impossible to come near him, he was so dejected. The following day he recovered and after that we could not have enough of listening to his music.'[4]

He recovered so well that he became the life and soul of the house party, plunging them into ecstasies with his improvisations or making them laugh to tears with his imitations of an Englishman speaking French. The younger Thun girl, Josephine or Jusa, was particularly taken with him. Chopin could never resist a pretty musician and before he left he dedicated to her a waltz he had composed during the holiday, copying it neatly into the album she kept jointly with her sister and dating it Tetschen, 15 September 1835. It was his Waltz in A flat major, later published as Op. 34, No. 1.

After five days he and one of the young counts left for Dresden where they were hoping to hear some good music. They had not been in town more than a day when on a street corner Chopin ran into an old Warsaw schoolfriend—he was always running into the right person at the right moment on a street corner—and fell into his arms. When they recovered from the pleasant surprise Felix Wodzinski took him to greet the rest of the family who were spending that year in Dresden.

Frederick's friendship with the Wodzinski boys dated back to the early 1820s, when they had boarded with the Chopins. When Countess Wodzinski came up from the country to visit her sons she used to bring her two lively little daughters Marie and Josepha with her and tell them to play quietly in the drawing-room. Far from being quiet, they would get the eleven-year-old Frederick to play them dances and gallops, romp about the house or demand a game of hide-and-seek. There was a happy nursery room atmosphere about the visits. When some time later the Wodzinskis set up house in Warsaw and no longer needed to board their sons out, the friendship with the boys continued. Chopin would call on them in his school uniform, indulge the little sisters with a game of hide-and-seek and sometimes show the eldest, Marie, how to run her fingers on the keyboard.

In 1831 the Wodzinskis left Poland and tried to settle down in Geneva. Marie was brought up by a string of governesses and given the education considered fit for a well-born young lady. She spoke French, German and Italian, was well-versed in contemporary Polish writing, played the piano and sketched. She even began to compose and her mother, like all fond mothers, would not rest until she had an expert opinion on her daughter's talent. She bethought herself of 'kind M. Frederick'[5] who had become such a celebrity in Paris and in 1834 sent him her fifteen-year-old daughter's Variations with a request to give his honest opinion of them. For a long time Chopin did not answer the countess's letter; then, suddenly remembering his good manners, he wrote to apologize for his apparent neglect, congratulated the family on Marie's composition and enclosed a copy of his newly-published Waltz in E flat major (Op. 18) with the courteous inscription: 'To Mlle Marie with respect from her former teacher'.[6] In his letter he charmingly referred to her as his 'esteemed colleague'.[7] The family were delighted.

Although there was no further communication after that, Chopin must have heard from Polish friends in Paris that the Wodzinskis had given up their Geneva residence and moved to Dresden; had he not run into Felix by accident he would have no doubt looked them up himself. Once he had paid his respects to the count and countess they threw their house open to him. He spent most of his time with them, had his regular place at the dinner table and in the evenings entertained them with his improvisations or with his hilarious imitations of Kalkbrenner and Liszt at the keyboard. He became like a member of the family; the countess declared he was like a fourth son to her and her youngest daughter Theresa clung to him with the touching confidence of a child and exercised a little sister's prerogative to be made a fuss of.

From Chopin's point of view the chief attraction of the family was Marie. The nine-year-old girl he remembered from Warsaw had grown into an accomplished young lady of sixteen. Her dark hair, olive complexion and flashing eyes—there was some Italian ancestry—enticingly contrasted with the demure manners of a well-brought-up Polish gentlewoman. Chopin was nothing if not impressionable; Jusa Thun of Tetschen castle went right out of his mind and Marie sparked off a new romantic fancy. True to pattern he presented her with a waltz he had just composed, dating it 24 September 1835 and inscribing it simply: 'For Mlle Marie'.[8] It was the Waltz in A flat major, posthumously published as Op. 69, No. 1 and entitled the Farewell Waltz.

After a week's stay he pushed off to Leipzig where he had arranged to see Mendelssohn. When the two of them had had their fill of playing their latest compositions to each other, Mendelssohn took his friend to the house of Friedrich Wieck whose fifteen-year-old daughter Clara was already an acknowledged concert pianist. At the Wiecks' Chopin had his first meeting with young Robert Schumann.

Schumann's name, a household joke apart, was familiar to Chopin not so much because of his compositions but because of his consistent championing of his own works in Germany. After his article in praise of *La ci darem* Variations which was published on 7 December 1831 in the *Allgemeine musikalische Zeitung* and included the famous words 'Hats off gentlemen, a genius', Schumann became the editor-proprietor of the *Neue Leipziger Zeitschrift für Musik* and went on lavishing praise on Chopin's growing output. Far from being pleased with the flattering comments, Chopin complained that they made him feel like someone who had been fed a large pot of honey. 'I dread Schumann's reviews as a Jew does a cross,' he once wrote to Delphina. 'He exaggerates so much he turns me to ridicule. I know he cannot change so just pray, my darling, that he leaves well alone. I nearly prefer Rellstab to him.'[9]

The meeting however was satisfactory. Clara played two of Chopin's Studies and elicited the rare praise that for a woman pianist she was his best interpreter yet. He too gave a sample of his art. Schumann remained unrepentently adoring. 'Chopin's playing, like his work, is unique,'[10] he informed the *Neue Leipziger Zeitschrift* subscribers, all five hundred of them.

Once back in Paris Chopin was engulfed in his usual round of activities. He just about remembered his promise to send Marie Wodzinska a copy of his song 'The Wish', which he wrote at the time of his yearning for Constance Gladkowska and which had since become so popular that it was sometimes taken for a Polish folk song. He had no time for letter-writing, but when Mme Wodzinska asked him to keep an eye on her irresponsible young son Anthony who was coming up to Paris, he obliged as a matter of course. He became Anthony's guardian, guide-about-town and banker; and when one evening, at his own place, he saw the young man writing a letter to his family in Dresden, he called to him: 'Don't forget to tell them that I love them terribly, I really do.'[11] That was all. The Dresden interlude was becoming a memory, another pleasant one in a summer that had been full of happy reunions.

He was still in love with Delphina and as jealous as ever of potential rivals. He, who could not see a pretty woman without becoming instinctively gallant, could not bear the thought of Delphina encouraging other men. It upset him to hear of her giving music lessons to some young man of their acquaintance and he was consumed with jealousy when he imagined the privacy of the sessions and the ensuing developments. 'For him it is only an excuse to be with you,' he wrote angrily, 'and the lessons would become an amorous adventure. In any case he has no talent for music and is not worth bothering about. Don't take me for a fool, I can see only too clearly what's going on, I am certain these lessons are only an excuse for an amorous adventure. If you want to break up with me say so openly and don't talk to me about so-called music lessons.'[12]

When the break-up did take place, in the summer of 1836, it was due to an entirely different cause and was effected without bitterness, leaving the way open for a renewal of friendship in years to come.

For some time past Count Potocki, Delphina's husband, had been asking her to come back to him and turn over a new leaf. Underneath her social independence Delphina believed in the institution of marriage and she had to admit to herself that her various emotional attachments had not brought her the longed-for happiness. By the standards of the day she was no longer young—she was nearing thirty—and she appreciated the advantages of stability and respectability. Having turned her husband's proposition over in her mind she decided to give it a try.

While she was putting her Paris house up for sale and getting ready for her departure, she and Chopin entered upon the final stage of their relationship. He, whose view of married life was based on his parents' happy example, was understanding and resigned; she was all tenderness and solicitude. She was moved when he dedicated to her, perhaps by way of a farewell present, his Piano Concerto in F minor which was published in

Leipzig in the spring and was due out in Paris and London in the autumn. In June they went to Enghien for the last time. In August Delphina left for Poland.

Even before her departure Chopin had been taking stock. He was twenty-six, he had sown his wild oats, he was ready to settle down. Delphina herself may have suggested that the time had come for him to get married; she was genuinely fond of him and, since she was rejoining her husband, wished to see him well taken care of. There was no question in Chopin's mind but that any future wife of his would have to be Polish, and of all the Polish girls he had met during his years of exile none seemed more desirable than Marie Wodzinska. His mind was made up. He looked up Anthony Wodzinski and learnt from him that the count had returned to Poland to supervise the reconstruction of the family mansion near Torun, but the ladies were still in Dresden and about to go to Marienbad to take the waters. In the second half of July, having bid his farewell to Delphina, Chopin travelled non-stop to Marienbad and put up at the White Swan where he knew the Wodzinskis were staying. On the registration form he described himself as a landowner from Paris, possibly so as not to look too lowly among the titled patrons of the hotel.

The Wodzinskis' surprise turned to alarm when they saw the state he was in. He was coughing badly, exhausted from the journey, too weak to get about. The weather that August was not favourable to his condition; dry and warm by day, chilly in the evenings, frosty in the mornings. A local doctor ordered complete rest and Marie constituted herself bodyguard and secretary, turning callers away and refusing in his name all requests to play even 'a single mazurka'.[13] She took advantage of his immobility to sketch him sitting upright in a red plush chair.

Under the joint ministrations of doctor and bodyguard he recovered sufficiently to join the promenade crowds but not enough to bring up the reason for his unexpected presence at Marienbad. After four weeks the family returned to Dresden; his attentions to Marie not having passed unnoticed, Mme Wodzinska was not surprised when he announced that he too was going to Dresden. This time his hotel registration form showed him to be a teacher of music.

He was better and in good form, but underneath the gay exterior he was tense. Time was running out and he had not yet made his intentions known, his inherent inability to take the initiative in matters of the heart making him put off a declaration of love. A fifth week passed, the date for his departure was set. On the very last evening, realizing that he was about to go away without having mentioned the object of his visit, he plucked up courage and formally asked Countess Wodzinska for Marie's hand in marriage.

The countess must have read the answer in Marie's eyes, but marriage was a social contract which could not be entered into without careful consideration. She explained that no definite answer could be given without first consulting her husband, whom she was going to join shortly in Poland. The young people must have looked dejected for the countess, somewhat repentant of her prudence, agreed to regard them as engaged. She insisted however that the arrangement should remain secret. The September sun had already set by the time the grave discussion reached its happy conclusion and the drawing-room was plunged into semi-darkness. In their subsequent letters to Chopin both mother and daughter would use the word 'dusk' to denote what had passed in their drawing-room that evening. The word engagement was never mentioned.

He returned to Paris in a mood of expectancy. 'I've seen our common friends, they are all asking if Mlle Marie is getting married,'[14] he wrote meaningfully to Countess Wodzinska. The countess remained non-committal. She reminded him to take care of his health and embarked on a long discussion of a pair of slippers, alas too large, which Marie had made for him. Marie herself was only allowed to enclose demure little notes which must have been submitted to her mother's censorship. In one she called her fiancé *'carissimo maestro'*,[15] in another she signed herself off as 'your very faithful secretary' and discreetly dated it 'dusk'.[16] That was the nearest she ever got to revealing what was in her heart.

Chopin was even more formal than Marie. He conducted his courtship—if courtship it was—solely through her mother and not once wrote to her directly. Perhaps he did not know how to write to a young maiden; perhaps he needed an intermediary even with his own fiancée, and expected the mother to translate his stiff expressions of respect into messages of love. The countess however was not the ally he had hoped for. She merely informed him that she and Marie were returning to Poland and would be calling on his parents to reassure them of his good health.

In all probability it was the visit to the Chopins in Warsaw which decided the Wodzinskis against the marriage. The Wodzinskis were gentry, with fifty thousand acres of land, a noble country seat near Torun and a distinguished place in society; Pan Chopin of Cracow Precinct, living in a rented apartment, was only a pensioned-off school-teacher. In Dresden Frederick's name shone like a jewel in the international cultural firmament; in Poland its lustre palled in the harsh light of convention. A marriage was a merger between two families of similar social background; Chopin's fame and genius could not make up for his humble background. Artists who were not gentry were not social equals. One invited them home, basked in their glory, treated them like sons, took them for lovers; but one did not marry one's daughters to them. The gulf was unbridgeable.

After their visit to Warsaw the Wodzinskis took up residence in their renovated mansion near Torun and settled down to the pleasant if somewhat dull life of the landed gentry. The count never involved himself with his wife's recent matrimonial aberration; the countess tried to extricate herself from a delicate situation by pretending it never existed. She continued writing to Chopin as to an old family friend, using the intimate form of address which he would never dare use to her, giving him motherly advice on matters of health. At the same time she never forgot to entrust him with new tasks; if it was not to transfer money to her good-for-nothing son Anthony who had gone off to fight in Spain, it was to select and ship a Pleyel piano to Torun, leaving him to pay for it. Of the secret engagement nothing was said and the code-word 'dusk' was no longer mentioned. Marie must have been persuaded that the Dresden episode was a summer fantasy best forgotten; seen from the perspective of a Polish country house, the four weeks at Marienbad and the one week in Dresden could have hardly seemed anything else. Marie was young and her heart still untouched; she demurred without apparent regret and her one or two further notes to Chopin, written at her mother's insistence, were as bored as they were boring.

By the beginning of 1837 the Wodzinskis regarded the chapter as closed while Chopin continued to act as if his prospects were still in the balance. He had written to his parents about his expectations and was copying eight of his recent compositions, some of them songs based on poems by Mickiewicz and Witwicki, into an album he was intending as a present for Marie. The news that he was aspiring to the hand of a young Polish countess had spread all over Paris. Some people made well-meaning enquiries, others gave him knowing winks and nudges. While Mme Wodzinska, from the depths of her country mansion, was congratulating herself on having broken off an undesirable engagement without alienating the famous Chopin, Chopin's matrimonial prospects were *salon* gossip.

Whether he was in love with Marie, after five weeks under her mother's chaperonage followed by several months of virtual non-communication, is a question which cannot be answered. He certainly wanted to marry her and settle down into a life which he hoped would give him domestic stability within the right social setting. In the spring of 1837 he sent her the album with his eight compositions, expressing in music the hopes and sentiments he was unable to put into writing. It fell on deaf ears. In the dullest of conventional notes, Marie thanked him for 'the nice album'[17] and conveyed the family's greetings. That was her last note.

Still there was no open breach, Chopin refusing to see the obvious, Mme Wodzinska anxious to retain the goodwill of a celebrity who was also such a useful errand boy. She kept asking him to render her all sorts of services, he kept obliging without a murmur, too proud to demand an explanation, too apprehensive of displeasing someone who might still be his mother-in-law. A year after the secret engagement at Marienbad he could no longer delude himself. When at the end of 1837 the countess wrote to him with yet another of her requests— this time she wanted him to find a publisher for a piece of music she was interested in—he had had enough. He simply did not answer, and Mme Wodzinska took the hint and left him alone. Some time later he put her letters and Marie's notes in a single envelope, tied a ribbon round it and scribbled on top the much quoted words *Moja bieda*, My Misfortune. Marie was out of his life.

Tradition has claimed for Chopin a broken heart and everlasting grief; the evidence available can hardly support such a romantic notion. There had been no time and opportunity for him to develop a deep attachment for Marie and throughout their brief unofficial engagement she must have remained for him what she had been from the beginning, an attractive and eligible young gentlewoman whom he wanted to marry for the sake of settling down. The failure of his project was a blow to his pride rather than his heart, for it was not the girl who jilted him but her parents who would not accept him as a son-in-law.

The lesson was all the more humiliating. Chopin believed he belonged in that genteel, titled society which ever since his childhood had prostrated itself before his genius and cocooned him with adulation. His rejection by the Wodzinskis brought home to him that in spite of his fame and popularity in the aristocratic circles of his choice, he would never be accepted as a social equal. It was a snub he was never to forget. Never again would he expose himself to another humiliation, never again would he seek to ally himself to a noble family, never again would he contemplate marriage. This, the most traumatic lesson he had yet learnt, was his real *bieda*.

As for Marie, she continued to live with her parents until in 1841, at the age of twenty-two, she married Count Joseph Skarbek, the son of Chopin's godfather. The marriage was a failure and in due course annulled. Later Marie married again. She died in 1896 aged seventy-seven, surviving Chopin by forty-seven years.

Preludes

In the last week of October 1836 Chopin called on Liszt and his mistress Marie d'Agoult, who had just set up house in Paris after a period of co-habitation in Geneva, and was introduced to a friend of theirs who was temporarily sharing their apartment. To his parents he wrote:

> I have made the acquaintance of a great celebrity, Mme Dudevant, known as George Sand. I did not like her face, there is something disagreeable about it. There is something about her which puts me off.[1]

Even before his first meeting with George Sand he had already heard enough *salon* gossip to prejudice him against a woman whose every action seemed to leave a trail of scandal behind her. He would have heard of her stormy affair with young Alfred de Musset, of her many other alleged liaisons, perhaps of her bid for Liszt's affections while professing friendship for his mistress. He knew that she had arrived in Paris in 1831, the same year that he did, having left an unloved husband in order to live her own life. That in itself should not have prejudiced him, for Countess Delphina Potocka and Countess Marie d'Agoult had done exactly the same. But while Delphina was feminine enough to pay lip-service to conventions even when it suited her to disregard them and d'Agoult's desertion of husband and children was partially redeemed by her absolute fidelity to her one and only lover, George Sand was reputed to make a virtue out of sin; her very name was a mockery of social decorum.

The way she carried herself that evening at Marie d'Agoult's confirmed everything he had heard about her. She lounged about in trousers, smoked cigars and addressed some of the other visitors in the familiar second person singular. Never in his life had he seen such unladylike conduct. To Hiller he said on their way out: 'What an unprepossessing woman that Sand is. Is she really a woman? I am inclined to doubt it.'[2]

Unlike Liszt and Marie d'Agoult who were familiar with George Sand's views on women's social status, Chopin had not read any of her novels; neither *Indiana* which had established her name in 1832, nor *Lélia* which caused a *furore* in 1833; not even her recent *Lettres d'un voyageur*, one of which was dedicated to Meyerbeer and another devoted to a holiday spent with Liszt and Marie d'Agoult in Switzerland. He was not a reader of contemporary French literature, let alone works which were alleged to call on women to neglect their traditional duty to hearth and home. To Liszt, who was curious to hear what impression George Sand had made on him, he dismissed her with the conviction of an unchallenged prejudice: 'Women writers'.[3]

To the lady herself he was perfectly charming. She was after all a celebrity, a baroness if not quite a countess, and on her father's side a fourth-generation descendant of a licentious king of Poland. A few days later, on 5 November, he had occasion to be even more charming to her when Liszt, with George Sand on one arm and Marie d'Agoult on the other, descended on him at his apartment in rue Chaussée d'Antin. A whole crowd came in with them, Heine, Meyerbeer, Nourrit, Hiller, Mickiewicz, Niemciewicz, Delacroix, Ferdinand Denis.

While Chopin was making his guests at home George looked around with curiosity. A grand Pleyel occupied one corner of the drawing-room, the rest of the furniture consisting of delicate chairs, a canapé and side tables. Heavy grey curtains were drawn back to reveal ample muslin curtains kept impeccably white, contrasting delicately with the dove-grey shade of the wallpaper. The walls were bare but for a portrait of a pianist playing to an admiring listener. There were knick-knacks everywhere and low vases with violets. The room was dimly lit, the candles round the piano leaving the far corners in semi-darkness and creating an impression of unexplored vastness. There were one or two rugs, allowing the polished parquet floor to reflect what light there was.

Chopin was a perfect host, putting himself out to please his guests, anticipating their every wish. Of the two ladies present he felt more at home with Countess d'Agoult, a *grande dame* of the old school, beautiful, musical, witty, always elegantly and expensively dressed, as gracious as any of his Polish countesses. George Sand, smoking again, was more intriguing than pleasant. When music-making was over he served tea and left her to the tender care of the writer Ferdinand Denis with whom she seemed content to spend the rest of the evening discussing moral philosophy.

George however felt in her heart that mounting excitement which she knew to be the precursor of love. Since it was common knowledge that Countess Potocka had vacated the field and Chopin's recent proposal to Marie Wodzinska was still a secret, she saw no reason why she should not try to charm an apparently unattached young man towards whom she was strongly drawn. She was thirty-two, many times disillusioned yet still hoping for an ideal love which would offer a perfect harmony of soul and body.

Her love life so far had been unlucky. A maidenly affection for the eligible Casimir Dudevant, coupled with a desire to escape her mother's caprices, had led her at eighteen to marriage and a year later to the birth of a baby boy. At that time she was still known by her given name Aurore. The young couple settled into her ancestral mansion of Nohant, in the region of Berry, and began leading the life of the landed gentry. Aurore was bored. She needed to exercise her mind; her husband was content with hunting and shooting. She formed a platonic relationship with a handsome idealist met on holiday, then, after several years of frustration, succumbed to a flesh-and-blood affair with a free-thinking intellectual who apparently fathered her second baby, a daughter. She had no more children.

She was a loving mother, with a tendency to over-anxiety and possessiveness; but as the children were growing out of babyhood her extraordinary energy and creative yearning drove her to seek fresh outlets. She played the piano, painted, wrote. She discovered that writing was her true vocation. The free-thinking intellectual was a loner who would not be tied down; she found consolation in a young law-student called Jules Sandeau and followed him to Paris. Her bemused husband agreed to look after the children and the estate during her absence, and allowed her three thousand francs a year drawn from her own dowry. She was free to stay away or return to Nohant whenever she wished. Within eighteen months she had written and published *Indiana* and won the acclaim of literary Paris. Since an early encounter with male prejudice had made her realize the risk of writing under her own name, Aurore Dudevant, she hid her sex under the pen-name George Sand, which was partly derived from an earlier literary collaboration with her student lover. Sandeau himself was jettisoned.

By 1836 she was one of France's best-known and best-paid writers, but her inner life was still disorientated. Having asserted her independence she longed to be attached. She sought love, found only affairs. After each new disillusion she was left unhappy, unforgiving, still avid for more, still dangerously irresistible.

She had always been musical, her piano-playing being one of her husband's earliest grievances against her. Liszt excited her, but he was bespoke and after her break-up with Musset her destiny carried her toward the brilliant republican solicitor Michel de Bourges who conquered her with his intellect then turned his back on her. The year 1836 was one of the most difficult in her life. She was litigating against her husband for a legal separation—there was no divorce—with possession of Nohant and custody of the children, throwing herself on the satiated Michel, being half-heartedly kind to the writer Didier, instinctively testing her power on any young man who seemed at all attractive.

Chopin seemed to be possessed of all the qualities she unconsciously sought in a lover: he was a creative artist of the highest calibre, dependent enough to bring out her protective instinct, reticent enough to become an irresistible quarry. It was in keeping with her character, dominating and never admitting defeat, that while she was unhappily chasing the vanishing phantom of Michel's love and sadly sharing the bed of the unwanted Didier, she should also try to draw into her orbit the young composer whom she sensed she could love.

Chopin found himself discreetly besieged. One evening he was invited to a dinner party at Countess Marliani's who was a good friend of George Sand's; another he was asked to a musical *soirée* given by Liszt and Marie d'Agoult whose apartment Mme Sand was still sharing. On 13 December he gave a musical evening at his own apartment which he was sharing with his childhood friend Dr Jan Matuszynski. The guests included Liszt and Marie d'Agoult, Nourrit, Eugène Sue, Ferdinand Denis, the Marquis de Custine, a Count Potocki who was Delphina's brother-in-law, another Count Potocki who was a distant relative, the newly-arrived Polish composer Brzowski and many others. Mme Sand was invited after she had hinted through Liszt that she would be grateful for a chance to make the acquaintance of the fashionable writer de Custine. It was more than a pretext; she was really curious about Custine, rich and middle-aged, who had been lavishing on the delicate young Chopin such attentions as gave rise to dark insinuations.

Again Marie d'Agoult and George Sand were the only two ladies present, Marie impeccably elegant, George unconventionally striking. Brzowski was perplexed by an outfit which looked half-male, half-female; only the widely-travelled Ferdinand Denis realized that a slit caftan over a tight bodice and baggy trousers was a Turkish peasant costume. That evening George was in one of her taciturn moods; she settled by the fire, listened to the music with her eyes half-closed and smoked 'like a chimney'.[4] When the music was over and tea served, Liszt monopolised the conversation. At midnight she took her leave and shortly afterwards returned to Nohant. Nearly sixteen months passed before Chopin was to see her again.

But he was not allowed to forget that she was interested in him. The first six of those sixteen months were punctuated by insistent little notes inviting him to come to Nohant. His polite aloofness having daunted even that most self-assured of hostesses, George Sand sent her invitations through Liszt and Marie d'Agoult who had already promised to spend a few weeks with her in the spring. Every time she wrote to discuss their coming, she asked them to bring Chopin down as well. 'Tell him I adore him,'[5] she wrote on 17 February 1837. 'Tell him I worship him,'[6] she wrote again on 3 April. She had ordered a new piano from Paris and, to make Chopin more inclined to accept, had instructed Marie d'Agoult to invite down some of his compatriots. 'I also want Chopin,' she reminded her on 6 April, 'and all the Mickiewiczes and Grzymalas in the world'[7]. Luck was not on her side. 'Grzymala is held up by two elderly princesses,' Marie d'Agoult reported, 'Mickiewicz likes to think he is a family man and Chopin keeps changing his mind, the only thing constant about him is his cough.'[8]

He was coughing badly. The good effect of the rest-cure at Marienbad the year before had been totally undermined by the never-ceasing round of activities which his life in Paris dictated. His friends were worried and the Marquis de Custine, amidst oblique protestations of love, begged him to look after himself. 'You must allow yourself to be taken in hand like a child and an invalid,' he wrote. 'You must bring yourself to see that at the moment there is only one task for you: your health. . . . Three months' rest and sensible treatment would be enough to arrest your illness; but you must do it.'[9] Chopin was not in the least tempted by the prospect of a month with Custine at his St Gratien villa and two more months with him at a watering place. He refused to follow any regular régime and was offended when Countess Wodzinska, instead of writing about his matrimonial prospects, kept asking whether he was taking his medicines like a good boy. When yet another invitation from George Sand was conveyed to him he began to wonder whether a few days at Nohant would not be a pleasant break after all. His instinct however warned him against the siren and in July, to everybody's surprise, he announced that he was going to London with the music publisher and piano maker Camille Pleyel.

The crossing on 11 July was smooth, but it did not stop Chopin feeling queasy. He and Pleyel put up at a hotel near Leicester Square and booked tickets for several operas. They behaved like well-to-do tourists, which indeed they were, hiring a carriage and doing the sights, first the City and Hyde Park, later venturing out into Richmond and Hampton Court. To Julian Fontana, another childhood friend who had emigrated to Paris, Chopin wrote:

To hell with you for saying that the mud in this place does not stick. Lovely grey mud. When I see you I'll tell you what pleasant thoughts and unpleasant sensations the crossing produced in me. Also what effect this 'Italian' sky has on my nose. It just will not breathe in so much greyness. But I'll leave this for another time and only tell you that I am really enjoying myself. Tell Jan [Matuszynski] that a visit to London can be quite enjoyable provided it is kept short. Tremendous sights, big urinals but nowhere decent to pee. And then the English women, the horses, the palaces, the carriages, the opulence, the splendour, the wide open spaces, the trees, everything from soap to razors is so different, yet so uniform, so tidy, so carefully washed, and with it as black as a gentleman's arse. I embrace you.

F Ch

Kozmian [a London compatriot] tells me that some signs display the name Duppa [Dupa in Polish being the equivalent of arse]. What do you think of London now?[10]

Tuesday 25 July found him watching a boisterous crowd from the top of a stage coach at Arundel. It was polling day in some parts of Great Britain and Lord Dudley Coutts Stuart, a patron and benefactor of the exiled Polish community in London, was contesting the Arundel seat from Lord Fitz-Allan. An excited Chopin gesticulated and called out encouragements like any native supporter. It was a brave façade; underneath he was still smarting under the Wodzinski snub, still tormented with hope. His health was precarious and the few acquaintances he met observed how sick he was. Mostly he confined himself to the company of Pleyel and Kozmian, declining to be introduced to the English aristocracy for fear of having to play before people who had not heard him before and would not make allowances for his indisposition.

There was one exception. One evening Pleyel took him to dinner at the house of his English counterpart, the piano-maker James Broadwood, at 49 Bryanston Square. Chopin, at his own insistence, was introduced as M. Fritz. Dinner was followed by music-making and Pleyel goaded M. Fritz into playing something. Nobody was particularly attentive when the languid young man walked to the Broadwood piano. What the guests saw was a well-dressed foreigner, thin even by English standards, of medium height—his 1837 passport gave it as 170 cm

—with auburn hair and sideburns one of which was somewhat thinner than the other, and sunken eyes which looked hazel to some, greyish-blue to others. But two or three bars were enough to send an electric shock through the audience; conversation stopped in mid-sentence, ears were cocked, knowing glances were exchanged with mounting excitement. When he stopped playing everybody crowded round the piano to shake him by the hand, the music having established M. Fritz's identity beyond doubt.

By the end of July he was back in Paris. Liszt and Marie d'Agoult were at Nohant, on the point of leaving for Italy, and Mme Sand had stopped issuing invitations. He accepted the Marquis de Custine's suggestion to go to Ems for his health and on his return fell back into the routine of lessons, calls and compositions.

He was working on his Preludes, some of which were begun a year or two earlier at the time of his liaison with Delphina Potocka. 'New themes assail me like a swarm of bees,' he had written to her. 'They will become my Preludes. I do not know yet whether I'll be able to write forty-eight like Bach. I probably won't be able to reach that number, it will be too much for my Polish patience. But even if they are short and small it does not mean that they have not cost me much effort to write.'[11] That year he also wrote the Impromptu No. 1 in A flat major (Op. 29), the Scherzo No. 2 in B flat minor (Op. 31), a song based on *My Darling* by Mickiewicz and various other pieces. Earlier compositions were being revised and prepared for publication.

The early part of 1838 brought the signal honour of a command performance at the Tuileries, where in February he played some of his works before Louis Philippe and the royal entourage. In the first week of March he joined forces with Alkan, Zimmermann and his own young pupil Gutmann in a performance of a Beethoven symphony which Alkan had transcribed for eight hands on two pianos. That same month he departed for once from his practice of shunning the public platform and took part in an orchestral concert held at the town hall of Rouen.

He had agreed to do so in order to set up his compatriot Orlowski who had just been appointed conductor to the Rouen orchestra. Rouen not being Paris, Chopin little imagined that some of the capital's best known music critics would travel one hundred miles to hear the elusive virtuoso that he had become. He played the E minor Concerto. There were five hundred people in the town hall and the success was 'immense, immense', as the critic Legouvé wrote in the *Gazette musicale* of 25 March. 'Chopin needed the call of a good cause and the love of his homeland to make him overcome his reluctance to play in public,' Legouvé explained, then went on:

> Come on, Chopin, come on! Let this triumph decide you. Stop being selfish, give your great talent to all, accept yourself for what you are, put an end to that great controversy which is dividing the musical world. Make it possible for people who are asked who Europe's greatest pianist is, Thalberg or Liszt, to say, as those of us do who have just heard you: It is Chopin.[12]

The call fell on deaf ears. For a second time Chopin retired into his shell, emerging to play only before intimate gatherings of friends and connoisseurs.

In April 1838 George Sand returned to Paris after an absence of nearly sixteen months.

Since she had last seen Chopin, in December 1836, she had obtained judicial separation from her husband with possession of Nohant and custody of her children, buried her mother, had a discreet liaison with the actor Bocage and was currently having a smooth if somewhat dull passage with Lucien Malle-fille, her son's tutor. With her inexhaustible energy she had also written and published two new novels, *Mauprat* and *Les Maîtres mosaïstes* as well as several long articles on women's status in society. Her initial gravitation towards Chopin had not been abandoned; it only awaited a suitable opportunity to be resumed and followed to its desired conclusion.

Since she no longer had a *pied-à-terre* in the capital, she put up at Countess Marliani's, the French-born wife of the Spanish consul in Paris, sometimes affectionately referred to by her friends as 'the ambassadress'. Unlike Chopin, who would bury his dreams of love deep in his heart and let months go by without breathing a word even to an intimate friend, George made her feelings known to anyone who might be of use to her. Not only Mme Marliani was expected to help but also Count Grzymala, a distinguished Polish *émigré* who had been taking a paternal interest in his young compatriot. Wherever George was, Chopin was sure to be invited; wherever Chopin played, George was sure to be present. One evening she passed him a fan-note which he was to keep for the rest of his life. '*On vous adore*', she had scribbled; the actress Marie Dorval added underneath with a theatrical flourish: 'Et moi aussi, et moi aussi, et moi aussi.'[13]

Chopin was disarmed. He no longer found Mme Dudevant disagreeable; he was discovering in her that assertive solicitude which agreed with his nature and allowed him to warm without taking the initiative. By the end of four weeks the proposition was clear though the conclusion still some way off. He knew himself attracted, yet was wary of that unfathomable French-woman who was so direct, so forthcoming and so unlike his idea of femininity and graciousness. While rushing to meet her whenever she beckoned—at Mme Marliani's or at Grzymala's—he was weakly wondering whether the relation-ship could not stop where it was; no crossing of barriers, no physical intimacy. He held out until mid-May, when George had to return to Nohant.

George was perplexed; it was unnatural for a man, when so obviously tempted, to shirk physical touch. She wondered if he was being romantically faithful to the vanishing memory of Marie Wodzinska or whether he had had some painful experi-ence which had put him off consummation. She never suspected that abstinence was his last stand in a losing battle against her terrifying magnetism. To Grzymala she wrote:

Until recently I thought it was beautiful that he should abstain, either out of respect for me, or timidity, or even fidelity to someone else. I thought it was a sacrifice which indicated strength of character and chastity. It charmed me and endeared him to me all the more. But the other day, as we were leaving your house, he said something about resisting temptation. . . . I do not remember his exact words. I think he said something about certain acts spoiling beautiful memories. This surely is nonsense. He cannot believe in what he said, can he? Who is that wretched woman who has given him such ideas about physical love? Has he had a mistress unworthy of him? Poor angel! Those women should be hanged who degrade in men's eyes the most respectable and holy thing in creation, the divine mystery, the most serious and most sublime act in the entire life of the universe.[14]

Her letter to Grzymala stretched over five thousand words. She was hoping that he would make Chopin see that she was offering him a selfless and unpossessive love and went to great lengths to rationalize her apparent promiscuity of the past. She was at her most persuasive but her sophisticated barrage failed to dissipate Chopin's fears. When a few days later he heard from Mme Marliani that George was returning to Paris at the beginning of June, he rushed round to Grzymala's for a word of advice. Grzymala was out. 'What is going to happen?' Chopin scribbled down in alarm. 'God only knows. I am really not well at all. I have tried to see you several times. Let's have dinner together somewhere.'[15]

It was his last attempt to escape. When George came up in June all doubts melted away before her tenacity and the longed-for conclusion became a fact. They were both discreet about their liaison; George stayed with the Marlianis and carried on with her writing while Chopin went on giving lessons at his Chaussée d'Antin apartment. Only their intimates were let into the secret, Count Grzymala, the Marlianis, Julian Fontana, Jan Matuszynski and Delacroix, who began to paint a double portrait of the happy couple. The summer exodus to the fashionable resorts had come and gone, but for once Chopin was content to stay sedentary. 'There is not one single little cloud in our sky, not one grain of sand in our lake,'[16] George told Delacroix after three months of bliss.

Her protective love brought out Chopin's own protective instinct. Never before had he been so considerate, so sensitive to someone else's moods, so anxious to smooth away worries. 'I am beginning to believe there are angels who come down to earth disguised as men,' George wrote to Delacroix, 'dwelling amongst us for a little while in order to comfort and take back to heaven those poor, weary, desolate souls who are about to perish down below.'[16] But the angel had a will of his own and while ministering to his mistress's needs imperceptibly made her renounce those of her habits which most offended his sensitivity. He did not have to say anything before George, divining his squeamishness, restricted her smoking in public and put away for good her male outfits. Alone among all her lovers and friends he eschewed the masculine name George and revived the use of Aurore, a beautifully feminine name which he translated into Polish. *Jutrzenka* he sometimes called her, his Dawn, his Morning Star.

When autumn came they were still walking with their heads in the clouds. 'You think this happiness cannot last?' an elated George wrote to Delacroix. 'If I consult my memory and my reason it certainly cannot; but if I consult the state of my heart and my elation, it seems to me it can never end.'[16]

Like a family

Chopin was twenty-eight at the beginning of his liaison with George Sand; she was thirty-four. For the second time in his life he was taken up by a woman older than himself in years and experience.

On the face of it they were poles apart or, as Marie d'Agoult was to say with ill-concealed malice, as far apart as the Antipodes were from France. Chopin was hesitant, George was domineering; he was reserved, she was outgoing; he was a stickler for proprieties, she flouted conventions to suit her whims; he shrank from controversy, she delighted in championing causes; he was at ease only in the opulent atmosphere of a society drawing-room, she was in her element striding along a country lane; he considered himself a connoisseur of *haute couture*, she contrived to lend a touch of the bizarre even to the most sombre of outfits. At the same time they complemented each other. Chopin liked to have somebody take off his hands the daunting decisions of everyday life, George was a born organizer. Chopin needed a prop, George liked nothing better than to feel needed. And above all she was musical, sensitive and capable of giving him loving support when he was tormented with the final shaping of a lightning inspiration.

Her instinct in love was primeval; she wanted to build a nest and live cosily like a family. But Chopin, however tolerant he might have been of the Liszt–d'Agoult *ménage*, would not hear of living openly with a married woman. He kept his apartment at rue Chaussée d'Antin and George, still staying at the Marlianis', called discreetly in the evenings.

She had so far avoided telling her former lover Lucien Mallefille that he had been deposed. On her instruction he stayed on at Nohant as young Maurice's tutor and when once

Frederick Chopin in Marienbad, 1836, by Marie Wodzinska

George Sand
(1804–1876)
by Delacroix

Frederick Chopin
in 1841,
by George Sand

he came up to Paris he was introduced to Chopin and persuaded to write an article about him for the *Gazette musicale*. Irritatingly he continued to find excuses to desert his tutorial duties at Nohant and come up to Paris until George, still avoiding an awkward explanation, instructed him to take her son on a fortnight's educational tour of Le Havre. Mallefille was not a hot-blooded Creole for nothing. He cut short the tour and with a lover's unerring instinct made straight for rue Chaussée d'Antin.

It was a warm August evening when the melodrama unfolded. Mallefille, pistol in hand, posted himself outside the house of sin and waited for the arrival of his faithless mistress. When she entered he rushed in after her and threatened to kill both her and Chopin. Fortunately the stalwart Grzymala was there to hurl himself between the rivals, disarm Mallefille and lead him out shouting threats of revenge. According to another version the scene was played out in the street. George was already indoors when the Creole arrived and concealed himself behind a lamp-post on the opposite pavement. When she eventually came out he began to cross over with his pistol at the ready. At that moment a large van emerged from a side street and blocked his passage. George gathered her skirts and ran as fast as her legs would carry her along her own side of the street until a passing *fiacre* stopped for her and drove with all possible speed to the safety of the Marlianis' residence.

Chopin's jealousy was easily roused. Having suspected nothing of George's past association with Mallefille, he now imagined a rival in every friend. One day he turned ashen when he saw George reading a long letter from Delacroix and regained his composure only after she had let him see for himself how innocent it was. To avoid further complications George suggested going abroad for an indefinite period, as Liszt and Marie d'Agoult had done. Chopin needed a rest cure and her children could also benefit from a change of air. It seemed a sensible idea for all of them to pass the winter in a milder climate and, once away from the limelight, set up house like a family. Manuel Marliani recommended his native country and thus Majorca was decided upon. 'I am leaving for Spain,'[1] George wrote to a cousin of hers in the first week of October, making it sound as if she was going off on her own to recuperate

from a hard summer's work. Shortly afterwards she returned
to Nohant to prepare her children for the journey, leaving
Chopin to tell Parisian society that he was thinking of spending
the winter in central France. Only the members of the inner
circle were let into the secret and perforce Pleyel, who was
instructed to ship a piano to Majorca as soon as possible. It
was going to be a long stay away.

After a separation of twelve days—the first since they had
become lovers—Chopin joined George at Perpignan, where
she had arrived from Nohant with her fifteen-year-old son
Maurice, her ten-year-old daughter Solange and a maid. The
weather was mild. On 1 November they sailed from Port
Vendres to Barcelona under an unblemished blue sky and after
a few days' stay boarded a ship due for Palma in Majorca.
The sky was still impeccably blue when they landed on 7
November. The harbour layabouts watched with curiosity as
El Mallorquín disgorged its few passengers. Chopin was wearing a coat buttoned up to the chin, tight trousers, silk cravat,
white gloves and a black top hat; Solange, obviously a girl, was
dressed in boy's clothes; Maurice, obviously a boy, had his
long hair falling loose on his shoulders like a girl; and George,
though demurely dressed in a lady's travelling outfit, was
demanding most aggressively to be conducted to a hotel. The
Majorcans stared, then shook their heads with determined
impassivity. No, there were no hotels in Palma, no inns, no
lodgings of any description.

It had never occurred to the travellers that there would be
no tourist facilities in Majorca. Chopin was totally unequal to
the situation. Used as he was to having the practical minutiae
of everyday life arranged for him by others, he let George do
battle for the whole party. With little Spanish and no experience
of the local dialect she knocked on every conceivable door in
search of a bed. At last two inferior rooms were found over a
barrel-maker's workshop. The din was deafening.

The following day the search continued. George had letters
of recommendation to the French consul Flury and the French
banker Canut and through them heard of people who might
have rooms to let. But even when going to view a house by
appointment she could not break the barrier of suspicion and
hostility which the locals put up against foreigners. There was

a whole set of rules she was not familiar with. 'At first they say it is impossible to view the place and advise *mucha calma* [patience],' she wrote to the French consul in Barcelona. 'Then, little by little, if you look honest and your shoes are not worn out, they crack open a window, then a door, then at long last make up their mind to show you the house. And what a house! I think that your Majorcan is an ill-disguised Jew, he has an honest air but he knows how to sniff your pocket without appearing to do so.'[2]

A few days later she triumphantly reported that for the first time within living memory a furnished house to let had been found in the countryside just outside Palma. It was owned by a Señor Gómez, clearly another ill-disguised Jew, who was willing to let it for a price. On inspection the furniture consisted of trestle-beds, rough chairs, kitchen tables and sooty braziers. Most of the windows had no glass, no panes, not even frames; those were fixtures which the tenants were expected to provide for themselves. They had hardly settled down in *So'n Vent* [House of the Wind] and hired a piano, when they heard that three guest rooms at the charterhouse of Valldemosa, a few miles east of Palma, were going to fall vacant very shortly. It was cheering news. Chopin was looking forward to a winter of inspiration in the lap of nature. He described his first impressions to his Polish friend and general factotum Julian Fontana:

> Palma, 15 November 1838
>
> I am in Palma, surrounded by date palms, cedars, cacti, olive trees, orange and lemon trees, aloes, fig trees, pome-granates etc. Everything they have in the hothouses of the *Jardin des Plantes*. The sky is turquoise, the sea a deep blue, the mountains emerald, the air like the sky. Sunshine all day, everybody goes about in summer clothes, it's warm. At night guitars and singing for hours on end. Huge balconies with overhanging vines. Moorish ramparts, the city, there is a touch of the Moorish everywhere. In short, life is beautiful. Do think of me. Please call on Pleyel, the piano hasn't arrived yet. Which route was it sent by? My Preludes should be with you soon. I shall probably move on to a marvellous monastery, in the most beautiful spot in the

world, sea, mountains, palm-trees, a cemetery, a crusaders' church, a ruined mosque, olive trees a thousand years old. Oh my dearest, I'm coming alive. I am close to all that is most beautiful. I feel better. Please pass on to Grzymala any letters from my parents and anything else you want to send me, he knows where to forward my mail. Give my love to Jan Matuszynski. He would get better so quickly if he were here [Matuszynski was tubercular]. Tell Pleyel he will receive the music soon. Please don't say too much about me to other people. I'll write more fully some other day. Say to those who ask that I should be back at the end of the winter. The postman calls only once a week. I'm sending my letter through the French consul here. Please forward the enclosed letter to my parents just as it is. Post it yourself.

Yours

Ch.[3]

He was intoxicated with the Mediterranean landscape, the exotic trees, the 'perpetual spring'.[4] He was bursting with musical ideas; alas he was still without a decent piano. 'My piano has not arrived yet,' he reminded Pleyel a week later. 'Which way have you sent it? Via Marseilles or via Perpignan? I dream music but I do not make any because they don't have any pianos here. In this respect it is an uncivilised country.'[5]

The creative mood was swept away by the first gust of winter gale. *So'n Vent* lived up to its name. The wind blew in through the unglazed windows, the thin walls soaked up the rain, the charcoal braziers filled the house with smoke. Chopin's cough became violent, he began to spit blood. Three eminent physicians examined him, solemnly shook their heads and pronounced him incurable. 'One sniffed my spittle,' Chopin wrote to Fontana with a touch of gallows-humour, 'the other tapped my chest to see where the spittle came from, the third felt me while I was coughing it out. The first said I was going to die, the second that I had breathed my last, the third that I was already dead.'[6]

Immediately the word went round that the gentleman up at *So'n Vent* had a contagious disease and was a danger to the community. Señor Gómez gave George notice to quit and

charged her an exorbitant sum of money for the infected sheets
he would no longer be able to use. The dream monastery at
Valldemosa was not yet vacant; the party had to spend a few
days at the house of the French consul. On 15 December, five
weeks after their arrival in the island, they at long last unpacked
their luggage for the last time.

They occupied three cavernous cells at what had once been
a Carthusian charterhouse. The order had been disbanded by
the government and the spacious building now served as a
state guest-house. In summer it was patronized by middle-
class merchants from the mainland but in winter it was quite
deserted. The last winter guest sold George the furniture he
had brought with him. It was still necessary to buy some essen-
tials like mattresses and a modern stove to keep the cold out.
The Majorcan piano was duly transported from *S'on Vent*
and installed in the large cell allotted to Chopin.

He was coughing badly, unable to get on with his work,
worried about the thousand francs which the banker Auguste
Léo had advanced him against the sales of the Preludes. George
dismissed the blood-letting doctors and undertook to cure
the patient with rest and a proper diet. Catering presented
unheard-of difficulties. The bread arrived at the charterhouse
kitchen door soggy with rain, the fish foul-smelling, the chicken
scraggy, the milk diluted. The staple food was pork, which
the Majorcan housekeeper served in a pride of varieties. There
was pork roast, pork stew, pork broth, pork pancake and
pork dessert. Chopin was nauseated. To make him take any
food at all George had to roll up her sleeves and do the cooking
herself. She also had to do the shopping in Palma, which
entailed several hours' travel by waterlogged roads and
haggling with the vendors who charged exorbitant prices and
refused to alter them except to raise them even higher. When
she noticed to her horror that the Majorcan maid-servants
were infested with vermin, she undertook cleaning and bed-
making as well. Both she and Chopin were forced to admit
that the Majorcan adventure was a failure and agreed to
return to France as soon as the patient's health would allow
him to brave the buffety crossing to the mainland.

In his better moments Chopin was a docile patient, touched
by his nurse's selfless devotion. 'She never tired of looking

after me,' he later wrote to Grzymala. 'She had to nurse me single-handed, for God preserve us from Spanish doctors. I saw her make my bed, tidy up my room, prepare beef-tea, deprive herself for my sake, not receiving any mail, looking after the children who needed her loving care more than ever in that unaccustomed way of life. And to think that she was also writing.'[7] But there were times, only too frequent, when the pain made him selfish and intractable. George never lost her patience.

Her sensible prescription of rest and careful diet proved more effective than the poultices ordered by the Spanish doctors. Chopin settled down to work at the inferior Majorcan piano while George, who wrote only by night, divided the daytime between domestic chores and giving the children their lessons. From time to time she took them on long walks to collect flowers and stones, returning after dark, guided home by a dim cloister lamp which beckoned like will-o'-the-wisp. One evening the three of them burst gaily into Chopin's cell to find him in a trance, his eyes wild, his hair on edge, his hands still on the keyboard. It took him several minutes before he came down to earth. In *Histoire de ma vie* George Sand recalled:

> He gave a forced laugh and then played us the sublime things he had just composed, or rather the terrible and heart-rending ideas which had got hold of him during that hour of solitude, melancholy and terror. It was there he composed the most beautiful of those short works he modestly named Preludes. They are masterpieces. Some call to mind those long-dead monks and the funeral chants which he heard in his mind; others are sad and sweet. They came to him in the hours of sunshine and good health, with the sound of the children's laughter under his window, the twang of distant guitars, the singing of birds among the rain-soaked branches.[8]

One day George and Maurice drove to Palma to do some shopping and on their way back were overtaken by torrential rain. Within minutes the whole countryside was flooded. The driver lost his way and after six hours' driving in the dark along non-existent roads refused to go any further. Mother

and son walked the rest of the way, miraculously reaching
the charterhouse about midnight, frozen, soaked to the bone
and *sans* boots. Chopin had gone frantic with anxiety. When he
could bear the strain no longer he withdrew into a world of
his own and spent the night playing with his eyes full of tears.
'At the sight of us coming in', George recalled, 'he uttered a
wild cry and said in a strange tone of voice: "I knew you were
all dead". . . . Later he told me that while waiting for our
return he saw in a dream what had actually happened to us
and, no longer able to distinguish between dream and reality,
was lulled to sleep by his own playing. He thought he too
was dead. He saw himself drowning in a lake and felt heavy,
ice-cold drops falling on his chest. When I suggested that
the regular sound of the raindrops on the roof had brought
on the dream, he said he had heard nothing.'[9]

In December word reached the charterhouse that the long-
awaited Pleyel had arrived in Palma. George drove down to
the harbour only to return empty-handed and indignant. It
took three weeks of hard negotiations to have the *pianino*
released from dock without greasing the palms of everybody
who had ever looked at it. Chopin swore mildly while George,
who did all the haggling, could not find harsh enough words
to describe the port bureaucracy. In *Hiver à Majorque*, written
three years after the event, she condensed her experiences
into a few hard-hitting sentences:

For a piano which we had shipped over from France we
were asked to pay 700 francs; it was practically as much as
the piano had cost to buy in the first place. We decided to
send it back, it was not permitted; leave it in dock until
further notice, it was forbidden; have it moved out of town
and thus avoid storage dues which came on top of customs
dues, it was contrary to regulations; leave it in town and thus
avoid exit tax which was not the same as entry tax, this
was impossible; throw it into the sea, that was the most
we could hope to do provided we proved our ownership
of the piano. After fifteen days of arguing it was agreed
that instead of moving the piano out of town by one gate,
we would be allowed to move it by another, thus getting
away with only 400 francs to pay.[10]

The stay at Valldemosa turned out to be beneficial after all. As the patient's health was improving, life fell into a pattern. George wrote, the children prepared their homework and played out-of-doors, Chopin was at the piano. In two months he revised and completed a remarkable number of works including Preludes No. 2 in A minor, No. 4 in E minor, No. 10 in C sharp minor, No. 21 in B flat major, No. 1 in C major (all from Op. 28). He may well have conceived the ideas for some others; the Raindrop Prelude, a title based on George Sand's reminiscences, is commonly thought to be No. 15 in D flat major, though at various times in history other preludes were credited with the title. Other works revised, completed or worked on during the Majorcan stay included the Mazurka in E minor No. 2 (Op. 41), the Scherzo in C sharp minor (Op. 39), the Polonaises in A major No. 1 and C minor No.2 (both Op. 40), the Ballades No. 2 in F major (Op. 38). It was a rich crop.

Like a true artist, once his inspiration had been captured on paper, Chopin applied himself to the important business of selling it to the highest bidder. Gone was the epistolary suavity which characterised his French correspondence. 'For the Preludes I want 1500 francs for the French and English rights,' he wrote to Pleyel who wanted to supplant Schlesinger as his French publisher. 'I am not bound to Wessel in London, he can pay more. When you have made up your mind pay the money to Fontana. . . . For the Ballades I want 1000 francs for the French and English rights, for the two Polonaises 1500 francs for world rights, for the Scherzo 1500 francs for world rights.'[11] When the stunned publisher tried to beat him down Chopin expressed horror at 'such Jewish practices on the part of Pleyel'[12] and instructed Fontana to take the music somewhere else.

The new year brought some pleasant diversions. One night a procession of masqueraders visited the charterhouse and performed folk dances to the sound of castanets. Sometimes George and Chopin drove down to Palma to spend the evening at the *salon* of the French consul. A Polish friend from Paris turned up unexpectedly and stayed for a few days. The weather was getting warmer. Nothing however would reconcile George and Chopin to the Majorcans, whom they continued to regard as thieves, money-grubbers and disguised Jews. They could not wait to leave the island.

In February 1839 Chopin felt fit enough to brave the sea crossing. Everything essential was packed, everything superfluous was left behind. The Pleyel *pianino* was carried back to Palma and put up for sale. None of the wealthy residents, not even the civilised French, would buy a piano which had been touched by a consumptive. At the eleventh hour Mme Canut, the wife of the local French banker, decided to risk her life for the sake of a good deed and bought it for twelve hundred francs. Chopin had had the use of it for only three weeks. Months later he was still writing to M. Canut to remind him that the outstanding amount had not yet been paid into his Paris account.

It was again *El Mallorquín* which took the party across. Since the tourist season had not yet begun, the space on deck was taken up by livestock. Wherever the passengers tried to sit down they were pushed out by pigs. George thought there were about a hundred on board; in retrospect, remembering how Chopin was denied a decent berth because of preferential treatment of pigs, she increased their number to two hundred. Chopin took the crossing badly and arrived in Barcelona coughing blood. George was outraged when the Spanish hotel owner, like Señor Gómez of *S'on Vent*, forced her to pay a replacement fee for the bedding he was going to burn after use. She did not realize that the law of the land imposed heavy penalties on anyone who failed to burn bedding used by people afflicted with a contagious disease.

At long last they reached Marseilles. The change from Spain was unbelievable. They had a good hotel, civilised food and the attentions of a French doctor. Nobody wanted to burn Chopin's mattress from under him, nobody recoiled when he offered to shake hands. The February weather was mild and promised the winter warmth they had set out to seek three months earlier. Chopin drank a lot of milk—no more of that revolting Majorcan goat's milk—abstained from coffee and wine and from time to time suffered himself to be vesicated though not, at George's insistence, to be bled. Now that his health was on the mend he was better able to appreciate the immense burden which she had been shouldering for the past few months. He watched her, somewhat relieved from the basic domestic chores, still running their daily life, teaching the children, looking after him, finding time to write; his heart swelled with love and gratitude. To Grzymala he described her as his angel and sometimes, to emphasize the extent of his feelings, as his angels, in the plural.

In March he heard that the tenor Adolphe Nourrit had committed suicide while on tour in Naples. They had been close friends, performed in each other's recitals and entertained each other at their homes until Nourrit, annoyed with the management of the Paris Opera for promoting another tenor, left in a huff. Now, at thirty-seven, he was dead, having jumped out of his hotel window in a fit of depression. His widow, with six children and a seventh on the way, arranged to have his coffin taken to Paris and when it passed through Marseilles had a memorial service held for him at Notre-Dame-du-Mont. During the Elevation Chopin played on the organ Schubert's *Die Sterne*, one of Nourrit's *pièces de résistance*. George suspected that the vast crowd which filled the church and had paid fifty centimes entry fee—an unprecedented practice—had done so not to honour the dead but to catch a glimpse of Chopin and herself.

Their relationship was no longer a secret. In Marseilles they were besieged by admirers who wanted to pay their respects and in Paris they were the subject of much gossip. Berlioz had discovered their address and wrote to ask Chopin when he was coming back and to remember him kindly to Mme Sand. But Mme Sand and Chopin were in no hurry. They decided to make the most of the mild climate of Marseilles and then go on to Nohant for an indefinite period. Fontana was instructed to wind up the agreement for the Chaussée d'Antin apartment, tip the servants, store the furniture, stall the tailor and the glove-maker. Above all he was to pursue publishers. Chopin was furious when Pleyel, Schlesinger, Probst, the banker Léo and other gentlemen concerned with his finances tried to have their own way and called them Jews, Huns, skin-flayers, riff-raff, scoundrels, Huns, Jews. The loyal Fontana must have transmitted the spirit of the invectives if not the verbatim text, for acceptable terms were finally arranged. How George, continuously badgering her own editor for more money, must have applauded.

On 1 June 1839 Chopin had his first glimpse of Nohant, the country mansion which George Sand had inherited from her grandmother and which she had barely managed to wrench back from her husband. 'Lovely countryside,' he wrote to Grzymala. 'Nightingales, skylarks.'[13] Nohant revealed to him a new dimension in George. The woman he had so far known as a Paris celebrity, and a lioness defending her young from hostile Majorcans, now showed him her *alter ego* as a châtelaine, running a large household, managing the estate, discussing bees and vegetables. He was charmed. He allowed himself to be embraced by her half-brother Hippolyte who came over from his nearby estate and shook hands with the Berry phalanx of admirers who wanted to see for themselves what the unpredictable George had in tow.

They were quick to sense that it was no passing whim on either side. George had reached that point in her tumultuous career when she wanted permanence while Chopin, independently of his drawing-room fantasies of romance, longed for the security and bustle of a family atmosphere. It is interesting to speculate what shape their life might have taken had there been divorce in France and Baroness Dudevant were free to remarry. In the circumstances they created for themselves a set-up which for nine years was as near a family as possible. Had it been possible for the relationship to become a formal bond, Chopin and George Sand may well have been more inclined to see their nascent differences in their true perspective and not allowed them to achieve the magnitude that they did.

George was a born home-maker. As soon as they arrived at Nohant life fell into a pleasant pattern. By day the family followed their respective occupations; Chopin worked at the piano in his room, the children prepared their homework, George gave them their lessons or saw to the running of the household. In the evening they assembled for an early dinner in the garden, received friends, discussed local news. Sometimes Chopin played, though none of the Berry neighbours was particularly musical. His health continued to fluctuate. 'Sometimes he is better, sometimes worse,' George wrote to Mme Marliani on 24 July, 'never actually ill, never quite well. I fear he is going to be slightly affected for the rest of his life.'[14] Surprisingly her childhood friend Dr Papet, who was called in

to have a look at Chopin, said that his lungs were clear and
that only an inflammation of the larynx was discernible. George
urged Chopin not to exert himself, sent him off to bed at the
same time as her children and spent the nights writing in the
solitude of her study. *Spiridion* had been written in Majorca
and Marseilles; now she was putting the finishing touches to
the revised *Lélia*, working on *Les Sept Cordes de la Lyre*,
Gabriel, various articles.

Chopin too continued the creative spurt begun in Majorca.
He completed the Scherzo in C sharp minor (Op. 39), composed
three mazurkas (from Op. 41), the Nocturne in G major
(Op. 37, No. 2), the Sonata No. 1 in B flat minor (Op. 35),
the Impromptu No. 2 in F sharp major (Op. 36). The quiet
country régime, away from the distractions of Paris and the
duties of teaching—young Solange being the only exception—
gave him the time he needed to put his inspiration into final
shape. He was amused when Titus Woyciechowski wrote all
the way from Poturzyn to advise him to compose an oratorio.
'Good old Titus still has his student's ideas,' he confided to
Fontana. 'I still love him as much as when we were at school.
He has a second son. He is calling him after me. Poor baby.'[15]

He was missing his compatriots. For the first time since
his arrival in France he was living in a purely French *milieu*
and meeting none but French people. It was a great joy when
Grzymala came down to stay, incidentally bringing with him
four pairs of boots Chopin had left in Paris and which he now
wanted for country wear. The Polish language came again
into its own and the Sand children, quick to pick up the sounds,
began to call Chopin *Chopinski*. When Solange was later sent
to boarding-school she signed herself once or twice with a
schoolgirl's sense of humour as *Solangeska Sandska*. George
too picked up a smattering of Polish and under Chopin's
guidance once began a letter to Grzymala with the words
'*Kochany mezu, lubie cie bardzo*'[16] [Dear Spouse, I love you well].
The term spouse was her normal form of address to him,
dating back to those early days when she liked to fancy herself
and Grzymala as Chopin's mother and father.

She was obsessed with maternal love. Countess Marie
d'Agoult, living with Liszt in a similar atmosphere of quasi-
marriage, regarded herself as a loving wife; George saw herself

as a loving mother. It did not occur to her that intimacy with
someone she called her child, and which she was never totally
to abandon, smacked of the incestuous. On the contrary, she
believed that the maternal element in her love lent respectability to an association which Chopin, with his fear of public
opinion, was anxious to disguise and which her children were
beginning to notice. Chopin, for his part, was the soul of
discretion. He avoided familiarity, formally addressed George
as *vous* and referred to her as Mme Sand or his hostess. For
the rest of his life he clung to the myth that he was a house-
guest at Nohant. Needless to say, none of their friends were
deceived.

Summer and health progressed together and in August Chopin's
thoughts turned to Paris. There was no question of sharing
with George a rented accommodation where the myth of a house-
guest would not be credited even by the most gullible. Two
separate apartments had to be found, and while Countess
Marliani was making enquiries about a place large enough to
accommodate George and the children, Fontana and Grzymala
were looking for a smaller one for Chopin. For weeks the
letters between Paris and Nohant discussed desirable neighbourhoods, rents, size and number of rooms, general amenities.
Chopin's touching helplessness spurred his friends to feats of
devotion and serviceability. Fontana inspected several apartments suggested by a reputable estate agent, sent detailed
descriptions to Nohant and was rewarded with the uncomfortable responsibility of making the final choice. Having decided
on 5 rue Tronchet he was asked to take charge of the interior
decoration as well. On 25 September Chopin wrote:

> Choose a wallpaper like the one I used to have, dove-grey
> but glossy and shiny, with a narrow dark-green border.
> Something different for the hall, but pleasant. If you see
> prettier or more fashionable wallpapers which you like, take
> them if you feel I might like them. I want something neat and
> quiet, not a shopkeeper's taste. That's why I like dove-grey,
> it is not brash or vulgar. Thank you for thinking of accom-
> modation for the servant, it is very useful. As for the furniture,
> I know it will be all right because you are dealing with it.

I was afraid to put you to all this trouble, but you have been so kind. I would like you to have my furniture collected from storage and installed in the new place. I'll ask Grzymala to give you money to pay for the removal van. I'll write to him about it. My bed and bureau will have to be sent to the cabinet-maker's to be repaired. Please take my papers out of the bureau and keep them somewhere else. Do what you think is best, I don't need to tell you what to do, whatever you will do is bound to be perfect. You have all my confidence.[17]

On 29 September he wrote again:

Please have the grey curtains which used to be in the study by the piano hung in the hall. In the bedroom those which used to be in the old bedroom, only have underneath the muslin ones which used to be underneath the grey ones. I should like to have the chest of drawers in the bedroom if there is a suitable place for it there, or else in the drawing-room if the space between the windows looks bare. If the red couch which used to be in the old dining-room can have white covers made of the same stuff as the chairs, it could be put in the drawing-room. This might be difficult, for you will have to find a needlewoman or an upholsterer willing to wait until I arrive. Let me know what happens.[18]

And again on 3 October:

I forgot to ask you to order a hat for me at Dupont's, up your street. He has my measurements and knows I like it lightweight. Let him make it according to this year's fashion, but not to overdo it. I no longer know what people wear these days. On the way you might also call on Dautrement's the tailor and tell him to make me a pair of grey trousers right away. Perhaps dark grey, you choose. Winter weight, good quality material, no faults, stretchy. Also a black velvet waistcoat, with a small inconspicuous pattern, something simple and elegant. If he has nothing suitable in velvet order something in black silk. I rely on you. Not too low cut, rather the opposite.[19]

On 4 October, when agreement, decorators and furniture were all under way, he had sudden misgivings about the apartment. 'Why is it so inexpensive?' he suspiciously asked Fontana. 'Is there something wrong with it? For Heavens' sake don't lose a moment, go at once to Mardel's [the estate agent], see if he has something better.'[20]

He felt happier when Grzymala inspected the apartment and assured him it was fine. Immediately he asked Fontana to find one for George and the children. He suggested two or three acceptable neighbourhoods, then went on to specify requirements in far greater detail than he had ever done for himself. There were to be no noisy workshops in the vicinity, no evil smells from the sewers, no fumes, smoke or soot. There was to be plenty of light and a view over gardens. He drew a plan of the ideal layout, indicated the number of rooms and the function of each, fussed and worried and all but drove himself into a state of nervous collapse. The unflappable Fontana, aided by Mme Marliani, came up again with the right solution and an apartment with two garden pavilions at 16 rue Pigalle was taken for George. Chopin, who used to tease Fontana about the English ways he had picked up during a long stay in England, paid him a handsome compliment. 'You have the heart of a real friend,' he wrote. 'Your soul is not English but truly Polish.'[21]

At long last the return to Paris took place. By the middle of October George and Chopin were settled into their respective apartments and ready to resume the social turmoil of a Paris they had left exactly a year earlier in search of warmth and peace in Majorca.

Years of Glory

One of the first invitations Chopin accepted on his return to Paris was to play after dinner at the house of the music-loving banker Auguste Léo. None of the guests listened to him more keenly than the host's kinsman Ignaz Moscheles who had recently arrived from London for a few weeks' holiday.

At a time when Frederick was still a schoolboy, Prague-born Moscheles was already one of Europe's leading pianists and composers. In 1821 he settled in London and for the next twenty-five years contributed greatly to the musical life of the British capital. From time to time he made trips to the Continent, where he gave concerts and lessons, one of his short-term pupils being the then fifteen-year-old Mendelssohn.

Moscheles had not taken to Chopin's music. In 1833, having tried out the Four Studies from Opus 10 which had just been published in London by Wessel's, he wrote to Mendelssohn: 'I am impressed with the originality and national flavour of his themes, but my mind, and therefore my fingers, boggle at those harsh, inartistic and to me unacceptable modulations. On the whole I find his music rather cloying, unmanly and hardly that of a profound musician.'[1] Two years later, when he had studied more of Chopin's published works, he reiterated his views. 'I am a sincere admirer of Chopin's originality,' he wrote. 'He has given piano players all that is novel and attractive. But personally I dislike his artificial and forced modulations, my fingers stumble at such passages. Practise as much as I might, I can never play them fluently.'[2]

As was his practice at private gatherings, Chopin played at Léo's only his own music, taking the opportunity to introduce some of the works composed during his year of absence. Moscheles was bowled over. 'For the first time I understood his music and why women go into raptures over it,' he noted in his diary in October 1839. 'Those harsh inartistic modulations which I have never been able to master, no longer shock me, for he glides over them imperceptibly with his elf-like fingers. His touch is as soft as a breath. . . . One never misses the orchestral effect which the German school demands of a pianist . . . In the world of piano players Chopin is unique.'[3] He told Chopin how impressed he was and the younger composer reciprocated the compliment by borrowing and practising Moscheles' Sonata for Four Hands in E flat major. When they next met they played it together. The joint performance became the talk of musical Paris and Count Perthuis, aide-de-camp to Louis Philippe, mentioned it at the palace. The result was a command performance at St Cloud. Chopin had hardly been back a fortnight.

On 29 October both he and Moscheles were called for at nine in the evening and driven in pelting rain to the palace where the royal family had already assembled in one of the smaller drawing-rooms. The 'Citizen Queen', as Moscheles referred to her, was so moved by his Sonata that she asked for the Andante to be repeated. 'Chopin played the bass part, something he always insists on,' Moscheles noted in his diary, adding generously: 'I think his enthusiasm throughout the Sonata must have infected the royal family for they showered us both with compliments. We took a brotherly pride in a triumph achieved through our combined talents; there was no showing off on either side, no jealousy.'[4] There was some individual playing as well, and at eleven-thirty, after refreshments had been served, the brothers were allowed to take their leave.

A few days later Moscheles was discreetly asked whether he would accept the *Légion d'honneur* as a mark of the royal favour. He intimated that he would prefer something less common and was promptly presented with a travelling-case inscribed with the words: 'Given by King Louis Philippe'.[5] Chopin could not help remarking that the nature of the gift indicated the king's desire to see the last of Moscheles as soon as possible. His own reward was a Sèvres porcelain cup embellished with bronze.

For the rest of Moscheles' stay they were asked everywhere

to play the Sonata which had so pleased the palace. One evening
George Sand gave a dinner party for Moscheles at rue Pigalle,
after which Chopin played his own Sonata in B flat minor
with the Funeral March (Op. 35). He was still weak and in
pain, frequently taking opium drops on lumps of sugar and
dabbing his forehead with a handkerchief dipped in eau-de-
Cologne. He was anxious for Moscheles to hear his recently
composed Scherzo in C sharp minor and asked his young pupil
Adolf Gutmann to play it for him. Moscheles was complimentary and Chopin, to show his gratitude to Gutmann,
dedicated the work to him when it was published (as Op. 39)
the following year.

Young pianists seemed to be more attuned to his music
than older ones, whose reactions were prompted by their own
early training. German-born Gutmann, who had been studying
with Chopin since he was fifteen, often astonished his listeners
with his delicate rendering of the master's music, so incongruous
in a person of his bulk and size. Chopin liked him and, alone
among all his pupils, addressed him in the informal second
person singular. When, shortly after George Sand's dinner
party, he heard that Gutmann was due for military service, he
wrote to the Grand Duke of Baden asking him to grant exemp-
tion to a pianist of such high promise. Gutmann stayed on in
Paris, graduating from pupil to friend and general factotum.

Another ardent admirer was a still unknown pianist of
seventeen, who was later to leave his mark on the musical
life of Manchester and be remembered by posterity as Sir
Charles Hallé. He had come to Paris from his native West-
phalia to seek tuition from the great Kalkbrenner, but failed
his audition. One evening he was invited to dine at Mallet the
banker's and found himself sitting next to Chopin. After dinner
Chopin played. 'I was fascinated beyond expression,' Hallé
later recalled. In his memoirs he wrote:

> It seemed to me as if I had got into another world, and all
> thought of Kalkbrenner was driven out of my mind. I sat
> entranced, filled with wonderment, and if the room had
> suddenly been peopled with fairies, I should not have been
> astonished. The marvellous charm, the poetry and originality,
> the perfect freedom and absolute lucidity of Chopin's playing

at that time cannot be described. It was perfection in every sense. He seemed to be pleased with the evident impression he had produced, for I could only stammer a few broken words of admiration, and he played again and again, each time revealing new beauties, until I could have dropped on my knees to worship him.[6]

Yet another young pianist who had an affinity with Chopin's music was Friederike Müller from Vienna, who later, under her married name Streicher, became a well-known exponent of his works. At their very first meeting he gave her his Preludes and Studies to sight-read and during her eighteen months' study with him he let her play many of his compositions before they appeared in print. His lessons however were by no means confined to his own works. He made his pupils play Clementi, Hummel, Cramer, Moscheles, Scarlatti, Hiller, Liszt, Thalberg, Beethoven and above all Bach. 'Bach will never age,'[7] he used to say. One day, when Fräulein Müller's lesson was over, he played to her fourteen of Bach's Preludes and Fugues off the cuff.

His physical infirmity made him evolve a technique which enabled him to preserve the dynamics without over-taxing his strength. 'If playing *forte* is difficult,' he used to tell his pupils, 'one should learn to shade one's *piano* and use the pedal so discriminately that the listeners would never notice the absence of a *forte*.'[8] Occasionally he had to send his manservant out with a message that he was too ill to see a pupil, but mostly the lessons had a therapeutic effect. 'Work, distraction and activity are essential to him,'[9] George Sand observed.

Their life had again fallen into a pleasant routine. During the day they followed their respective occupations in their respective abodes; at four in the afternoon, when Chopin had done with his lessons, he drove to rue Pigalle where George, looking matronly in ample skirts and the beginning of a double chin, was ready to receive callers. The early part of the evening was domestic. George embroidered or hemmed handkerchiefs, Maurice sketched, Solange tugged impatiently at her needlework and Chopin talked Polish to a little stray dog who had made his home at rue Pigalle. He called him Mops, which is the Polish for pug-dog; and George, like any other long-suffering housewife, sometimes went down on her knees to clear up the mess that the untrained Mops had left on the carpet.

The later part of the evening usually brought a flow of callers. Rue Pigalle became a place of reunion for some of the most illustrious names of the time. George Sand entertained Balzac, Heinrich Heine, Leroux, Lammenais, Delacroix; Chopin entertained Berlioz, Meyerbeer, Franchomme and a host of distinguished Polish *émigrés*. Sometimes George invited her friends to a musical evening at Chopin's at rue Tronchet. On one such occasion, when the guests included the statesman Emmanuel Arago, the engraver Calamatta, Delacroix and Grzymala, George gaily threatened: 'The first one who fails to enjoy himself will be thrown out of the window.'[10]

The only friend who felt *de trop* in the face of such obvious domestic bliss was the Marquis de Custine. He wrote Chopin a note reminding him of his own 'constance'[11] and when Chopin failed to answer, he sent him an antique inkstand and pen with a telling New Year's message:

> Goodbye, bad year 1839! And you, inconstant sylph, promise me a better one to come! That is all I wish for myself. As for what I might wish for you, it is not for me to give it to you. I am delighted from the bottom of my heart that you have found it, but I shall be less pained by it if, in spite of all your happiness, I could still mean something to you.[12]

By that time the sylph must have heard from George, if not from other sources, the savoury story which fifteen years earlier had both shocked and titillated Paris society. The Marquis had made an assignation with a handsome guards officer in a secluded stable when, instead of his paramour, the young man's comrades-at-arms turned up and all but whipped him to death. Since then society matrons struck his name off their lists of acceptable bachelors and Custine had to pursue his quest of beauty among artists and musicians. It was not however in Chopin's nature to rebuff the flattering advances of an aristocrat, even one with a shady reputation like Custine's. He contrived to steer a cautious course between acquiescence and indifference and in the summer of 1840 spent a week at the

Marquis' villa at St Gratien, duly chaperoned by Mme Sand, Delacroix and Grzymala. None of his letters to Custine—if indeed he ever wrote any—have survived. Custine, for his part, continued to write in his usual vein until the last year of Chopin's life.

The year 1840 saw George Sand's début as a playwright. She had long been attracted to the theatre and was delighted when the Théâtre Français, the precursor of the Comédie Française, commissioned a play from her. She offered them *Cosima*. There followed a period of intensive arguing about who should play the title-role, the theatre management making various suggestions, George discarding them one by one in favour of her old friend Marie Dorval. The Théâtre Français was not happy with the play in any case and seized on every possible excuse to put off rehearsals. George was furious and thought of offering *Cosima* to another company but desisted on Chopin's advice. When a further postponement was announced she no longer knew whom to blame. 'I am annoyed with my damned little Chopin,' she wrote to her half-brother Hippolyte in February 1840, 'for having persuaded, dissuaded and re-persuaded me, as Duplomb the lawyer used to do, to offer my play to that infamous shop.'[13]

After several more postponements the first night of *Cosima* was firmly fixed for 29 April. George refused the services of a hired *claque* and relied on the merits of the play to win the audience. But even a well-paid *claque* would not have saved a play whose alleged flouting of moral conventions had antagonized bourgeois and aristocratic theatre-goers even before they saw it. The two-thousand-strong audience hissed and booed, the disconcerted actors fluffed their lines; even Marie Dorval could not carry off the part of a faithless middle-class wife abandoned by a fickle aristocratic lover. When the curtain came down there was no doubt that the play was a fiasco and after seven performances it was taken off never to be revived.

Throughout that bad patch Chopin was virtually the only one in George's entourage who knew how to comfort her. Having witnessed the humiliating scenes of the first night, he discharged all his hatred of public audiences in his attempt to soothe her wounds. He reiterated his views on the coarseness

of the public and the deterioration of good taste until he
succeeded in restoring her ebullience. 'He is as kind as an
angel,' she wrote to Hippolyte after the failure of *Cosima*.
'Without his perfect and delicate love I would often lose
heart.'[14]

She could no more visualize life without him than without
Maurice and Solange. He became one of her 'three children'[15]
and she had pet-names for him as she did for the other two.
While Solange was Fatty and Maurice was Bouli, Chopin was
Chopino, Chopinet, Chop, Chip, Chip-Chop, Chip-Chip, even
Chippette. Sometimes she mentioned him in her letters to
friends as Fritz, the more convenient spelling of the Polish
Fryc; and sometimes, because he was never quite well, she
called him her 'regular patient'.[16] The intimacy of the past
two years had taught her to admire him all the more. 'He is
still the most gentle, modest and reserved amongst all men
of genius,'[17] she told Hippolyte.

But admiration and loving care could not fill the vacuum
created by the ebbing away of passion. George needed to be
excited, resisted, buffeted, yielded to, subjected all over again
to that exquisite suffering she called love. The person who
unwittingly set her heart on fire was the young singer Pauline
Garcia who had made her Paris début only a year or so earlier.
Fortunately for all concerned George was wise enough to
channel her new passion into an acceptable social form.

Pauline was the daughter of the Spanish composer Garcia
and the much younger sister of La Malibran. George and
Chopin first heard the eighteen-year-old mezzo-soprano at
the Théâtre des Italiens shortly after their return from Majorca;
but while Chopin merely admired the singer's musicianship,
George felt the upsurge of a new love. She inundated Pauline
with invitations to rue Pigalle and baffled her with extravagant
expressions of adulation. She was perfectly aware of the
interpretation which evil tongues might put on her insistent
courtship and therefore established it from the very start on a
firm mother-daughter basis; Pauline was after all hardly older
than her own son Maurice. She called her 'Dear daughter'[18]
and 'Dear child of my heart'[19] while Pauline, engulfed by
George's forceful personality, acquiesced by respectfully addressing her as 'Dear maternal friend'.[20] Neither ever deviated

from the formal *vous*. Although Pauline had a mother, it was George who brought about her marriage to the forty-year-old writer and theatre manager Louis Viardot. Chopin, Maurice, and even Solange, adored her.

In August 1840 Pauline Viardot accepted an engagement to give a series of recitals at Cambrai, in the north of France. She was accompanied by her husband who had given up his post as manager of the Théâtre des Italiens in order to act as his wife's impresario, but George announced that she would be coming along as well. Such was the force of her passion that neither the Viardots nor her own 'three children' could resist it. For a few days she was carried away by that old familiar excitement. She laughed off the discomforts of provincial hotels, suffered with Pauline from the coarseness of the audiences, battled with managers of inferior halls. She was in her element.

During her week's absence Chopin assumed the role of head of the family. He took Solange for afternoon walks and once, to amuse her, had her weighed as well as himself. At twelve she weighed 84 pounds (six stones) while he, still alarmingly thin, weighed 97 pounds (six stones and thirteen pounds). He spent the nights at rue Pigalle in what he called the *gabinetto bianco*, the better to keep an eye on house and family. The three children felt orphaned. 'If you only knew how sad the house has become since you left,' seventeen-year-old Maurice wrote to his mother on 14 August. 'Chopinet and I stare at each other in the evenings, with only two bits of candle to light the room, with wide-open eyes and a big mouth which opens from time to time to say *Ah mon Dié mon Dié* [Maurice's rendering of Chopin's Polish accent in French] *I am missing someone here*. To which I answer: *Ah mon Dieu mon Dieu, that's right, we are both missing someone here*. Then I yawn, Chopin stretches and soon we bid each other goodnight.'[21]

Chopin added a few lines in his schoolboy's made-up Italian. Addressing George reverently as *Ma padrone*, he assured her that he was well, that Solange was behaving herself and that Mme Marliani was helping to keep an eye on her. None of George's friends ever wrote to her as impersonally as he did in that letter, written under the surveillance of an adolescent son who was beginning to resent another man's place in his mother's heart. When that same year Chopin gave Maurice an expensive watch and chain, it was only the mother who was pleased, not the boy.

In the spring of 1841 Liszt returned to Paris in between tours abroad and gave several successful concerts. He had brought George a pipe, not having heard that since her association with Chopin she had given up pipe-smoking in favour of the more ladylike cigarettes. The conversation at rue Pigalle was full of Liszt's new triumphs and Chopin's friends pressed him to give a public performance of his own. He would not hear of it. His friends went on badgering him and one day his resistance gave way and he agreed to play at the Salle Pleyel. 'My poor Chopinet', George wrote to Hippolyte, 'is well enough. He has got it into his head to give a concert. I do not know whether he will have the courage and perseverance to go through with it.'[22]

She was right to question his perseverance. No sooner had the preparations got under way than Chopin regretted his decision and wanted the concert cancelled. It was too late. Three-quarters of the tickets, at the very high price of fifteen to twenty francs each, had been snatched up as soon as the word went round that the elusive virtuoso was going to appear in public. Then began what George amusedly described as 'the Chopinesque nightmare'.[23] Chopin refused to allow any display of posters, the printing of programmes, the sale of the remaining tickets. When he learnt that the adored Pauline Viardot had a previous engagement in London and would not be free to appear with him as a guest artist, he wanted to call the whole thing off. No one was allowed to mention the word concert in his presence. By dint of much cajoling and persuasion, George obtained for him the participation of the celebrated singer Mme Damoreau-Cinti and the violinist Heinrich Wilhelm Ernst. Chopin felt trapped. 'You cannot imagine anything funnier than the meticulous and irresolute Chip-Chip forced not to change his mind,' George wrote to Viardot. The affectionate little jokes were only for her intimates. At home she was a tower of strength and it was largely thanks to her encouragement that Chopin was able to go through with what he regarded as an ordeal.

The concert, on 26 April 1841, was a dazzling social occasion.

Carriage after carriage drew up in front of the Salle Pleyel at rue Rochechouart and dropped elegant women, fashionable young men, artists, financiers, 'the élite of high birth, wealth and talent'.[24] The carpeted wide stairs leading to the concert hall were decked with flowers, the concert organizers bowed over dainty hands as if they were receiving guests at a private reception. The grand piano had been placed on a large raised platform, with chairs all round it, offering the most coveted seats in the house. Most of the four-hundred-strong audience were either friends or people who could claim some personal acquaintance with Chopin. Liszt sat in the front row, having persuaded the editor of the *Gazette musicale* to let him review the concert instead of the regular critic Legouvé. Legouvé managed to take Chopin on one side to inform him of the change.

'I would rather have you as my reviewer,' Chopin said anxiously.

'You must not say that, *mon cher ami,*' Legouvé protested. 'A review by Liszt is a boon for the public as well as for you. Trust his admiration for your talent. I am sure he will proclaim you king among musicians.'

'Quite,' said Chopin, 'Keeping for himself the style of emperor.'[25]

The printed part of the programme included some of his recently published works: the Ballad in F major (Op. 38), a Polonaise from Op. 40, Four Mazurkas (Op. 41) and the Scherzo in C sharp minor (Op. 39). In between items Mme Damoreau-Cinti sang and M. Ernst played the violin. Chopin forgot it was a public performance and played inspiredly as if he were surrounded by an intimate circle of friends. Each item was received with tumultuous applause and when he took the final bow there were insistent calls of *bravo* and *bis.* He gave one encore after another, playing studies, preludes, nocturnes. The audience went berserk. Even sedate and digni-fied matrons joined in the frenzied foot-stamping which enhanced the hand-clapping. A few days later the *Gazette musicale* published Liszt's review of the concert. He proclaimed Chopin not king but poet, describing him as 'elegiac, profound, chaste and dreamy'.[26]

The *France musicale* went even further. 'Chopin has done for
the piano what Schubert has done for the voice,' its anonymous
reviewer wrote. 'One might say that Chopin is a founder of a
new school of piano playing and piano composition. Nothing
equals the lightness and sweetness of his touch, nothing as
yet can be compared with his works; they are original, distinguished and charming. He is in a class by himself, and there
is no comparing him with anyone else.'[27]

The success was so complete and the public performance, in
retrospect, so much less of an ordeal than anticipated, that
Chopin began thinking of his own accord about giving more
concerts at some suitably distant date in the future. For once
the success was also financial. The proceeds were enormous,
well over six thousand francs. George was delighted, while the
poet Witwicki, some of whose poems Chopin had set to music,
sighed with envy. 'Try to recite poetry for an hour or so,' he
said, 'and see if you get six thousand francs for it.'[28]

Two months after the concert George took Chopin to spend
the summer at Nohant, where they had not been since their
move to Paris eighteen months earlier. Chopin dropped his
bags in his old room, ran his fingers over the disused piano and
immediately wrote off to Fontana to send him a new Pleyel.
Although Nohant was not so far off as Majorca, it took nearly
two months before the piano arrived.

The early part of the summer was wet, but life at Nohant
was as gregarious as ever. Maurice and Solange were down
for the holidays, Hippolyte came to stay with his wife and
daughter, the Berry regulars called at all times. In August the
Viardots came down for a fortnight, their arrival miraculously
coinciding with that of the new piano and the warm weather.
Chopin practised with Pauline Viardot little-known songs by
eighteenth-century composers; Louis Viardot wrote articles
about Spanish literature, Maurice sketched and Solange made a
show of practising the piano. Some mornings the entire house-
party went for a walk in the woods, George and the young ones
striding energetically ahead, Chopin, with his hair meticulously
waved and his hands in white gloves, following daintily on a
donkey.

The summer of 1841 gave Chopin and George Sand the
congenial working conditions they had vainly sought in Majorca

several years earlier. They had few distractions, comfort, company when they wanted it, and each other. Chopin, who usually worked during the day, sometimes stayed up by the piano until two or three in the morning while George, true to a lifelong habit, wrote from midnight to dawn. They helped each other. George, who was working on *Consuelo*, the story of an opera singer inspired by Pauline Viardot, leaned heavily on Chopin for the musical background of the novel; while Chopin, who disliked the drudgery of making a fair copy of a recently completed composition, entrusted George with the demanding task of copying out several of his works.

He was working well, the comparatively quiet life at Nohant releasing those marvellous ideas which during the busy season in Paris had to be left in abeyance. With no lessons or social engagements to take up most of his time, he completed the Polonaise in F sharp minor (Op. 44), the Ballad No. 3 in A flat major (Op. 47), the Fantasia in F minor (Op. 49), the Prelude in C sharp minor (Op. 45), and the Tarantella in A flat major (Op. 43). The rough copy of the Tarantella was sent to Fontana in Paris, with instructions to go through it, add the occasional sharp or flat which might have been left out, decide whether the work should be written in 6/8 or 12/8 time, make three fair copies with the repeats written out in full, and finally offer it to a suitable publisher. As always, Chopin was anxious to sell his work to the highest bidder and instructed Fontana what to ask for each item or collection of items. The magic figures flowed from under his pen like music, building up into a tremendous *crescendo*: 300 francs, 500 francs, 600 francs, 1200 francs, 2000 francs, 3000 francs.

There were other requests as well. Fontana was to buy and send down to Nohant a favourite brand of soap, some scent, a bottle of patchouli, an ivory hand with a black handle for scratching one's head, two pairs of Swedish gloves. He was also asked to call at rue Tronchet and retrieve a cushion and a hot-water-bottle. When the parcel arrived without the last-mentioned article, Chopin sketched it so that Fontana should be able to identify it without further difficulty and send it down by the next post.

Towards the end of the four-and-a-half months' stay at Nohant he decided that he no longer liked his apartment at

rue Tronchet and asked Fontana to find him another. Before
the house-hunting assumed the agitated character of two years
earlier, George stepped in and offered Chopin the use of one
of the two pavilions situated in the back garden of her apartment
at rue Pigalle. It only remained for Fontana to pay off the
outstanding bills for rue Tronchet and take charge of the
removal. Inevitably he was instructed to call urgently at the
hatter's and order a new fashionable hat to be ready for collection on the day of Chopin's return to the capital.

The move to the garden pavilion at rue Pigalle was beneficial.
George was at hand when Chopin needed attention. She made
him start his day with a warm drink and insisted that he saw a
doctor when he spat blood. She arranged for him to be fetched
and returned in style when he was asked to give lessons at
pupils' homes and, being the shrewd businesswoman that she
was, obtained for him a fee of thirty francs an hour instead of
the twenty he charged when he was teaching at the pavilion.
In December he played again before Louis Philippe and the
royal entourage, this time appearing on his own and in a
white cravat.

He was preparing for a public concert which was to be held
early in the new year. His favourite singer Pauline Viardot
was available to participate, and so was his old friend the cellist
Franchomme. Even so the last few weeks before the scheduled
date were a nightmare. All the old fears returned, the tension,
the irresolution. One of his newly-accepted pupils, Wilhelm
Lenz, recorded a conversation they had on the subject of
public performances.

'Do you practise much before a concert?' Lenz asked.
'I go through a terrible time before a concert,' Chopin told
him. 'I do not like appearing in public, but it is expected of a
person in my position. I shut myself away for two whole
weeks and play Bach. This is how I prepare for a concert, I
never practise my own compositions.'[29]

Once the date of a concert was settled, Chopin's indecision
found an outlet in clothes. His intimates were only too familiar
with an agonizing routine which preceded even a private
performance. Days before the set date he would order a new

outfit from his regular tailor and, to give himself freedom of choice, a second complete outfit from another fashionable tailor. On the day of the performance he would stare helplessly at the array of clothes laid out for him and mutter that he had nothing suitable to wear, would someone please lend him a jacket. On one such occasion he made Gutmann lend him his own, several sizes too large, and thus attired, pathetically reassured under the semi-disguise, he gave a splendid performance. It is perhaps significant that Chopin, with all his phobia of public appearances, once expressed a wish to be buried in his concert outfit.

On 21 February 1842 the Salle Pleyel again opened its doors to Paris high society. Chopin played some mazurkas, the Ballad No. 3 in A flat major (Op. 47), some studies from Op. 25, some nocturnes. The *Gazette musicale* gave him unstinting praise. 'Under Chopin's fingers,' the journal said, 'the piano is transformed into a new instrument which obeys the feverish impulse of a tender and passionate genius.' The Ballad had moved the reviewer to tears. 'It is sheer poetry superbly translated into sound,'[30] he concluded.

The rival *France musicale* reviewed the concert in the style of a gossip column, rhapsodizing over the dazzling beauty of the ladies in the audience, the lovely white hands, the opulence of the *grandes toilettes*, the prevalence of *bon goût*. 'The first success of the evening', the paper reported, 'went to Mme George Sand. The moment she arrived with her two charming daughters [in his ecstasy over the charms of the two young ladies the reporter omitted to verify that only Solange was a daughter, the other young lady being a cousin] all eyes turned on her. Anyone else may well have been embarrassed by so many eyes gazing at her like so many stars, but George Sand only lowered her head and smiled.'[31]

In his gauche way the reviewer of the *France musicale* paid Chopin the highest compliment of all. He was Chopin; his name was synonymous with greatness, he was above praise. All that a worshipful reporter could do was to point out that the best people in Paris had come to pay him homage. That was also George's view of the evening; in a letter to Hippolyte she said that the proceeds, five thousand francs, were proof that 'everybody' in Paris wanted to hear 'that most perfect

and exquisite of musicians'.[32] She was preparing a surprise for
him. His room at Nohant was being altered by expert builders
so as to improve its acoustics and turn it into a study worthy
of his music.

His triumph was tinged with sadness. News reached him
that on 21 February, the very day he played at Salle Pleyel,
his first piano teacher Zywny died in Warsaw at the ripe old
age of eighty-six. Other news from home was not calculated
to cheer him up. His father, at seventy-one, was coughing in a
way all too familiar and his mother's eyesight was failing. He
had not been writing to them as regularly as he used to and
the entire family, particularly his adored mother, felt hurt at
not having had first-hand information about his latest concert.
Justina, who very rarely added anything in her own hand to
her husband's letters, felt it necessary to put her reproaches
on paper and on 21 March she wrote:

> Dear Frycek,
> At last, after three whole months, we received a letter
> from you. You gave a concert, we read in the papers that
> you were going to give one and later that you had actually
> given it; it was embarrassing for us not to have heard it
> directly from you. It simply is not possible that all this time
> you have not had a free moment to write to your parents
> about yourself and also ask how they are getting on. You
> have hurt us, but I am sure it was not intentional. You
> forget, dear child, that your parents live only for you
> children and that every day they pray God to give you health
> and blessing.[33]

Chopin's silence was uncharacteristic, but it indicated a
change in his emotional bearings. He was no longer the dependent son who needed the reassurance of his faraway parents,
but a mature man sharing his life with a woman who gave him
a sense of belonging. Still, he was attached to his family, and
although he was no longer lonely for them as he used to be
during his first years abroad, he continued to miss them and
hope for another reunion. Every returning Pole was entrusted
with messages and presents for them; glasses for Nicholas,
engravings for the sisters, books for Louisa's husband, a gold

chain for Isabel's husband, toys for the young nephews and nieces. Once he sent his mother a ring with three diamonds of the finest cut. She knew he could refuse her nothing and in the same letter she reproached him for his negligence she also asked him to send her in secret three thousand Polish florins to help her pay a debt she had contracted without her husband's knowledge.

His mother's letter found him prostrate with a fierce attack of rheumatism and George spent three anxious nights by his bedside. He was hardly better when news reached him that Jan Matuszynski was dying of consumption. Jan had been a close friend ever since their schooldays in Warsaw. He knew of Frederick's unexpressed love for Constance and later, when he emigrated to Paris and shared Chopin's flat, was one of the first to know of his liaison with George. Although a doctor of some note, Jan knew no more than the rest of the medical profession of the time how to treat tuberculosis and had had recourse to regular blood-lettings. His end was agonizing. George and Chopin spent the last two days and nights of his life by his bedside, desperate at not being able to alleviate his pain. Chopin was calm and spared no effort to be of use, but when Jan died he broke down. They were the same age, they had the same illness. The thought was frightening.

George knew the cure. She collected her brood and in early May took them back to Nohant. Within two days Chopin was beginning to lose his pallor and within two weeks he was complaining that life in the country was too dull. He gave Solange piano lessons, joined in the reckless games she played with the village urchins and submitted to a course of treatment by Dr Papet. Another new Pleyel arrived and was promptly inaugurated. 'Chopin has composed two admirable mazurkas,' George wrote to Delacroix on 28 May, 'which are more worthwhile than forty novels and have more to say than the entire literature of the century.'[34] She herself was completing the second part of *Consuelo*, letting Chopin read it page by page as they came from under her pen, waiting for his comments.

They were eagerly awaiting the arrival of Delacroix, who was not only George's friend and Maurice's art master, but virtually the only Frenchman with whom Chopin had ever formed a close friendship. 'Come,' George had pleaded in a joint invitation, writing the word eight times and arranging it to look like a verse of poetry. 'Come,' Maurice reiterated, writing the word twenty-two times and also arranging it to look like a verse. 'Multiply the first verse by the second,' Chopin added, 'and put the total to the power of a thousand.'[35]

He began to know Delacroix in the summer of 1838, when he and George sat for a double portrait at the artist's studio, leaning against a piano which had been specially borrowed for the purpose from the firm of Pleyel. (The canvas has since been sliced in two, the half with Chopin finding its way to the Louvre, and the half with George to the Hansen Collection in Copenhagen.) Delacroix was already at the height of his fame. He had exhibited in many *salons* and in 1831, the year that an unknown Frederick Chopin and an ambitious Aurore Dudevant arrived in Paris, he was awarded the *Légion d'honneur*. Twelve years older than Chopin, he cultivated a touch of dandyism which was bound to appeal to the fashion-conscious musician. Friends who witnessed the growing affection between the two men jokingly remarked that what brought them together was their love of clothes. Indeed they used to spend hours seriously discussing fabrics, tailors and trends of fashion. Whatever slight jealousy Chopin might have felt at first at the friendship between George and Delacroix totally disappeared on closer acquaintance. Delacroix became one of those rare people with whom Chopin sometimes, though only sometimes, discussed music.

Artistically, it was an uneven friendship. Delacroix, who in his early youth had trained to be a violinist, was open to music; Chopin, who could still sketch like an inspired amateur, had little interest in art. 'Delacroix understands and admires Chopin,' George observed; 'Chopin does not understand Delacroix. He thinks highly of him as a person, likes him and respects him; but he loathes the artist in him. Delacroix is a man of parts, he appreciates music, understands it and knows it; his taste is sure and delicate. He never tires of listening to Chopin. He relishes him, he knows him by heart. Chopin accepts the homage and is touched by it, but when he looks at a painting by Delacroix he is pained and has nothing to

Nohant, George Sand's country estate, by her son Maurice Sand, 1850

A hitherto unpublished letter from George Sand (Aurore Dudevant) to her cousin Clotilde (postmarked Paris 8 October 1838), in which she lets slip her secret plan of going to Spain. Shortly afterwards she and Chopin left for Majorca say to him. He is a musician; nothing but a musician. His thoughts can only be translated into music. He has much wit, subtlety and malice, but no understanding whatever for painting or sculpture. Michelangelo frightens him, Rubens horrifies him, anything which seems eccentric scandalizes him. He shuts himself in what is most narrow and conventional. Strange anomaly in one whose genius is the most original and individual there has ever been.'[36]

Delacroix came down at the beginning of June and was slightly dismayed by what he described as a monastic régime. At certain hours of the day there was no one about: George was shut up in her study, Chopin's presence was felt only through whiffs of music which floated through the open window and mingled with the twitter of the birds. Social entertainment was confined to country walks and a game of billiards. Even the neighbouring squires seemed to prefer minding bullocks to paying calls. Chopin, however, was not an assiduous worker and the two friends were often lost in endless discussions: the relation between sounds and colours, the art of the fugue, the superiority of English tweed over French wool. Delacroix fell into the leisurely rhythm of Nohant and stayed a whole month, returning the following summer and for many years to come.

There were other house-guests that summer: the actor Bocage, with whom George had once had a fleeting affair and with whom she had uncharacteristically retained a lasting friendship; Countess Marie de Rozières, a former pupil of Chopin and thanks to him Solange's piano mistress; and finally Pauline and Louis Viardot. Chopin continued to cough and George suffered from severe headaches and eye-trouble. Sometimes they changed roles as patient and nurse, caring for each other with exemplary devotion which looked to all but the shrewd Mlle de Rozières as the expression of unflagging love. After quietly observing them for a week or two she found herself agreeing with Marie d'Agoult who had been suggesting for some time that it was compassion rather than love which still bound Mme Sand to an ailing, jealous and difficult man of genius.

The summer at Nohant again brought forth new compositions, including the Three Mazurkas (Op. 50), the Impromptu

7

No. 3 in G flat major (Op. 51), the Ballad No. 4 in F minor
(Op. 52), the Polonaise in A flat major (Op. 53) and more.
Chopin's source of inspiration seemed inexhaustible. His
genius had reached the most perfect stage of its development,
radiating with all the intensity of its romantic nature. At
thirty-two he was at the zenith of his power.

The glory and the agony

In the summer of 1842 George and Chopin decided with one accord to move out of rue Pigalle and find a place more suitable to their style of life. Since the stalwart Fontana was on the point of emigrating to America, the unenviable task of house-hunting fell to Countess Marliani who promptly recommended an elegant complex into which she herself had recently moved. George and Chopin came up to inspect the premises and returned to Nohant well pleased with what they saw. Square d'Orléans, as the complex was called, became the most permanent of their joint Paris abodes.

Situated near the present rue Taitbout, it had been built by an English architect in the style of an Italian *palazzo* and was owned by another Englishman living in London; hence perhaps the ascendance of the English name *Square* d'Orléans over the French variants of *Cité* d'Orléans, *Cour* d'Orléans and *Place* d'Orléans. The complex overlooked a well-kept lawn and consisted of nine numbered blocks with a large number of apartments, studios and mews for residents' equipages. The rents were high. Chopin paid six hundred francs a year for a small apartment on the ground floor of No. 9 while George paid three thousand francs a year for a larger one on the first floor of No. 5 and eight hundred francs for a penthouse studio for Maurice in the same block. The move took place in September.

The first few days were chaotic: furniture was moved in, windows were measured, curtains were made up, carpets laid, pianos tuned, pictures hung. Maurice hammered nails, George was in three places at once. 'The *maestro* is also exerting himself,' she told Hippolyte, 'and is preparing at No. 9 a magnificent drawing-room fit for his magnificent countesses and exquisite marchionesses.'[1] He had two pianos moved in, a grand and an upright.

The other residents of Square d'Orléans were mostly well-to-do musicians and artists. There were the Kalkbrenners, the Viardots, Alkan, Marmontel, the dancer Taglione, the sculptor Dantan who a year earlier had made a bust of Chopin, and many others. The exclusiveness of the place gave the residents a sense of community. Some made a habit of assembling every evening at Mme Marliani's at No. 7 for a communal dinner at shared costs. Neighbours dropped in on one another without ceremony and George hired a billiard table in order to provide entertainment. At times she imagined she was back at her beloved Nohant, playing the hospitable châtelaine to neighbouring squires.

She was well content with an arrangement which kept all members of the family within reach: Solange often home from her *pension*; Maurice in his studio high up, Chopin in his den a few doors away. But the composition of the family was undergoing a change. Partly to placate Maurice, who could not bear his *Maman* to be anything but chaste, and partly to justify her own creeping frigidity, she insisted that she loved Chopin like one of her children and referred to him as 'my other son'.[2] In her autobiography, published after his death, she neglected no opportunity of emphasizing the mother-son nature of their relationship and called attention to his proverbial susceptibility to feminine charm in words which a fond mother might use to describe the exploits of a naughty little boy. In the course of one evening, she wrote, he was known to fall in love with three different women, leave each of them with the impression that she was his one and only muse, only to forget all three by the following morning. There was not a trace of jealousy in her account; she knew full well that her so-called maternal hold over him was stronger than any drawing-room fancy.

The jealousy was all on his part. He had once been jealous of Delacroix; he was still jealous of Bocage, of the editor of the *Revue indépendante* which George had founded, of any man she drew into her orbit. In her characterization of Prince Karol, the tormented hero of her novel *Lucrezia Floriani*, George Sand had Chopin in mind when she wrote: 'One day

Karol was jealous of the parish priest who called to collect charity. Another day he was jealous of a beggar he suspected of being a lover in disguise. Another day he was jealous of a servant who, spoilt like all the servants in the household, answered with impudence. Then it was the pedlar, then the doctor, then a slow-witted cousin.'[3]

There is no reason to believe that George was anything but physically faithful to Chopin until the final phases of their liaison, but her freedom of association was bound to make him feel uneasy. Furthermore, her repeated affirmation that she loved him like a son was a slur on his manhood. When he was not jealous he was bitter. After four years of intermittent and unsatisfactory intercourse, his thoughts turned again to Countess Delphina Potocka who had recently returned to Paris.

Delphina, it will be remembered, left Paris in the summer of 1836 to rejoin her estranged husband in Poland. The Potockis' attempt to patch up their marriage proved unsuccessful and a year later Delphina left her husband again and divorce proceedings were instituted. She joined a married sister in Italy and in 1838, just as Chopin was entering upon his long association with George Sand, she embarked on hers with the young playwright and poet Sigismund Krasinski.

Born in Paris in 1812 while his father was a general in Napoleon's army, Krasinski was later taken to Warsaw and sent for a year to the Warsaw Lyceum. He was a precocious child and at fifteen became a law student at Warsaw university. It was probably then that he first met Chopin, two years his senior and a student at the conservatoire. Tradition has it that the two youngsters, each precocious in his own way, politely disliked each other; Chopin yawned ostentatiously whenever Krasinski recited a poem; Krasinski fidgeted noisily whenever Chopin played.

Krasinski's career at the university was short. His father was a strong supporter of the Russian régime and on one memorable occasion, when the entire studentship turned out for the funeral of a Polish patriot, Sigismund was the only one who, obeying his father's command, reported for lectures. There was a nasty reaction and the young count was promptly sent off to Geneva to continue his studies. He did not return to Warsaw until after the insurrection, by which time his father was branded as a Russian collaborator. For a long time after that Krasinski wrote under a variety of pen-names to avoid using a name he was ashamed of. In 1835 he published *The Undivine Comedy* and later *Iridion*, both plays which reflected his deep concern for Poland. Later he published the patriotic poem *Dawn* and many others. Together with Mickiewicz and Slowacki he was to become one of the great poetic trinity of Polish romantic literature.

He was twenty-six when he met Delphina in Naples; she was thirty-one. For both the meeting sparked off the greatest love affair of their lives; Krasinski's letters to Delphina fill volumes. But the families disapproved and the old Count kept reminding his son of his duty to marry and continue the line. After four years of pressure Sigismund yielded and agreed to marry the very attractive Countess Eliza Branicka.

Towards the end of 1842 Delphina returned to Paris where another of her sisters was married to the Prince de Beauvau. She took an apartment in rue des Mathurins and threw her *salon* open to the élite of French and Polish society. Her singing, like her powers of seduction, had improved with experience and her company was keenly sought. In whose *salon* Chopin first met her after her return it is not known; possibly at her sister's, the Princess de Beauvau, with whom he was on cordial terms and to whom he had dedicated a year earlier his Polonaise in F sharp minor (Op. 44). He found Delphina as desirable as ever and the sound of her singing carried him several years back. In due course he found an opportunity to tell her of his re-awakened interest and her reaction prompted a long explanatory letter which forms part of the vehemently disputed Chopin–Potocka correspondence. The date suggests that it was written in the privacy of his new sumptuous drawing-room at Square d'Orléans:

Paris, 19 November 1842

My own sweet life,

You want me to write an explanation or an apology, I am only a few steps away from you in Paris, still you want it in writing. May I then remind you of your promise that if my explanation is satisfactory you will forgive me and grant me your supreme favour. Let me explain everything.

About Mme Sand, people make up lies rather than stick to the truth. My liaison with her lasted less than a year, the moment I fell ill everything was over. I swear on my love for you and for my mother that that is the truth. Apparently I could not satisfy her, she wanted it five times a night and I couldn't. My illness served her as a pretext to break up with me. After that she tried to prove at great length and with learned arguments that my health did not permit love, then she went off and found herself another lover.

From then on she has been giving me true maternal love, she has been nursing me with devotion, you cannot imagine how kind she has been, and I accept it, you know how much I need tenderness and solicitude. But to say that I have been her lover all these years is a lie. All those who go to Nohant know about her lovers and everybody knows who her favourite is in Paris. At Nohant she writes all night, then during the day she shuts herself in her bedroom with a lover and everybody knows it. With her even the strongest of men will soon grow weak because she makes great demands, that's why she has been changing lovers so often. Her passion is insatiable, it is really a sickness, one must understand and forgive. After our break I still loved her, I wanted her, I found her attractive, but when I saw her relations with other men I lost my desire for her. Today I feel only friendship for her, I love her like a mother.

After the break with Mme Sand I had some affairs which did not last long, they were passions without love, hardly worth mentioning. Don't believe it if people say I am quick to fall in love. You have known me so well so long, I have not changed. Those pretty women, I always look at them with admiration and if any of them excites me and arouses my desire, I pull her to bed, but I do not give my heart that easily. Only you and Mme Sand had my heart, and you more than her, because I felt more passion for you, because you know me and understand me as no one else does. To her, a foreigner, I could not lay my soul bare because I knew she would not be able to understand me. The other women in my life were youthful dreams long since buried or winds of passion which swept over me for a short time. To those women I gave my bed, my body and a little of that life-giving fluid, no one ever possessed my heart.

When a violent love gets hold of me temptation and desire tear at me like wild dogs, the whole world ceases to exist, as it was with you. I am then ready to give up everything for a woman, even sacrifice my life and my creative power.

It was not like that with those other women, I never lost my head and took care not to exhaust myself so as not to use up my creative power, I spared my strength and the life-giving fluid. Except for Mme Sand, there has been no other love and passion in my life. My work will prove it best. When you and I were together I could only revise old compositions or prepare for the printers those which had been lying around. I could write new ones only when you were away for a long time and I was not spent dry making love to you. Now for the past few years I have composed a great many works, and not bad ones either, so you must clearly see it was not love which has been taking up my energy. And seeing that all these years I have loved only you and Aurore, you must admit that I do not easily fall in and out of love.

I feel I have explained everything so clearly that even a child would understand it. I have had one mistress who mattered, and then some affairs which hardly counted. After we parted you too had one lover who mattered, and no doubt several smaller affairs, so I think we are even with each other.

I have told you everything, I repent of my trespasses and await to be restored to favour. Oh Phindela, I have never loved anyone as much as you. You have always kept the tenderest spot in my heart and memory, I have never lost my inclination and desire for you. Even in Mme Sand's arms I always felt I would rather be in yours. Please forget the lies people tell about me and the evil gossip which comes between us. I swear I shall be better now for life has taught me forbearance, never again will I torment you with my jealousy. I have never loved anybody as deeply as you.

You were my first mistress, be my last. There will never be another after you.

I hope I have convinced you and that you will let me know if I can come to you tonight. But if this clumsy letter, sincere as it is, fails to move you, let me ask your forgiveness and try to soften your heart with music. Tonight, when I ask your pardon, I shall put a new improvisation at your feet, and perhaps my music will open your arms to me as before. Do you remember how you used to say I was a virtuoso in the art of love, I knew how to satisfy. My romance with Mme Sand has taught me much more, you'll see, now you will be the pupil and I shall teach you some little love games which are absolutely new and exciting. Have pity on me, Phindela, don't refuse, I want you so much, my desire is driving me mad, and then you will always have me on your conscience.

My heart is always with you.

Oh my poor heart, it has known more sorrow, sadness and yearning than happiness! Those tears which I have been fighting back for so long, I would like to shed them on your bosom. I now feel like playing and crying, I shall play for you as I have never played for anyone. Tears fill my eyes when I think you might refuse. You, the first and last love of my life . . . forgive me . . . my tears stain the paper . . . I beg of you!!! Answer me, I await your call as the dying await the sacrament.

With all my heart unto death,
Your Fritz[4]

Delphina's heart would have had to be of steel to resist such pleading. Whether she credited Chopin's allegation of George Sand's insatiety is another matter. She was woman enough to sense the hurt and jealousy behind his accusations, experienced enough to question a tale of passion turned into filial devotion. On the other hand her own moral code did not preclude overlapping, and with Krasinski about to be married, there was all the more reason to be kind. The old intimacy was revived, though there is no telling how long it lasted and with how many rivals it was shared; in due course it mellowed into loving tenderness which endured until Chopin's

death. In 1848 he dedicated to her the Waltz in D flat major
(the so-called 'Minute Waltz') from Opus 64. It was perhaps
during that Indian summer of their love that she gave him the
handsome purse he was to use during his pathetic stay in
England in 1848.

But Delphina's kindness was only a faint ray of sunshine in
a darkening sky. Chopin's heart was for ever fettered to George.
His sisters, believing his association with her to be the hostess-
house guest one he had made it out to be, rubbed salt into
his wounds when they hinted how happy they would be if he
found himself a wife. For him there was no more question of
getting married than of embarking on a new liaison. He had
bound up his life with George's and could visualize no other.
There were the precious moments of tenderness which made
up for everything; there were the bad patches when he was
prepared to believe the worst. Delphina was a refuge, but she
was often on the move, and Krasinski had not ceased to play
a part in her life even after his marriage. Chopin kept an
impenetrable façade; but the frustration and hurt, combined
with his longing for Poland and the unadmitted realization
that he would never go back, resulted in an over-riding sense
of guilt. At times the agony was unbearable. Gutmann once
heard him sobbing behind the closed doors of his study and
calling on God to forgive the poor sinner that he was.

His health fluctuated alarmingly. Some nights he coughed
so violently that there seemed nothing left inside him to be
coughed out except his life; he gasped for breath, was on the
point of choking. Doctors came and went, one treatment was
tried after another. In the autumn of 1843 he had a fierce
attack at Square d'Orléans while George was held up at Nohant.
He concealed it from her so as not to bring her rushing back
and she heard about it from Grzymala only when the worst
was over. It brought home to her, if indeed she needed it
brought home, how much they were part of each other's life.
'I miss him as much as he misses me,' she wrote to Grzymala
before starting back for Paris. 'I need to watch over him as
much as he needs my attentions. I miss his person, his voice,
his playing, his melancholy, even the heart-rending sound of
his coughing. Poor angel! As for me, he will never have to

go without me, you may be sure of that, my life is consecrated to him for ever.'[5]

She meant it; she could not see anything or anybody coming between them. If she tried to deny herself to him, she did no more than many a wife would do in her place when the initial zest had been lost. She loved him in the only way she could love lastingly—like a matriarch: overbearing as well as gentle, generous as well as demanding gratitude, wise as well as blind, self-righteous as well as reliable. It was not the sort of love that Chopin would have ideally wished for himself, but it was not one he could do without. He came to terms as best he could.

From 1842 onwards Chopin's main source of income came from teaching, since he again shunned the public platform. During the season he gave as many lessons as his health would permit so as to have enough money to live on during the long annual retreat to Nohant. At the same time he was choosy about pupils and disinclined to audition anyone without a strong personal recommendation. He was particularly wary of pupils who had already given public performances. Wilhelm von Lenz was a case in point.

Lenz arrived in Paris from his native St Petersburg in the summer or late autumn of 1842, and while waiting for Chopin to return from Nohant, took lessons with Liszt whom he had met many years earlier. One morning Liszt informed him that Chopin was back and gave him a card on which he had grandly written: '*Laissez passer*—Franz Liszt'. Lenz presented himself at Square d'Orléans at two in the afternoon and was confronted by a valet who informed him that the master was out of town. 'A manservant in Paris is an article of luxury, for a pianist to keep one is something unique,' von Lenz reflected while discreetly pressing something into the servant's palm. He was ushered into the drawing-room and a few minutes later Chopin appeared, card in hand, 'a young man of medium height, slim, haggard, worn with suffering and dressed in the most elegant Paris fashion'. Chopin did not ask the visitor to sit down and the following exchange took place with Lenz standing upright as if in the presence of royalty.

'What can I do for you?' Chopin said, his eyes on the card. 'You are a pupil of Liszt's I see, a pianist.'

'A friend of Liszt's,' Lenz corrected. 'I would be most grateful if I could work on your mazurkas under your guidance. I have already studied some with Liszt.'

'You have? In that case what do you want with me?' Chopin pulled out a small watch from his waistcoat pocket and consulted it. 'I still have a few minutes to spare. Be good enough to play what you have studied with M. Liszt. After that you will have to excuse me. I was about to go out and have instructed my servant to admit nobody.'

'So I am being auditioned like a novice,' thought Lenz, who, at thirty-eight, six years older than Chopin, enjoyed a professional reputation in St Petersburg. He strode to the grand piano, struck a defiant chord and then played a mazurka with an embellishment he had learnt from Liszt. It was a mistake.

'This added trait isn't yours, is it?' Chopin said in his soft voice. 'It's his, isn't it? He will meddle with everything.' Then, to Lenz's astonishment, he added: 'Very well then, you may take lessons with me, but only twice a week. It is difficult enough as it is to find a three-quarters-of-an-hour period which is not already taken up.'

He consulted his watch again. 'What do you do apart from playing?' he asked. 'What do you read?'

'My favourite authors are George Sand and Jean Jacques Rousseau,' Lenz answered quickly.

'It's Liszt who has told you what to say, I can see that,' Chopin said with a smile, his face suddenly looking very young and handsome. 'You have obviously been initiated. So much the better. But remember to be punctual, I start on the hour, my house is like a dovecot.'[6]

It was no vain boast. There was always someone waiting in the ante-chamber while another pupil was still in the drawing-room. Lenz made a habit of arriving early and thus met several of Chopin's pretty pupils on their way out. In his memoirs he recalled how the master used to escort the most beautiful amongst them all the way to the front door.

In 1842 the star pupil in the dovecot was a young Hungarian boy by the name of Karl Filtsch. 'When the boy starts touring,' Liszt said after he had heard him play, 'I might just as well close shop.'[7] The following year, at thirteen, Filtsch went to London and played at Buckingham Palace. Chopin had eyes for nobody but Filtsch and treated him with the respect and admiration due to a genius. 'Chopin allows the boy to play whichever way he feels,' Ferdinand Denis wrote in his diary in April 1843. 'I hear that all he says to him is: *We two understand this piece differently, but go your own way, play it as you feel it should be played, your interpretation is also right.*'[8] It was old Elsner speaking from Frederick's mouth.

One day pupils and friends were invited to Square d'Orléans to hear Filtsch play the E minor Concerto with Chopin providing the accompaniment on the second piano. It was like a command performance, no levity and few handshakes. The guests tiptoed to the far end of the drawing-room and sat down as unobtrusively as possible. After the performance, during which both pupil and master surpassed themselves, Chopin announced that he had to go out and the guests scuttled out without further ado. Only George Sand and Lenz were allowed to stay behind. The four of them drove to Schlesinger's music shop and Chopin bought Filtsch the score of Beethoven's *Fidelio*. 'I am grateful to you for today's performance,' Lenz remembered him saying to the boy. 'You have given me much pleasure. I was a happy young man when I wrote this Concerto. Accept Beethoven's masterpiece from me as a token of my esteem and in years to come, when you look through it, do think of me sometimes.'[9] Filtsch was too moved to speak and kissed Chopin's hand. He did not live to fulfil his master's hopes, for he died not long afterwards, aged only fifteen.

There were many other gifted pupils, though none so promising as young Filtsch. There were those princesses and countesses whose names grace the dedications of Chopin's works: Princess de Chimay, Countess Esterhazy, Countess de Kalergis, Countess Branicka, Countess d'Est, Mlle de Noailles. There were the professionals of all nationalities: the English Lindsay Sloper and Brinley Richards, the German Caroline Hartmann, the French Mme Dubois and Georges Mathias, the Russian Mme Rubio, the Italian Mme Peruzzi, the Polish Mikuli, the Norwegian Tellefsen. There were those who became close friends: Princess Marcellina Czartoryska née Radziwill who lived with her husband in Vienna but spent long enough periods in Paris to become an outstanding Chopin exponent; Countess Marie de Rozières whom Chopin recommended as

piano mistress for Solange and who gradually became a sort
of unpaid social secretary; and Miss Jane Stirling, the rich
Scottish spinster who constituted herself his guardian angel
when George Sand was no longer there.

Chopin had no worked-out method like Kalkbrenner, and
on the whole maintained, echoing his old master Elsner, that
the best way of teaching was to let the individuality of a
talented pupil assert itself. On the other hand he did toy with
the idea of producing a complete method of his own and from
time to time jotted down ideas for his projected *Méthode des
méthodes*. Many of his tips were included in his letters to
Delphina; some survived in fragmentary notes which after
his death passed into the hands of his sister Louisa and which,
after several changes of ownership, were acquired in London
by Alfred Cortot. His favourite dictum was that feeling and
intelligence—the two qualities he valued most—could not be
taught; what could be acquired were the mechanics of playing.
His tips therefore centred mainly round the use of the pedal,
to which he brought hitherto unknown subtleties, and the art
of fingering, where he introduced some daring innovations.
He scandalised traditionalists like Kalkbrenner when he
declared it was no mortal sin to place the thumb under the
little finger, let the middle finger cross over the thumb or
even—horror of horrors—make the middle finger cross over
the little finger. 'An accomplished virtuoso', he once wrote
to Delphina, 'may indulge in the most diabolical tricks.'[10] In
one of his unpolished jottings he tried to explain how he saw
the task of each individual finger:

> The aim is not to play everything with an equal tone. I
> believe the aim should be to shade with a tone of good
> quality. Piano players have long acted contrary to nature
> when they sought to give each finger equal strength. Since
> each finger is individually shaped, it is best not to seek to
> destroy the charm of the individual touch of each finger;
> on the contrary, it is best to develop it. We have the thumb,
> the strongest, and the little finger, at the other extremity
> of the hand; the middle finger, the freest, as a point of
> support; the forefinger; and the fourth finger, the weakest
> of all, the Siamese twin of the middle finger, to which it

is bound by the same ligament. Some piano players want to detach the fourth one from the middle one at all costs, an impossible task and, thank Heavens, an unnecessary one. There are as many qualities of sounds as there are fingers. The main thing is to know how to make the most of them as they are.[11]

In his Warsaw days young Frederick once expressed admiration for the pianist Rembielinski whose left hand was as flexible as his right. In his maturity he assigned to each one a different task. The left hand, he often said, was meant to act as a band leader, beating time and never wavering; while the right was there for the pianist to do with what he would and could. His own hands could apparently do whatever he asked them to do. Thin and rather small, they had an astounding capacity of stretching, opening up like the mouth of a snake about to swallow a rabbit.

During lessons he made his pupils sit at the grand piano, while he sat by the upright, ready to demonstrate a point or improvise an accompaniment for a piano concerto by Hummel, Beethoven, or himself. When carried away he went on with the lessons well past the appointed period. He expected his pupils to practise at home—though never more than three hours a day—and acquaint themselves with the theory of music, attend chamber music concerts and singing recitals, even take singing lessons. When he was pleased with a pupil's rendering of a set piece, he pencilled a cross in the margin of the pupil's copy. He rarely awarded more than three crosses of honour to any one person.

The legends about his lessons are legion. Once, we are told, a pupil played the opening *arpeggio* from a Study by Clementi. Chopin started violently in his seat. 'What was that?' he called. 'I thought it was a dog barking.'[12] He taught with prophetic zeal and, like a true prophet, was sometimes driven to exasperation when a pupil failed to grasp the message. Lead pencils broke in his hands like so many reeds, sheets of music were snatched and flung in the air, a string of extraordinary expletives sallied forth. But no sooner did a pupil's eyes fill with tears than the storm subsided and the lesson proceeded with infinite gentleness. His pupils worshipped him. They brought him flowers, ran errands for him, protected him from unsolicited callers. He held court like a prince.

One of his great admirers, though never a pupil of his, was the pianist Hallé. To him we owe much of the information we have about Chopin's musical idiosyncrasies during his years of glory.

'From the year 1836 to 1848, a period during which Chopin created many of his most remarkable works,' Hallé wrote after Chopin's death, 'it was my good fortune to hear him play them successively as they appeared, and each seemed a new revelation. It is impossible at the present day, when Chopin's music has become the property of every schoolgirl [this, in *c.*1895], when there is hardly a concert programme without his name, to realize the impression which these works produced upon musicians when they first appeared, and especially when played by himself. I can confidently assert that nobody has ever been able to reproduce them as they sounded under his magical fingers. In listening to him you lost all powers of analysis; you did not for a moment think how perfect was his execution of this or that difficulty; you listened, as it were, to the improvisation of a poem and were under the charm as long as it lasted.'

'A remarkable feature of his playing', Hallé continued, 'was the entire freedom with which he treated the rhythm, but which appeared so natural that for years it had never struck me. It must have been in 1845 or 1846 that I once ventured to observe to him that most of his mazurkas, those dainty jewels, when played by himself, appeared to be written not in 3/4 but in 4/4 time, the result of his dwelling so much longer on the first note in the bar. He denied it strenuously, until I made him play one of them and counted audibly four in the bar, which fitted perfectly. Then he laughed and explained that it was the national character of the dance which created the oddity.'[13]

Hallé was lucky to get off as lightly as he did; Lenz recalled how ill Chopin took the same criticism when it came from another quarter.

During a lesson, Lenz was playing the Mazurka in C major (Op. 33, No. 3) when Meyerbeer came in unannounced and sat down to listen. Suddenly Meyerbeer exclaimed:

'That's not three crotchets, that's 2/2.'

Chopin shot Meyerbeer a dark look and made Lenz play the mazurka all over again, beating time on the piano frame with the blunt end of his pencil.

'Two crotchets,' Meyerbeer persisted.

The blood rushed into Chopin's pale cheeks, his eyes were aflame. 'Three crotchets,' he said very loudly.

'Let me take it to the ballet dancers of my opera [*L'Africaine* was then in rehearsal],' Meyerbeer sneered, 'I'll prove it to you.'

'Three crotchets,' Chopin shouted, beside himself with rage. He pushed Lenz out of the way and played the mazurka over and over again, counting aloud, beating time with his foot. It was no use. Meyerbeer insisted that he was playing three crotchets like two. At last Chopin could take it no longer. He rose from the piano and shut himself in his study, leaving an embarrassed Lenz and an unrepentant Meyerbeer to see themselves out. Twenty years later, when Lenz met Meyerbeer in Berlin, they both recalled the incident. 'I meant no harm,' Meyerbeer explained. 'I thought he wanted it that way.'[14]

George Sand wrote in her autobiography that Chopin's feelings for Nohant were ambivalent; he longed for it while in Paris, was bored with it while in residence. That was not altogether true. He would not have returned to Nohant year in year out, for four or five months at a time, had he not found there what he needed: a family atmosphere.

He was familiar with George Sand's genealogy all the way back to the licentious Augustus the Strong, King of Poland, and was aware of the contemporary ramifications of his French quasi-family. In Paris there were the aristocratic Villeneuves, George's relatives on her grandmother's side, and the plebeian Braults, the relatives on her mother's side, with their presentable young daughter Augustine. In the country there was the half-brother Hippolyte Chatiron, born out of wedlock to a servant girl, drunk, boisterous and reeking of the stables, yet not unlovable; and there were his well-born wife and daughter. There were of course Maurice and Solange and their young friends, many of whom were sons and daughters of George's old admirers. Chopin liked the company of the young and, when not entertaining them with his mimes, he was improvising at the piano so that they could dance or play charades. It was like being taken back fifteen or even twenty years to the country houses in Szafarnia or the nursery at Cracow Precinct.

He was as fond of children as he had always been, particularly if they happened to be strong-minded young ladies under the age of two. He was completely captivated by Pauline Viardot's baby daughter, whom the mother had left at Nohant while she went on tour. He and George petted her like two doting parents and could refuse her nothing, as George wrote to Pauline in June 1843:

> She babbles in such a funny way and calls me Mummy if you do not mind and says 'Little Chopin' in a way which melts all the Chopins in the world. Naturally Chopin adores her and spends his life kissing her hands. It must be admitted that the young lady does not play hard to get. As a matter of fact she is an outrageous flirt and compromises him publicly. There are no pouts, funny gestures or monkey tricks which she does not practise on him. When she has had her soup there follows the scene of running round the dinner table with a leg of chicken in her hand. Pistolet [the dog] follows her lovingly, keeping an eye on the bone which is his by right. But the little one hands it to me for preference and I must accept the gift with good grace or else have my sleeves pulled out of shape.[15]

It is tempting to suggest that the sight of little Louise Viardot in her cot inspired Chopin to compose his Berceuse in D flat major, that gem of grace and delicacy, which he began that summer and which was later published as Opus 57; it is certainly the only lullaby he ever wrote. That year he also composed his Three Mazurkas Op. 56 and the Two Nocturnes Op. 55, dedicating the latter to his Scottish pupil Jane Stirling. He never dedicated any of his works to George Sand.

Since Fontana's departure for America he had been obliged, much to his distaste, to conduct his business transactions with publishers without an agent and—even worse—watch out for errors or omissions in his manuscripts. He was in Paris, preparing some recent work for the printers, when news reached him that in May 1844 his father had passed peacefully away at the age of seventy-three. They had not seen each other since their one and only reunion at Carlsbad nine years earlier.

The news told on his health and George rushed him to Nohant, the only place where she knew he might revive physically and mentally. She wrote to Mme Chopin a warm letter of condolence and assured her that she was looking after Frederick as if he was her own son. From the family's replies, either directly to her or to Frederick, it was obvious that they regarded her as a generous matron who had taken their frail Fritz under her wing and was looking after him like a real mother. Their gratitude shone from every line. When George learnt that Louisa and her husband had decided to come to France to visit Frederick, she offered them the use of her comfortable apartment at Square d'Orléans and the hospitality of Nohant.

Louisa and her husband arrived in Paris in the second half of July 1844 and were met by Chopin who had travelled up from Nohant. He had not seen his sister since he left Poland fourteen years earlier. He settled the visitors in Mme Sand's apartment, introduced them to his many friends, showed them the sights of the capital and arranged a musical evening in his own drawing-room. But the physical exertion began to tell and when he learnt that Professor Jedrzejewicz had some academic business to attend to, he left the couple in the good care of Mlle de Rozières and returned to Nohant to await their arrival. The reunion in the country, he later wrote to her, was every bit as wonderful as the first reunion in Paris. George took to Louisa instantly and the result was a period of perfect bliss, with Chopin acting the courteous host side by side with Mme Sand. There were animated conversations between the two women about every topic under the sun, pleasant walks in country lanes and a general feeling of well-being. When at the end of August it was time for the Jedrzeje-wiczes to start on their return journey, it was a real wrench. George invited them to return to Nohant as soon as possible and extended the invitation to the rest of the family in Warsaw. Her parting present to Louisa was a couple of sketches she

had made a few years earlier of Chopin at work; he was said
to prefer them to any professional portrait ever made of him.
That was not all. The following year, when she completed
—in four days—the novel *La Mare au diable* which was based
on local folklore, she dedicated it to Chopin and later sent
the original manuscript to Louisa in Warsaw.

The meeting of the two families marked the beginning of
a new phase in the relationship between George and Chopin.
The grievances of the past few years were submerged and a
renewed feeling of tenderness pointed to continued stability.
It was as if the old bond had been brought back to life by the
affection and approval of the Warsaw relatives. At the beginning of the winter, when he returned to Paris ahead of George
who was held up by some unfinished improvements on the
estate, he was aglow with tender recollections.

Of his twenty-odd extant letters to George Sand, two were
written in December 1844. Without deviating in any way
from the formal style of the other extant ones, he still managed
to infuse them with concern and longing. There was no form
of address; he plunged straight into the first paragraph and
never departed from the respectful *vous*. But although he
wrote deferentially and discussed nothing more intimate than
their respective states of health, the weather and mutual friends
recently seen, his tone was unmistakably loving. He begged
George not to worry about his health and told her how worried
he was about her plan to travel to Paris in extremely bad
weather. He missed her. He told her how he imagined her
at Nohant in her house frock, surrounded by her *chers fanfi*—
their pet name for the children—and asked her to give them
his love.

Ironically it was those *chers fanfi* who were to upset the
newly-found placidity and subject it to their own nascent
passions and jealousies. Maurice and Solange shattered George's
maternal Utopia and forced her to reassess her relations with
Chopin. In the delicate situation which already existed between
them, any new tension was bound to cause irreparable damage.

Parting

The early part of 1845 brought a further deterioration in Chopin's health and at thirty-five the thought of death was never far from his mind. One day he heard that the violinist Artot had died. 'To see us both together,' he wrote home, 'nobody would have thought that he would be the first to go, and of consumption too.'[1] He was careful, however, not to alarm his mother and sisters. 'I have survived so many people who were younger and stronger than me,' he wrote with levity, 'I am beginning to think I shall probably live for ever.'[2] In fact he was spared for only four more years; years of suffering, distress and decline.

The summer found him back at Nohant, listless and disinclined to work. He spent hours, sometimes days, writing enormously long letters to his family about nothing in particular. He discussed the newly-installed telegraph service between Washington and Baltimore, the tunnel under the Thames, the latest story about Victor Hugo caught *in flagrante*. Sometimes he peppered his letters with jokes he had heard in Paris, rendering them in French since they were as untranslatable into Polish as they are into English. 'Do you know why Godfrey of *Bouillon* was so called?' went one of them. 'Because he was the most *consommé* commander of his time.'[3]

His letters were so devoid of any real news of himself that at times it seemed as if he was trying to avoid an awkward subject. He was probably hoping to conceal from his family that he and Mme Sand were no longer the tender friends that Louisa had seen at Nohant the summer before. The winter months had introduced a new element of discord between them and although he refused to recognise it, his position in the Sand household was becoming increasingly untenable.

With all her love for her children, George Sand had never succeeded in giving them a sense of security. It was not so much her chosen way of life and her occasional delegating maternal duties to unsuitable substitutes as her blissful assumption that the love of the heart made up for any disorders in the family pattern. The children rarely had the reassurance of a domestic routine and for many years were buffeted between mother and father, mother and lovers, mother and tutors. They grew up self-centred and maladjusted. Maurice, a dabbler and his mother's darling, never detached himself from her apron-strings while Solange, self-willed and a snob, indulged in acts of spite to call attention to herself.

They were not the happy, outgoing youngsters who would welcome a stranger into their midst, but George, driven by her compulsive need to lavish love, was blind to their antagonism. She expected them to accept her 'other children', as she liked to think of Chopin and Pauline Viardot, as if they were their own brother and sister. It was a matriarchal pipe-dream. Maurice developed a crush on Pauline—married and a young mother as she was—and treated Chopin as an intruder. Solange tolerated Pauline and strutted round Chopin with all the un-innocent guiles of an awakening young girl. Chopin, for his part, could not see himself as a child with the children and claimed their mother's love as a man, while George, her passion spent, could no longer view him uncritically. All the elements for a family feud were there, only a *casus belli* had to be found.

It was provided, ironically enough, by George's own generosity, or rather, by her impulse to do good regardless of the effect it might have on her real children. She had long been showing kindness to Augustine Brault, the poor relative who in 1842, when taken with Solange to Chopin's concert at the Salle Pleyel, was mistaken by a rash reporter for a second daughter. At that time the thought of adopting Augustine had not yet occurred to her, but in 1845, when she learnt that M. Brault, a tailor's assistant, was about to bestow the girl on a rich protector, she offered to take charge of her and bring her up like her own. Legal complications ruled out adoption but George regarded Augustine none the less as her adopted daughter and set aside a handsome dowry for her.

To friends she happily said that she now had four of her children about her: Maurice, Solange, Chopin and Augustine.

Augustine, however, was no more acceptable to the Sand children as a sister than Chopin was as a brother. Solange hated her, Maurice fancied her. Solange began making insinuations and used her growing ascendance over Chopin to make him see the girl through her own eyes. Father Brault demanded to know whether M. Maurice's intentions were honourable and Mme Sand assured him that her son loved and respected Augustine like a sister. Solange insisted that she could prove what she had been insinuating while Chopin felt called upon to open George's eyes. He went as far as to suggest that Augustine should be sent away. Maurice told him to mind his own business, accused him of being a snob who could not forgive a poor girl for not being a countess, and finally informed him that he was no longer wanted in his mother's house. The entire household was plunged into fierce battle.

George was in a difficult position. She was fond of Augustine and wanted to do the right thing by her, but at the same time she would not hear anything against Maurice; and since she was unable to silence Solange who had gleaned some incriminating information from the servants, she turned the full brunt of her displeasure on Chopin, who had dared voice disapproval of Maurice's conduct. Chopin was indignant. He had always been consulted on the children's misdemeanours and was convinced that his past arbitrations in family quarrels had had a staying effect on all concerned. He totally failed to understand that, in Augustine's case, an enraged George was bound to defend a favoured son rather than listen to an irksome lover whom—whether he accepted it or not—she no longer regarded as one. He suspected other motives. They had stormy arguments which, in his state of frustration, degenerated into ugly scenes of jealousy. At such moments, as during some of his lessons, he let his temper fly and shouted hurtful accusations, blind to the presence of children, servants and even house-guests.

George argued, warned Solange, cajoled Augustine. After a thorough investigation and the dismissal of an old servant who seemed to know too much, the affair was hushed up and the hatchet buried. The rest of the summer passed amicably enough. In September 1845 Augustine came down to Nohant while Chopin returned to Paris for a few days. All was well again between him and George. As she was preparing to take Augustine on a few days' excursion in the country she found time to send him a note so that he would not feel lonely during his three or four days' absence from home. She was discussing nothing more romantic than the arrangements to procure Hippolyte a mount for the excursion, but her tone was genuinely affectionate. Suddenly, perhaps moved by her own memories, she switched from the formal *vous* to the second person singular and added swiftly: '*Aime-moi, cher ange, mon cher bonheur, je t'aime*';[4] with which she enclosed a lock of her hair.

But such moments of tenderness, tinged as they were with a shade of remorse, were infrequent; they certainly did not prevent her from viewing the crumbling realtionship with the speculative eye of a writer in search of material. She had always derived inspiration from personal experience, and her association with Chopin had given her fresh insight into the complexities of a lover's mind. In the early part of 1846, while Chopin was painfully dallying over the Barcarolle in F sharp major (Op. 60), the Polonaise Fantasy in A flat major (Op. 61) and the Sonata for Piano and Cello in G minor (Op. 65), George Sand effortlessly turned out *Lucrezia Floriani*. Situation and protagonists had been closely drawn from life.

Lucrezia of the novel was a well-to-do actress with four children born out of wedlock. Prince Karol of the novel was an ailing young man who had just lost his adored mother. His initial disapproval of the actress' morals melted away at the sight of her exemplary love for her children, and when he fell ill and she nursed him back to life with her selfless devotion, he fell deeply in love with her. She pledged him a mother's love and sealed the pledge with total capitulation. Unfortunately Karol was suspicious by nature and tormented her with his insane jealousy. In the end she could take his suspicions no longer and died of a broken heart.

George Sand had given Lucrezia all the virtues she admired most: compassion, devotion to children, constancy and the courage of her convictions. She was clearly an idealized version of herself. Prince Karol—a Polish name—was clearly modelled on Chopin. She had drawn him larger than life and the result was a devastating portrait of a tormented lover turned tormentor.

His chief crime was jealousy. He was jealous of the priest, the tradesmen, the servants. 'Karol was even jealous of the children. *Even,* did I say?' George Sand asked addressing herself to her readers in the manner of the day. 'I should have said *above all.*' Then she proceeded with the indictment:

> He did not understand his own feelings when he saw them devour their mother with their embraces. But since a jealous man's imagination is as presumptuous as a bigot's, he soon developed an aversion for the children, not to say real loathing. He said they were spoilt, noisy, obstinate, self-willed; he maintained that other children were not like that. He was annoyed to see them nearly always between him and their mother. He felt she gave in to them, let herself be their slave. . . .
>
> But in his lucid moments, when he was not obsessed with jealousy, he spoke and felt differently. Then he adored the children and admired everything they did, even when there was nothing to admire. He spoilt them even more than Lucrezia, let them make a slave of him without suspecting his inconsistency. Then he was happy and showed the angelic side of his character. . . . Oh what a cherub, what an archangel he could have been had he always stayed like that. At such moments, which sometimes lasted hours, sometimes several days, he was benevolent, charitable, compassionate and accessible. . . . But then what a fall, what a terrible cataclysm when joy was succeeded by anguish, suspicion and spite.[5]

George Sand made no attempt to disguise her model and went on to describe other give-away faults, together with some hitherto unsuspected ones:

> Since he was predominantly polite and reserved, nobody ever suspected what went on inside him. The more exasperated he was, the colder he grew and the extent of his fury could only be gauged by his icy courtesy. It was then that he was at his most unbearable. He wanted to have an

argument and subject life, which he did not understand, to principles which he was not able to define. He then became witty, sporting that false and carping wit of his, in order to torment those he loved. . . . And when he did not have the courage to contradict or poke fun, he shut himself away behind a wall of disdainful silence and pathetic sulkiness.[6]

It has often been asserted, from 1846 to the present day, that *Lucrezia Floriani* was George Sand's diplomatic way of telling Chopin to go out of her life. Nothing could have been less in character. George was not one to prefer long drawn out tactics to speedy handling and had she wished to end the association she would have found a surer method of having her intentions conveyed. She was not one to mince her words either. During one of their rows she actually warned him in no uncertain terms that if he did not become more amenable she would have to send him away. The truth was she did not want to send him away; she wanted to keep him on her own terms. After she had offered *Le Courrier français* the serial rights of *Lucrezia Floriani* prior to its publication in book form, she made a point of telling Chopin that it was not worth his while reading it. That was not the advice of a woman who wanted her novel to serve as an implied dismissal.

But although she probably never intended *Lucrezia Floriani* as a notice to quit, she was guilty of selfishness and insensitivity, allowing her lust for writing to set aside any thought for the humiliating repercussions the book was bound to have. Artistic Paris could hardly fail to identify the long-suffering Lucrezia with Mme Sand and the impossible Prince Karol with Chopin. Each new instalment was awaited with mounting suspense and Liszt, on one of his tours abroad, was annoyed when he could not get hold of the latest issue. Paris society watched avidly for Chopin's reaction. He remained impassive. Even as *Le Courrier français* was bringing out one instalment after another, from June to August, he was staying at Nohant as usual, with the subject of *Lucrezia Floriani* delicately avoided and the unruly children temporarily subjugated.

It was a beautiful summer, with rich foliage, fragrant flowers and a splendid crop of fruits. Mme Sand went into her seasonal jam-making. In August the twenty-four-year-old Matthew

Arnold made a tour of Berry in the wake of George Sand's rural novels and addressed her a letter of homage. He was invited to call and was astonished to find a traditional country-house atmosphere, with the hostess, in a comfortable house-frock, presiding over family and guests. 'The midday breakfast at Nohant was not yet over when I reached the house,' he recalled many years later, 'and I found a large party assembled . . . among them her son and daughter . . . and Chopin with his wonderful eyes.'[7] There were many house guests that summer, old friends of Mme Sand's as well as friends of the young generation. There were excursions, swims in the Indre, puppet plays and sessions of mimicry. Chopin gave his family an account of a visit to a neighbouring *château* and George added an affectionate postscript for his sister and mother.

That summer the eighteen-year-old Solange announced that she was engaged to a handsome squire called de Préaulx. Her choice seemed eminently suitable. The young man was well-born, well-to-do, well-mannered and clearly in love. Both George and Chopin were delighted and the pleasant preoccupation with Solange's forthcoming marriage helped to sink their recent differences. George, too, had an announcement to make. After fifteen years of dividing her life between Paris and Nohant, she decided to give up living in the capital and stay permanently in the country. Solange was due to leave the parental home in any case while Maurice, at twenty-three, was going to be given his own bachelor establishment in Paris. The understanding with Chopin was that he would spend the winter at Square d'Orléans on his own and rejoin Mme Sand in the country for the customary summer term of four or five months. The parting in November 1846 was all affability and solicitude. Nobody had any foreboding that Chopin would never see Nohant again.

On his return to Paris he was immediately confronted with a wave of speculations about the alleged rift between him and Mme Sand, substantiated by her ostensible decision to live away from him. One evening he found himself in a literary drawing-room where part of the evening's entertainment consisted of reading of excerpts from *Lucrezia Floriani*. He kept a straight face and had nothing but praise for the novelist's skill. Still the rumours about the alleged rift persisted and eventually reached Warsaw; but when his family tactfully asked what he was going to do with himself the following summer, he answered: 'But what I always do. I shall leave for Nohant as soon as it gets warm.'[8]

For the first time in many years he was living again like a bachelor, without the comfortable domesticity which George Sand had created around him. His beautiful titled pupils rushed in to fill the gap and Countess Delphina Potocka, involved as she still was with the married Krasinski and other men, became dearer than ever. In February 1847 George and Solange came to Paris to draw up the marriage contract and see to the trousseau. The visit lasted nearly two months. Chopin and Mme Sand went to the Luxembourg Gardens to admire Delacroix's new ceiling and called together on Mme Marliani who was no longer living at Square d'Orléans. One evening he gave a recital in his drawing-room to which he had invited his nearest and dearest. 'Mme Delphina Potocka whom I dearly love as you know,' he wrote to his family, 'left for Nice a while ago. Before her departure I played her my Sonata for Piano and Cello with Franchomme. I had invited Prince and Princess Czartoryski, Princess Würtemberg [sister of the former] and also Mme Sand. A warm and pleasant occasion.'[9]

With all the cordial restraint in their relations, he could not suppress a twinge of jealousy when he learnt that Mme Sand and daughter were having their busts done in marble by a notoriously lascivious sculptor called Clésinger. His suspicions proved right, although not in the way he had imagined. After three or four sittings Solange announced that she was breaking her engagement to de Préaulx and marrying Clésinger instead. Chopin was appalled and George withheld permission. When Solange remained intractable, she whisked her off to Nohant, hoping that distance would cure her of her caprice. Clésinger followed in hot pursuit, stormed both mother and daughter and eventually made it quite plain that an instant wedding was the best possible course for all concerned. George gave in. Chopin, in Paris, could not understand her change of heart and continued to express strong disapproval. The bride's mother, distressed as she was, felt that the least he could do was to trust her judgement and stop giving unwanted advice. Even when he eventually accepted her decision and offered Solange his felicitations, Mme Sand could not forgive what she regarded as unwarranted meddling in family affairs. She avoided communicating with him and he learnt the date of the wedding from the Forthcoming Marriages column of the Paris *La Presse*. It was held at Nohant, hurriedly and with little ceremony, on 19 May.

After the wedding George went up to Paris to relinquish the lease of her large family apartment at Square d'Orléans. Chopin helped her to choose a pied-à-terre at No. 3 and again they parted with the understanding that he would be joining her at Nohant later in the summer. Her first summer visitors, however, were the Clésingers, who, in seven weeks of marriage, had gone through most of Solange's dowry and needed free board and lodgings for as long as they could get it.

An early pregnancy and her husband's intemperate conduct had only increased Solange's pathetic need to make mischief. She got hold of an eligible young artist who was honourably courting pretty Augustine and whispered in his ear that his intended had been deflowered by Maurice. The result was catastrophic. The young man fled, Maurice was furious, Augustine miserable and George at the end of her tether. She told Solange off and home truths began flying backwards and forwards. Nohant again became the scene of ugly family brawls. During one such brawl, Clésinger hit his mother-in-law in the chest and Maurice rushed at him with a gun. When she recovered George told the Clésingers to leave Nohant and never darken her doors again.

Solange was not going to let her mother have the last word. From her hotel room at the nearby village of La Châtre she wrote to Chopin in Paris to ask whether she might borrow his carriage which was permanently stabled at Nohant, since she was in no fit state to use any other form of transport. Chopin, crediting her brief account of the recent scene at home, wrote directly to Mme Sand with instructions to put his carriage at Mme Clésinger's disposal. George felt as if she had been slapped on the face, but worse was to come. Immediately on reaching Paris, Solange gave Chopin her own full version of the quarrel, throwing in for good measure that *Maman* had been unfaithful to him. Prince Karol needed to hear no more.

He cancelled his projected visit to Nohant and stopped writing. George sent a barrage of anxious enquiries about his health —a dignified way of keeping in touch—and finally, when she had had no reply, she wrote angrily that he need never come back to Nohant unless he stopped taking Solange's side against her mother and promised never to mention Clésinger's name in her presence. Chopin was greatly agitated and for once throwing his customary reticence to the winds, rushed over to Delacroix and read him the full text of the ultimatum. Delacroix did not know what to say since he was as fond of Mme Sand as he was of Chopin; but he was appalled by the cruel tone of the letter. In his diary he noted that the novelist seemed to have taken over from the woman.

Chopin was faced with a terrible dilemma. He could not give up George, yet he did not have the heart to turn his back on Solange whose tale of woe brought out his sense of chivalry and whose insinuations made him feel the wronged party. He saw his entire world crumbling around him. After much deliberation he sent George his considered reply, using the formal *vous* and omitting any form of address:

Paris, 24 July 1847

I am not going to speak to you of M. Clésinger. I began to get used to the name only after you had given him your daughter.

As for her, I cannot be indifferent to her. You will recall how I used to intercede with you for both your children without favour whenever there was occasion to do so. I was certain that you were going to love them *for ever*, since this kind of love never changes. Unhappiness may cloud it but not alter its nature.

This unhappiness must be very deep indeed to forbid your heart to take an interest in your daughter when she is about to become a mother, and at a time when her condition requires maternal care more than ever.

In view of the gravity of what concerns your most sacred love, I shall not discuss today what concerns me. Time will act. I shall wait. *Always the same.*

Your very devoted
Ch.

Regards to Maurice.[10]

If Chopin hoped to re-awaken George's tenderness for Solange with his reference to maternal love, he had misjudged his tactics. Mme Sand needed nobody to tell her where her maternal duties lay, least of all Chopin who had more reason than most to appreciate how sacred they were to her. She sent her reply by return of post:

Nohant, Wednesday 28 July 1847

Ill as I am, I had ordered a seat on the mail coach and was about to set out by gig in this atrocious weather; I was going to Paris for a day just to find out how you were. That is how worried I have been about your health while you kept silent. During that time you thought things over and your letter is very calm. Very well, my friend, do what your heart now tells you to do and take its bidding for the voice of conscience. I understand perfectly.

As for my daughter . . . she has acted with ill grace when she said that she needed the love of a mother whom she detests and maligns, whose most saintly actions and home she defiles with atrocious talk. It pleases you to listen to what she says and perhaps to believe it. I will not engage in a battle of this kind; it appalls me. I would rather see you go to the enemy camp than defend myself against an enemy grown in my womb and nurtured on my milk . . .

Do look after her since you feel you have an obligation towards her. . . . I shall not grieve over that extraordinary *volte-face* of yours. Farewell, my friend. I hope you will recover from all your ailments, I have good cause to wish you better; and I shall thank God for this bizarre conclusion of nine years of undivided friendship. Let me hear from you from time to time.

There is no point in going over the rest.[11]

If George had hoped to shame Chopin into an act of contrition, she too had misjudged her tactics. He took her letter for a categorical dismissal and was too proud to beg readmission into grace. Like any rejected lover, he kept hoping against hope that his cruel mistress would realize the error of her judgement and take the first step towards reconciliation. When some time later he heard that Solange—though not her husband—was received at Nohant before going to stay with her father in Gascony, his spirits rose. He kept a regular correspondence with Solange and sometimes enquired what news she had from Nohant, no doubt expecting her to pass on his enquiries; but Solange was not the person to serve as a messenger of peace nor was she going to risk losing Chopin to her mother. George, for her part, did not appreciate the humiliating finality of her last letter and waited for a reply. 'I have not heard from him for three whole months,'[12] she bitterly complained to Mme Marliani in November. While each of them was waiting for the other to make a conciliatory gesture, time was splitting them further and further apart.

Chopin could not get her out of his mind. As the months went by, he tried writing to her, then burnt everything he had written. In February 1848, some six months after the break-up, he discussed it for the first time in a letter to his sister Louisa, giving his own analysis of the situation:

Mme Sand is in the country with Borie [a young journalist and, although Chopin could not be sure of it, her lover], her son, Lambert [Maurice's friend] and Augustine who is to be married, definitely this time, to a friend of Borie's, an arts master in the small village of Tulle. She has not written a word to me, nor I to her. . . . She has turned her daughter's nuptial chamber into a theatre and is putting on comedies there; she is trying to forget, to stun herself. She will only wake up when her heart, which today is dominated by her head, will hurt too much. As for me I have put a cross over all that. May God guide her and protect her, for she cannot tell a true attachment from flattery.

But then perhaps it is only I who sees some people as flatterers, perhaps her happiness is where I cannot see it.

For a long time her friends and neighbours could not understand what happened; perhaps they are used to it now. In any case nobody can follow the twists and turns of such a capricious soul. Eight years of a more or less settled life, that was too much for her. God has willed that the children would grow up during those years. Had it not been for me, her son and daughter would have long left her and gone over to their father. It is to his father Maurice will go

Jane Stirling (1804–1859), engraving by Achille Deveria

Frederick Chopin's visiting-card during his stay in London in 1848. The site now houses Aeroflot

Chopin's letter from London to Marie de Rozières, dated 19 November 1848: '. . . The weather in England this time of year is absolutely unbearable . . .'

at the first opportunity. But maybe these are the circumstances necessary for her life, her talent as a writer, her happiness. Do not let all this worry you, all this happened quite a while ago. Time is a great healer. Until now I have not come to myself yet. . . . All that has happened between us is that we have not seen each other for a long time, there has been no battle between us, no scene. And I have not gone down to see her only because she made it a condition that I should not mention her daughter.[13]

He concluded his confused account with a brave assurance that he was well and that there was no need to worry about his health. In fact he was getting weaker and weaker, his emotional distress accelerating the inexorable progress of an illness for which nineteenth-century medicine knew no cure. At times he was so weak he could no longer sit at his piano, and gave his lessons—when he did give them—reclining on a couch. When he dined at friends' he had to be carried upstairs, even when the dining-room was on the first floor. Drops of opium on lumps of sugar no longer alleviated the pains. The only thing which carried him through the cruel physical suffering was his music. One evening he invited some friends to Square d'Orléans to hear him and Franchomme play his Sonata for Piano and Cello. Hallé, who was one of the guests, recalled:

On our arrival we found him hardly able to move, bent like a half opened pen knife, and evidently in great pain. We entreated him to postpone the performance but he would not hear of it; soon he sat down to the piano and as he warmed to his work, his body gradually resumed its normal position.[14]

Partly to tear him away from his sorry state of mind and body, partly from their usual admiration for his art, friends like Franchomme, Léo, Perthuis and Pleyel began pressing him to give a public performance. After six years of retirement from the public platform, he agreed.

The single announcement in the press brought in such a rush for tickets that Pleyel, at Chopin's insistence, grudgingly

8

agreed not to put up any posters. The concert had been announced for 16 February 1848; two weeks before the date all three hundred seats of the Salle Pleyel, at twenty francs each, were sold out. Louis Philippe, the Queen, the Duke of Montpensier and the Duke of Orléans bought ten tickets each for their entourage, although a court mourning prevented them from attending personally. The Marquis de Custine bought two tickets and sent a note reproaching the 'Sylph of the piano'[15] for having failed to notify him in person of the forthcoming rare event. There was no George Sand to steer Chopin through the pre-concert tantrums, but his former pupil Jane Stirling, having quietly asserted herself as his guardian angel, shielded him from all possible vexations. She arranged for the concert piano to be sent to Square d'Orléans so that he could practise on it at home until the very last day; gave instructions for the Salle Pleyel foyer to be properly heated and the concert hall aired during the interval and finally, on the day, had the place filled with flowers to make it look like a drawing-room. On 16 February, at half-past eight in the evening, a weak and pale Chopin, as immaculate as ever in his dark concert outfit and well-groomed hair, walked unassisted to the platform and sat down to play.

As usual, the programme was lent variety by the participation of guest artists. There were two noted singers, one male and one female, who had brought along their own accompanists and sang well-known airs. Chopin opened the evening with the Trio in E major by Mozart which he played with Franchomme and the violinist Alard. His own compositions included his Sonata for Piano and Cello with Franchomme, a nocturne, a study, a waltz, some preludes and mazurkas, the Berceuse and the Barcarolle. Many of his listeners were familiar with one or more of these works, which had been published in previous years, and were eagerly awaiting to hear his own rendering of them. They had at least one surprise in store for them. Knowing himself too weak to play the Barcarolle with the force and volume he had originally conceived for it, Chopin altered the dynamics to suit his physical condition. 'He played the latter part of the Barcarolle, from the point where it demands the utmost energy,' Hallé recorded with admiration, 'in the most opposite style, *pianissimo*, but with such wonderful nuances, that one remained in doubt if this new reading was not preferable to the accustomed one. Nobody but Chopin could have accomplished such a feat.'[16]

The recital had taxed all his strength. As soon as he had taken his last bow he walked, still unassisted, to his dressing-room and collapsed into Jane Stirling's arms. The *Gazette musicale* proclaimed him the Ariel of pianists and Pleyel prevailed upon him to agree to two repeat performances in the early spring. Neither was to take place. Within days of the concert the barricades went up and what came to be known as the February Revolution broke out. There were no more public performances for Chopin in France but, in the wake of the revolution, an unexpected meeting with George Sand.

She was at Nohant when he gave his concert at the Salle Pleyel and deeply immersed in her *Histoire de ma vie* when the glorious news reached her of Louis Philippe's abdication and the birth of the Second Republic. Immediately she dropped her work and rushed off to Paris to see her socialist dream come true. The Republic had her in thrall. She offered her services to the new government and was entrusted with the writing and editing of a political column in the newly-founded official organ *La République*. She had no time or thought for private griefs.

She had put up at Maurice's, having given up her pied-à-terre at Square d'Orléans for fear of running into Chopin. Solange was at her father's in Gascony, expecting her baby any day. A few days after her arrival in Paris George called on Mme Marliani. She had just climbed the flight of stairs leading to Mme Marliani's apartment when the door was flung open to let Chopin out. They had not seen each other for eight months and not written to each other for seven, ever since George's dismissive letter the previous July.

There was no way of avoiding each other; besides, there were others present: the young artist Lambert who had escorted Mme Sand from Nohant, the explorer and diplomat Edmund Combes who was going to help Chopin down the stairs, the doorman. Chopin, his manners always impeccable, greeted Mme Sand with respect and when his greeting was acknowledged felt impelled to prolong the meeting for a moment or two. His account of the conversation was given in his letter to Solange the following day:

> Paris, 5 March, Sunday, 1848
>
> Yesterday I called on Mme Marliani and when I was about to leave I found myself in the entrance hall face to face with *Madame votre mère* who had just come in with Lambert. I said good afternoon to *Madame votre mère* and asked if she had had any news from you lately.
>
> 'I heard about a week ago,' she said.
>
> 'You have not heard anything yesterday, or the day before?'
>
> 'No.'
>
> 'Then I can tell you that you are a grandmother. Solange has a baby daughter and I am happy to be the first to give you this good news.'
>
> I then bowed and walked downstairs. The Abyssinian [Combes's nickname] walked down with me, but as I had forgotten to mention that you were well, a detail of particular importance to a mother (now you will be able to appreciate this, Mother Solange), I asked him to go up again as I did not have the strength to climb those stairs again, and tell her that both you and the child were doing well.
>
> I was waiting for the Abyssinian to rejoin me when *Madame votre mère* came down with him and asked me many questions about your health. I told her that you were fit enough to have written to me in pencil two days after the baby's birth, that it had been a difficult childbirth but that the sight of your little daughter made you forget all the pain. She asked whether your husband was with you and I said that the envelope seemed to have been addressed in his hand.
>
> She asked me how I was and I said I was well, then told the porter to open the front door for me. I bowed and the next thing I knew I was at Square d'Orléans, having walked all the way with the Abyssinian at my side.[17]

He never saw her again. Shortly after that chance meeting he left for England and when he returned to Paris, a dying man, she was firmly entrenched at Nohant, shutting her heart and mind to the call of the past.

George Sand had been the greatest emotional influence in Chopin's life. She had given him home, roots, a sense of belonging and, even when her passion had died down, companionship and loving care. Her dominating personality complemented the dependent element in his character. He leaned on her, loved her and benefited from her possessive generosity, accepting without regret that she was a Frenchwoman and therefore someone who would never penetrate the innermost folds of his Polish soul. What he could not accept was that her love for him, which he had not sought and which he had allowed to become the pivot of his emotional life, should cool off while he remained 'always the same' in his feelings for her. He did not understand the complexities of a heart which needed frequent rejuvenation and was constant only in a matriarchal sense; and he therefore misinterpreted her well-intentioned, though totally unrealistic, attempt to transform him from lover into son. He bore the humiliation of unrequited yearning with a mixture of bitterness and hope, clinging achingly to the vestiges of a love which had once shone so brightly for both of them. No woman had been so much part of his life, no woman had so much wrung his heart. He did not live long enough to put the bitterness of the separation behind him; perhaps he would have never been able to do so even if he had been spared for as many years as George Sand had.

A London season

Long before the February Revolution, which induced many artists to leave Paris and seek their fortune elsewhere, Chopin had been making plans to go to England.

His imminent departure had been mentioned in the press announcement about his forthcoming concert at the Salle Pleyel; his destination, however, remained undisclosed. Acquaintances not in the know began speculating. The Marquis de Custine wondered what the sylph was up to while George Sand discreetly instructed Maurice to find out whether he was returning to Warsaw or simply going to Gascony to see Solange. His family, having seen a copy of *Le Courrier français*, feverishly debated whether he was going on tour to Holland, Germany, Petersburg or, miraculously, to Warsaw; and his sisters even started a happy dispute over which of them should have the privilege of putting him up.

Once he began collecting letters of introduction to the English nobility and compatriots living in London, the secret was out. Even then only few people realized that his departure for Great Britain, in preference to all other possible destinations, had been prompted and engineered by Jane Stirling, the enamoured Scotswoman who had once been his pupil.

Jane Wilhelmina Stirling was born in July 1804—the same month and year as George Sand—at Kippenross House, near Dunblane in Perthshire. She was the youngest of thirteen children; by the time she was two one of her sisters was married and by the time she was twelve her mother was dead. Her father died when she was sixteen and she passed into the care of a widowed sister, Mrs Katherine Erskine, thirteen years her senior. Although Mrs Erskine was unencumbered by children and still pretty, she never remarried and spent the rest of her life as chaperone and companion to her young sister.

To her native Scottish clear-headedness, Jane Stirling added a strength of character entirely her own. At an age when society expected a young lady of quality to attend hunt balls and ply her charms on eligible bachelors, she preferred to remain single as long as she had not sighted her ideal match. She was accomplished, attractive and well-provided for; family tradition has it that she had had anything from sixteen to thirty-three proposals. She declined them all. Instead of limiting herself to conventional social interests, she showed curiosity for matters of the spirit. Kippenross House had a library, an art collection and a Scottish harp; she took an interest in all three. She was musical and, unlike many of her contemporaries, regarded her piano playing as more than a mere social accomplishment.

In 1826, when she was twenty-two, widow Erskine took her to Paris. They were well-connected and the aristocratic *salons* were open to them. From that year on the two sisters divided their life between Scotland and Paris, Jane becoming as proficient in French and as at home in the French capital as any other well-to-do francophile. And well-to-do she was, having inherited well from her parents, apparently without irritating legal restrictions on the management of her wealth.

It is difficult to ascertain in what year the two Scottish ladies made Chopin's acquaintance, but the likelihood is that it was some time in the 1840s. Jane Stirling came to Chopin as a pupil and, apart from her ability to pay his high fees, so pleased him with her admiration for his genius, that in 1844 he dedicated to her his Two Nocturnes (Op. 55). He was as gallant with her as with any other of his court admirers, but there was never any indication that she was more to him than a middle-aged, if well-preserved, rich spinster with whom it was agreeable to be on good terms. He recommended her to Franchomme, from whom she desired to have cello lessons and once, from Nohant, asked him to give her and Mrs Erskine his regards should he happen to see them.

Jane Stirling's adulation, which had been kept in check while George Sand reigned supreme, began to gush forth in the winter of 1846, when Chopin returned to Square d'Orléans and resumed a bachelor existence. She willingly shouldered all those chores he was so good at leaving to others and slowly but firmly asserted herself as his main prop, her mature age and social independence giving her an advantage over other benevolent rivals. On the face of it she was a sensible and practical Scotswoman; underneath she must have been lonely and aching to give. Most of Chopin's pupils had a sentimental crush on him; with Jane Stirling the sentiment flowered into belated love.

To judge by her portraits, she looked much younger than her forty-odd years and even when allowing for the artist's flattery, she must have been a bonnie lass. She was several years older than Chopin; like George Sand, like Delphina Potocka. And again like George Sand and Delphina Potocka, she was determined to win him for herself. What their relations were *in camera* is a matter for conjecture. It is not unlikely that for a short while they might have been lovers. What man, rejected by his partner of many years, would not have allowed himself to be comforted by an attractive and persistent woman who made no secret of her eagerness to serve? Friends and pupils soon sensed that Jane Stirling had become an integral part of Chopin's entourage and accepted her for whatever the two of them wished her to seem—a benevolent patroness, an unpaid business agent or a devoted general factotum. Nobody disputed her authority when she took it upon herself to direct operations before the Salle Pleyel concert.

She was discreet about her new role; the only person she took into her confidence was widow Erskine who accompanied her unmarried sister on her various missions of mercy and whose name Jane Stirling always coupled with her own when issuing instructions on Chopin's behalf. At the same time she took the trouble to win the approval of the family in Warsaw. She had met Louisa during the latter's visit to Paris and, after Chopin's break-up with George Sand, neglected no opportunity to be remembered to her. There must have been a tacit and grateful acceptance of her benevolent presence in dear Frycek's life, for at the end of 1847 she felt confident enough to send Louisa a New Year's present, an English *Lady's Companion*. Chopin, forwarding it on her behalf, called her his 'good Scotswoman'.[1] He rarely referred to her in any other way, except when he called her one of the two Erskine ladies. In none of his references was there any shade of tenderness; only uneasy gratitude for a tremendous devotion he found as indispensable as it was overbearing.

Jane Stirling rightly thought that the best way to tear him away from the clutches of the past was to thrust him into an entirely new environment. Through her numerous brothers-in-law and sisters-in-law she was well-placed to open doors for him in London and assure him of a warm welcome in the houses of the great. Deep down, however, she was prompted by an entirely personal motivation. She ardently hoped that once Chopin had met her illustrious relatives, he might well come to realize the good sense of marrying her. That loving hope overrode any sensible consideration of the obvious risk of taking a consumptive to a country whose climate was notoriously unfavourable to tuberculars.

Chopin probably never gave a thought to the health risk of the plan. He was only too happy to have somebody care for him and make decisions for him. There was nothing much to hold him to Paris apart from lessons and the prospect of concerts he did not really want to give. There were no draft manuscripts waiting to be revised and sent to the publishers, no new themes to be captured and developed in the privacy of his study. For nearly eighteen months, ever since his final summer at Nohant, he had written no music, the physical decline and the ravages of the heart combining to dry up that mysterious fountain which had once seemed inexhaustible. England held out a promise of rejuvenation. He began toying with the idea of settling there permanently, and the London *Athenaeum* of 8 April, announcing his forthcoming arrival, mentioned it as a distinct possibility.

On 20 April 1848 Chopin crossed the Channel, and after a few hours' rest at Folkestone, continued his journey to London where his Scottish guardian angels had already booked him lodgings at 10 Bentinck Street, near Cavendish Square. He went straight to bed. The following morning his heart sank when he looked out of the window and saw a grey sky and deserted streets. It was Good Friday. After Easter he moved to a beautiful apartment at 48 Dover Street, Piccadilly, with a noble staircase and a vast drawing-room, where he stayed until

the end of the London season in July. Jane Stirling had thoughtfully provided him with his favourite brand of drinking chocolate
and a supply of notepaper with his monogram. His old acquaintance Broadwood sent over one of his pianos, as did the London
representatives of Pleyel and Erard. The drawing-room
accommodated all three grand pianos with ease and elegance,
but the landlord, sensing that his tenant was no ordinary
person, immediately doubled the rent.

On May Day the sun came out and Chopin ventured for the
first time into 'that abyss which is called London'.[2] The capital
was full of Paris celebrities, Berlioz, Kalkbrenner, Thalberg,
Hallé, Pauline Viardot, all busy giving concerts. He heard both
Pauline Viardot and Jenny Lind sing the part of Amina in the
rival productions of Bellini's *La Sonnambula* at Covent Garden
and Her Majesty's. 'A Swede without an equal,' he wrote to
Grzymala of Jenny Lind. 'Her singing is sure and pure, her
piano as sustained and smooth as a hair.'[3] The twenty-nine-year-
old Queen Victoria had also attended that performance. 'The
Queen was more loudly applauded than Jenny Lind,' he wrote
to his family. 'They sang *God Save*, with everybody standing
up, also Wellington and all the nobles. Very impressive, this
esteem and sincere respect for the throne, law and order. There
was such enthusiasm, they could not settle down.'[4]

The news that he was in London spread fast and music
lovers were eager to hear the illustrious Chopin whose works
had been regularly published by Wessel's and whose piano
concertos had been performed once or twice by the Philharmonic
Society. The conductor of the Philharmonic paid him the signal
honour of inviting him to play during the current season, in
the face of Kalkbrenner and Hallé who had been vainly trying
to secure just such an invitation. Appearing with an orchestra
was, however, the last thing Chopin had in mind; for him it
was a nightmare magnified *ad infinitum*. He went to see the
orchestra in rehearsal and came away convinced that it was not
for him. 'Their orchestra is like their roast beef and turtle soup,'
he wrote to Grzymala. 'Solid, strong, but nothing else. And
the worst thing is that they never rehearse properly, for time
costs money. There is only one rehearsal, and even that one
is open to the public.'[5] The practice seemed to him so unreason-
able that three months later he again mentioned it with indigna-

tion, this time to his family. 'These gentlemen have only one rehearsal,' he wrote, 'and the public is admitted by complimentary tickets. How was I expected to rehearse and try things out?'[6] He tactfully turned down the offer on grounds of ill-health, but his refusal rankled.

He accepted, however, invitations to play socially, and was heard in the drawing-rooms of Lady Gainsborough, the Marquess of Douglas, Lady Blessington of Gore House, Kensington, Mr Henry Chorley, the music critic of the *Athenaeum*, and a few others. On 15 May he played in the presence of Queen Victoria and Prince Albert who were being entertained by the Duke and Duchess of Sutherland at their magnificent home Stafford House (now better known as Lancaster House, Stable Yard). Every one of the eighty guests was highly distinguished and the setting was dazzling. Chopin, who had played before French royalty and seen the interiors of the Tuileries and St Cloud, was none the less tremendously impressed. To his family he wrote:

> The staircases are famous for their magnificence. They do not lead from a vestibule or an ante-chamber, but rise in the middle of the rooms, like part of a huge hall, with most splendid paintings, statues, galleries, carpets, all of the loveliest design and the loveliest perspectives. You should have seen the Queen on those stairs, under the dazzling light, covered with diamonds and ribbons, and the noblemen wearing the garter, all descending the staircase with the utmost elegance, conversing in groups, lingering on the various landings, where at every point there is something to admire. What a pity some Paul Veronese could not have seen such a spectacle, he would have painted another of his masterpieces.[7]

Other performers that evening included the singers Lablache, Mario and Tamburini, but the royal attention focused on Chopin. Prince Albert walked over to the piano to talk to him, and the Queen, after he had been presented to her, addressed him twice, an unprecedented honour for an itinerant musician. A few days later the *Illustrated London News* reported that 'Chopin's playing before Her Majesty at Stafford House on Monday created a great sensation'.[8] He felt confident that he would soon be summoned to the Palace. When no word came, he thought it was due to court mourning; only too late did he realize that he had given offence. He had turned down the invitation of the Philharmonic Society, little suspecting that the conductor was also in charge of court concerts.

In the meantime he was being introduced to all the best people. His letters read like a page from *Debrett* or *Burke's Peerage*: the Duchess of Cambridge who was the Queen's aunt, Lady Lincoln who was sister to the Marquess of Douglas, the Duke and Duchess of Sutherland, Lady Dover who was a niece of the Duchess of Sutherland, Lady Shelburne née de Flahaut, Lady Jocelyn, Lady Granville, Lady Cadogan, Lady Stanley, the Duchess of Argyll, Lady Norton, Lady Molesworth, Lady Peel, Lady Byron. Of the latter he wrote home: 'We seem to get on well, talking to each other without understanding, she in English I in French. I can well see why she bored Byron so.'[9]

While impressed with the English aristocracy's love of culture he was disappointed with their attitude to music. 'It is all the same to them whether the music they hear is good or bad,' he complained to Grzymala, 'since they feel obliged to have it about them from morning till night. In this country they have flower shows with music, dinners with music, charity sales with music.'[10] He was astonished to learn that in England he was not to describe himself as an artist. 'By art they mean here painting, sculpture and architecture,' he explained to Grzymala. 'Music is not an art and is not called art; and if you say you are an artist, the English think you are a painter, a sculptor or an architect. Music is a profession, not an art, and no one ever speaks or writes of a musician as an artist, for in their language and customs music is something apart from art, it is a profession. Ask any Englishman you like.'[11] He felt his music was regarded as a service and was not a little taken aback when old Lady Rothschild asked him point blank how much he cost. When he replied that his fee was twenty guineas an appearance, her ladyship tut-tutted and counselled moderation.

He was much worried by his dwindling resources. His Dover Street apartment, the wages of a good-for-nothing Italian manservant, the hire of carriage and coachman, all dug deep into his purse. He made it known that he was prepared to accept pupils at a guinea a session, but found his patronesses unbelievably calculating. Lady Peel, whose daughter had been taking two lessons a week with a local musician at half-a-guinea a time, transferred her to Chopin; but to make up the difference in the fee, restricted her to one lesson a week. The Duchess of Sutherland did the same. An unnamed lady who took lessons throughout the season, left for the country without paying for the last nine. Yet another, who was booked for two lessons a week, often skipped both without notice or offer of compensation. It was all undignified and belittling. He missed the adulation of the Paris *salons*, the sensitivity of his Paris audiences and, last but not least, the musicality of his Paris pupils. He poured out his heart to Delphina Potocka, to whom he wrote:

> I cannot understand what the English expect from music. They admire old as well as new music, but it must be written by foreign composers. They pay for music because it is a form of luxury, but they do not feel it or love it. Today, when I asked my new English pupil to sing me a phrase, she squealed like a mouse which had been trodden on until I felt sick. I have never heard an English person sing in tune, they are always off pitch. I think the English have wooden ears and will never create anything noteworthy in music.[12]

After the unintentional slight to the Philharmonic Society, no more offers to play in public came his way. A small but influential côterie seemed to be forming against him, headed by J. W. Davison, the editor of *The Musical World* and the music critic of *The Times*. Davison had never taken to Chopin's music and although he conceded that it was not devoid of originality, he described it as early as 1841 as crude and limited. In 1843 he had a change of heart, or so it seemed; for when commissioned by Wessel's to write notes for the English edition of Chopin's works, he produced an 'Essay on the Works of F. Chopin', which was couched in the most fulsome language. His real admiration, however, went to Mendelssohn and it was after the latter's premature death in 1848 that his dislike for Chopin took on a distinctly personal form.

What brought matters to a head is not altogether certain, but it had something to do with a letter of condolence which some German musicians in Paris proposed to send to Mendelssohn's widow. When asked to add his name to the list of signatories, Chopin refused, explaining it would be incongruous for a Pole to sign a letter beginning with the words 'We German musicians'. The *Musical Times* reported the refusal though not the reasoning behind it, plainly insinuating jealousy and prejudice. Later Davison further exceeded his capacity as music critic by accusing Chopin of priggishness and obsequiousness, while Chopin, from his Dover Street drawing-room, retaliated by calling Davison 'a creature of the late Mendelssohn'. 'Davison does not even know me,' he indignantly wrote home, 'but he imagines that I have something against Mendelssohn, or so I am told. It does not really matter, it only goes to show how people all over the world will say things which are not true.'[13]

He was beginning to despair of ever making his mark on London. 'I am being introduced to lots of people,' he wrote to Grzymala, 'but I hardly know who they are and I do not know my way about London society. Twenty years in Poland, seventeen in Paris, it's not surprising that I am slow to get on here, particularly that I do not speak the language.'[14]

After several weeks' wait, two semi-public performances were arranged for him through the good offices of the Broadwoods. Though involving publicity and the sale of tickets, the concerts promised to be intimate since they were due to be held at private homes. The first took place on 23 June 1848 at three o'clock in the afternoon at the house of Mrs Sartoris at 99 Eaton Place, where a Blue Tablet commemorates the occasion; the second was held on 7 July at four in the afternoon at the Earl of Falmouth's at 2 St James's Square. Mrs Sartoris, born Adelaide Kemble, was a singer before her marriage and had heard Chopin in Paris. Her drawing-room had the ambiance of a Paris *salon* and was a meeting-place for the cultural élite of the time—Browning, Thackeray, Dickens, Leighton, Watts, Wilkie Collins, the Carlyles. The Earl of Falmouth was a different proposition altogether. A music-loving bachelor, walking about town in such beggarly clothes as made Chopin wonder why nobody stopped to give him a penny, he had a sumptuous house and a generous heart. Both *matinées* were publicized in *The Times* and both, at a guinea a seat, were sold out days in advance. The total number of people who heard Chopin publicly in London did not exceed however three hundred and fifty, the Earl of Falmouth's house accommodating two hundred and Mrs Sartoris' about a hundred and fifty.

The supporting artist on 23 June was the opera singer Giovanni Mario who sang three times, while Chopin appeared four times, playing some of his studies, mazurkas, nocturnes, waltzes and the Berceuse. On 7 July he again played the Berceuse, as well as the Scherzo in B flat minor (Op. 31), and more studies, preludes, mazurkas, ballads and waltzes. This time he had two supporting artists, one being Pauline Viardot and the other her young cousin Molina di Mondi, who had sung for him at his last appearance in Paris. Physically he was totally unfit to give concerts, spitting blood in the mornings, coughing so violently that with each attack he thought the end was coming, unable to get about without support; yet, once at the piano, he achieved what Hallé described as the triumph of the spirit over the flesh, playing with that sylph-like touch which had come to be identified with his name.

He had some excellent reviews. The *Athenaeum* wrote after the first concert: 'We have had by turns this great player and the other great composer, we have been treated to the smooth, the splendid, the sentimental, the severe in style, upon the pianoforte, one after the other. M. Chopin has proved to us that the instrument is capable of yet another "mode"—one in which delicacy, picturesqueness, elegance, humour, may be blended together so as to produce that rare thing, a new delight'. The reviewer had also noticed how well Chopin expounded in practice one of his pet theories. 'Whereas other pianists', he continued, 'have proceeded on the intention of equalizing the power of the fingers, M. Chopin's plans are arranged so as to utilize their natural inequality of power.'[15]

The second *matinée*, at the Earl of Falmouth's, happened to fall on an afternoon when Chopin was feeling less sick and consequently able to put some vigour into his playing. The *Athenaeum* reported that the second concert was even better than the first and the *Illustrated London News* observed that 'the delight of the auditory was unbounded'.[16] The most detailed review, and the one which pleased Chopin most, appeared in *The Daily News* of 10 July. Mentioning the 'numerous and fashionable assemblage' and indulging in a witticism about the English way of calling a *matinée* a performance given well past noon, the reviewer listed the works performed and then went on to say:

> In these various pieces he showed very strikingly his original genius as a composer and his transcendent powers as a performer. His music is as strongly marked with individual character as that of any master who has ever lived. It is highly finished, new in its harmonies, full of contrapuntal skill and ingenious contrivances; and yet we have never heard music which has so much the air of unpremeditated effusion. The performer seems to abandon himself to the impulses of his fancy and his feelings—to indulge in a reverie, and to pour out, unconsciously as it were, the thoughts and emotions that pass through his mind. We have never heard any public performance so remote from anything like exhibition or display. M. Chopin does not seek to astonish by loudness of sound or mechanical dexterity. He accomplishes enormous difficulties, but so quietly, so smoothly, and with such constant delicacy and refinement, that the listener is not sensible of their real magnitude. It is the exquisite delicacy, with the liquid mellowness of his tone, and the pearly roundness of his passages of rapid articulation, which are the peculiar features of his execution, while his music is characterized by freedom of thought, varied expression, and a kind of romantic melancholy which seems the natural mood of the artist's mind.[17]

The Times did not review the concerts, Chopin having taken the precaution not to send any press tickets to Mr Davison; but the latter, in his capacity of editor of *The Musical World*, had his own back. The issue of 8 July mentioned them as the fourth item in a column entitled *Miscellaneous*; and Davison, hinting at a current drawing-room gossip about a budding attachment between the unmarried Jenny Lind and Chopin, ended his reportage with what he no doubt hoped would be a lethal flourish:

M. Chopin has lately given two performances of his own pianoforte music, at the residence of Mrs Sartoris [the writer had not bothered to verify his facts], late Miss Adelaide Kemble, which seem to have given much pleasure to his admirers; among them Mlle Lind, who was present at the first, seems to be the most enthusiastic. We were not present at either, and, therefore, have nothing to say on the subject. *Vivat Regina!*[18]

The two concerts left Chopin with three hundred guineas in pocket; a handsome profit, considering that a full house at the opera, with takings of one thousand guineas an evening, netted only one hundred after overheads. He reckoned that in Italy he might have lived on the proceeds for a whole year; in London he felt he could hardly last six months after paying his rent and carriage. The short London season was over, his pupils were leaving for the country, there was no more playing for a fee in the great houses. He was dogged by the fear of having nothing to live on. 'What will become of me?'[19] he kept asking Grzymala. He became thrifty in small matters, refusing to pay one pound and fifteen shillings excess postage for a bundle of newspapers which Grzymala had sent from Paris and which were charged at letter rate, since the sender had scribbled a couple of words on the back of the envelope. 'Next time please don't write anything on the back of the envelope,' he begged Grzymala. 'The English are very strict about things like that.'[20]

He was frustrated. During the three-months'-long season he had given only two semi-public performances while Thalberg, whom he had never admired, had given twelve in a row. His hopes of establishing himself in London were receding. 'If I had the strength to run all day from one influential person to another,' he explained to Grzymala, 'if I had not been spitting blood, if I were younger and if I were less tied down by social obligations, perhaps I could have started life all over again.'[21] His heart was in Poland, where an insurrection had been crushed in the region of Poznan, and in Paris, where there had been bloody clashes between demonstrators and the new Republican government.

He kept scanning French papers for a mention of George

Sand, whom he knew to be in the service of the government, and often asked Grzymala if he had any news of her. He gloated over reports of M. Brault accusing Mme Sand of having procured young Augustine for Maurice; felt jealous at the thought that she might be gallivanting round with Clésinger whom she said she hated but whom gossip gave her for a paramour. One day Pauline Viardot mentioned that she had received a letter from Mme Sand asking after him. 'How she must be playing the part of the righteous mother,'[22] he wrote bitterly to Grzymala.

Jane Stirling was always at hand, smothering him with her attentions, relentlessly tightening her gentle hold over him. The more she hovered around, the less attractive he found her. She tired him with her adulation, put him off with her obvious expectations. 'My Scottish ladies are kind and loving,' he wrote to Grzymala time and again, 'but they bore me to death.'[23] At the same time he could not do without their protection and dined at their place whenever he had nothing else to do. London society watched the ménage with curiosity and Jane Carlyle, taking things as she found them, addressed herself to Jane Stirling as the accepted intermediary when she wanted to convey her admiration for Chopin. Indeed Jane Stirling did all she could to lay claim to him, discreetly suggesting that he was her intended. She made him drive round with her and Mrs Erskine to leave visiting cards at friends' houses—*en famille*—refusing to see that after three or four hours' jolting in a carriage he was more dead than alive. For his part he did not have the heart, or the strength, to point out that those calls were killing him, guiltily feeling that it was the least he could do to please a devoted woman he did not love.

He needed company. When left on his own, even for a moment, he was beset by dark thoughts. Every evening he went out to see people he did not much care for in order to stun himself with the noise and glitter of society. He had acquired a new manservant, Daniel, a French-speaking Irishman, who escorted him on his outings, carried him upstairs, eased him into a seat and waited to take him back to Dover Street when he was ready to leave. As soon as he was alone he did not know where to turn. He could no longer compose, he hardly felt like playing. A page in his pocket diary shows that one day he whiled the time away playing noughts and crosses with himself. On another page he drew a gate leading to a churchyard, with one large tomb and a cross overshadowing several smaller ones. He wrote letters, to his family, to Solange, Marie de Rozières, Gutmann and, above all, to Grzymala.

Even at the best of times he found it difficult to take decisions. Now, in his distressed condition, he left decision-making entirely to Jane Stirling who, with one eye to his welfare and another to her own matrimonial hopes, suggested that he should spend a few weeks in Edinburgh as the guest of her brother-in-law Lord Torphichen. It mattered little to him where he went. London after the season was becoming a social desert. There was no reason for him to stay behind, no reason why he should not avail himself of the hospitality arranged for him by that serviceable, influential, if boring, Scotswoman. He allowed himself to be planned for without much interest or regret. 'I can feel neither grief nor joy,' he wrote to Grzymala before his departure for Edinburgh. 'I no longer feel anything, I am just vegetating and waiting for it all to end quickly.'[24]

In Scotland and England

Calder House, twelve miles west of Edinburgh, was an ancient castle where three hundred years earlier John Knox had celebrated his first communion. From his bedroom window Chopin could see a beautiful park, acres of woodland, ruined fortifications and a range of distant mountains. In the drawing-room he found a Pleyel, which Jane Stirling had had dispatched from London. The two sisters, who had travelled ahead of him, must have given their brother-in-law to understand how much depended on the success of the visit, for the seventy-eight-year-old Lord Torphichen went out of his way to be affable to the young foreigner with whom he had little in common. He dragged him round the long dark corridors hung with portraits of ancestors, tapped the eight-feet-thick walls of the castle and told blood-curdling stories of the resident ghost. He was not particularly musical but, to make his guest relish his stay all the more, he regaled him with Scottish songs which he sang in a gruff, ageing voice.

Unfortunately the guest was in no condition to enjoy anything. The twelve-hour train journey from Euston on 5 August had brought on another fit of blood-spitting and the Highland air seemed to make things worse. His lungs refused to acclimatize. 'I can hardly breathe,' Chopin wrote to his old friend Fontana. 'I am just about ready to give up the ghost.'[1] He kept thinking of old friends who had been carried off in their prime and imagined the mournful scenes round his own grave. One day he made his will.

What distressed him most was not the thought of death but the feeling that he had nothing to live for. He was a composer who could no longer compose. The move to England had not worked the hoped for miracle and the blank music sheets on top of the Broadwood piano in his bedroom remained untouched. 'Not a single decent musical idea in my head,' he wrote to Franchomme from Calder House. 'I have lost the knack.' He felt that if there was a prize to be won for not composing, not even bad music, he would have surely won it. 'I wish I could compose just a little,' he concluded without hope, 'if only to please the good Mrs Erskine and Miss Stirling.'[2]

But he could no more compose than a donkey could dance at a fancy dress ball, to use his own pathetic words. He wondered whether to stay on in Scotland, as Jane Stirling intended him to do, or return to London to avoid the rigours of a Highland winter. In either case he was not in his element. His inability to take part in any English conversation above the level of ordinary civilities irked him, the table talk which regularly revolved round family trees bored him, Jane Stirling's maddening solicitude drove him to the solitude of his bedroom, where only his manservant Daniel had the freedom of entry. 'I am lonely, lonely, lonely,'[3] he cried out to Grzymala. He longed to be back in Paris, but he was too sick and dependent to break out of the protective cocoon which Jane Stirling had woven round him. Besides, post-Revolution Paris was not the capital he had known and loved. For the second time in his life he felt homeless and uprooted, only this time he had no youth to urge him on, no faith in his ability to create. At times he felt he no longer remembered those haunting Polish peasant songs which had been the basis of his inspiration and which he believed indelibly engraved on his heart. His only Polish contact was Dr Lyszczynski, the Calder House family doctor, who was a resident of Edinburgh. Chopin clung to him as to a lifeline and during the next three months availed himself several times of the Lyszczynskis' invitation to stay in their house in between visits to various Scottish manors.

What kept him going—and that in spite of his phobia of public performances—was the prospect of giving concerts and making enough money to keep his head above water. Even before he left London he had already agreed to take part in a motley concert in Manchester, where he was to share the honours of the evening with three Italian singers and an orchestra. The concert was organized by the Gentlemen's Concert Society, one of the oldest and wealthiest musical societies of Manchester, whose programmes, ambitious as they were, included such tell-tale announcements as 'The Committee earnestly request the co-operation of the Subscribers in maintaining silence during the Performance'.[4] Hallé, who had just accepted a post in Manchester, groaned when he first heard the orchestra at work; Chopin, however, no longer cared very much about other musicians' standards of performance and was prepared to play some of his piano compositions mainly to earn the agreed fee of sixty guineas.

He was still resting at Calder House when his Scottish ladies arranged to call *en famille* on a kinsman who lived in a castle by the sea. They drove along the cliff road in two coupés, the sisters in one, Chopin and Daniel in the other. Suddenly one of the horses in Chopin's carriage reared, the reins snapped and both horses began careering madly down the slope. The coachman was hurled out and sustained severe injuries while the horses tore on uncontrollably. Mercifully the carriage was dashed against a tree and came to an abrupt standstill on the very edge of a cliff, its chassis shattered and one horse buried under the debris. Daniel leapt out unharmed and pulled the bruised and shaken Chopin after him. 'To tell you the truth,' Chopin wrote to Grzymala a few weeks later, 'I envisaged my last hour with equanimity, only the thought of having my hands and legs fractured terrified me. All I need is to be an invalid.'[5]

The accident did not put him off the concert any more than his sickness did, but his natural irresolution made it difficult for him to decide which works to play. The organizers kindly attributed his frequent changes of mind to the accident which, they thought, prevented him from practising the works he had originally suggested. Eventually a list was agreed upon and the programme went to press. That did not prevent him from changing his mind again and a last-minute notice had to be inserted. He went to Manchester by train and was installed in the spacious house of a rich German Jewish manufacturer renowned for his hospitality and love of music. Jenny Lind was another house guest.

It was an evening performance. Twelve hundred people, the largest audience Chopin ever had, assembled on August 28 at Manchester's Concert Hall. The orchestra played overtures by Weber, Rossini and Beethoven and the singers sang excerpts from Italian operas. In between items Chopin played the Andante Spianato (Op. 22), the Scherzo in B flat minor (Op. 31), the Berceuse, a waltz, a ballad, some mazurkas. The audience watched wide-eyed as the celebrated artist, too feeble to walk, was carried on and off the stage. His playing, which even in his heyday tended to be lost in a large hall, was barely audible at the back of the house and the co-operation of the subscribers in maintaining silence during the performance was apparently not fully given. The front rows, however, applauded persistently and made him give an encore. Two days later the *Manchester Guardian* raved about the singers but remained somewhat guarded about Chopin, suggesting that both his music and manner of execution had 'subtle elaboration rather than simple comprehensiveness of composition'.[6] The *Manchester Courier* and *Lancashire General Advertiser* was more forthcoming, writing that Chopin's music was 'perfectly original' and that although he was no Thalberg, his execution was unsurpassed for 'brilliancy of touch and a delicate sensibility of expression'.[7] Press reviews apart, Chopin's participation seemed to have made little impact. George Osborne, who was the singers' accompanist, said that the music was not suitable to the hall, and Hallé summed up briefly and sadly: 'Chopin came, played, but was little understood.'[8]

Chopin kept a brave face. He informed Grzymala that the concert had been successful and that two more were in the offing. Jane Stirling was indefatigable. She clinched the arrangements for a concert in Glasgow and in the meantime took him back into the family fold, this time to Johnstone Castle, just a few miles outside Glasgow, to stay with her widowed sister Mrs Houston. As usual, Chopin could not make up his mind what to play. The musical director of the Glasgow concert came up to discuss the items, returned to town satisfied that he had a final list in hand, only to receive an urgent message to go back to the castle to discuss some vital changes. The other participant, a lady singer, was far less capricious.

The concert was held on 27 September at the Merchants' Hall at two thirty in the afternoon. The printed programme proclaimed the patronage of ten titled gentlewomen headed by the Duchess of Argyll, and the audience included some of the most distinguished names of the Scottish nobility, amongst

them several members of the Stirling clan who had foregathered
to support their kinswoman's protégé. Even so, the hall was
only one-third full, and the number of people present could be
counted in dozens; presumably the charge of half a guinea a
ticket for a matinée was too high by local standards. The
gentlemen of the press were impressed, however, by the
formidable array of illustrious names and moulded their reportage to suit the occasion. The *Glasgow Herald*, though it found
Chopin 'difficult to understand',[9] pronounced him a refined
musician; the *Glasgow Courier* pointed out that Chopin's style
blended 'the elegant, the picturesque and the harmonious',[10]
borrowing both phrase and view from the London *Athenaeum*
of 1 July; and the *Glasgow Constitutional*, after some pleasing
banalities, concluded with a list of the nobility present.

The proceeds were disappointing, but there was an unexpected boon from another quarter. Prince and Princess Czartoryski, who had had to leave their Vienna home in the aftermath
of the 1848 European upheavals, were in London. When they
heard that Chopin was in Scotland they made a point of
travelling up. He met them in Edinburgh and invited them to
his Glasgow concert. The effect on him of a reunion with two
compatriots, particularly with the beautiful princess who had
been one of his most brilliant pupils, was miraculous. He came
alive again, chatted excitedly in Polish, forgot how ill he was.
After the Glasgow matinée Mrs Houston gave a grand reception at Johnstone Castle to which the Czartoryskis were invited.
It was one of the few social occasions in Scotland he unreservedly
enjoyed.

A week later he was to play at the Hopetoun Rooms in
Edinburgh. The flicker of life lit by Princess Czartoryska's
presence died down with her departure and he was too weak
and depressed to be driven to town to inspect the hall and
piano. Still he approved the advertisements in the local press
for a programme which unaccountably departed from common
practice and was to present him on his own, without a guest
artist to sing in between items. The tickets were again priced
at half a guinea each and Jane Stirling, fearing another poor
attendance, discreetly bought a hundred and distributed them
among friends and members of the Edinburgh Polish community.

The evening recital on 4 October included an *andante et impromptu,* studies, preludes, mazurkas, a ballad. The Scots in the audience were appreciative, while the Poles were carried away by the sound of their native melodies embroidered into Chopin's compositions. 'That they went home to the hearts of such of the performer's compatriots as were present', the *Edinburgh Evening Courant* wrote a few days later, 'was evident from the delight with which they hailed each forgotten melody, with all its early associations, as it rung in their ears'. The reviewer's own favourite was the Berceuse, composed at Nohant during the summer of 1843 when little Louise Viardot had Chopin in thrall. 'The recurrent air in the minor key', the reviewer wrote, 'conveyed to the mind the idea of night with its silence and repose, while the introduced *motif* fell on the ear as a lullaby, the beautiful simplicity of the melody, with all its sleepy softness, prompting the idea of a cradle song. It was, indeed, a charming morceau, exquisite alike in its composition and in its performance'.[11]

Not all papers had a music critic equal to the task. 'Our limits will not admit of our entering into a lengthened description of Chopin's system,' the *Edinburgh Advertiser* excused itself, then plunged into a crib from that well-thumbed article in the London *Athenaeum* of 1 July: 'But one may mention that, while all other pianists strive to equalize the power of the fingers, M. Chopin aims to utilize them; and in accordance with his own ideas, are his treatment of the scale and the shake, as well as his mode of sliding with one and the same finger from note to note, and of passing the third over the fourth finger.'[12] *The Scotsman* cautiously limited itself to a factual account of Chopin's recital, informing its readers that 'he played his own music, which is that of a musician of genius'.[13]

That was Chopin's last public appearance in Scotland. He continued to play in the drawing-rooms of his various hosts and hostesses, sometimes to an audience of four or five, sometimes to as many as thirty. He never refused a request to play before those intimate and adoring audiences, for playing, as always, momentarily carried him away from physical and emotional suffering. But he did not think much of their musicality. His final verdict on the English and their attitude to music was given in a letter written to Grzymala on 21 October 1848:

> Lady — , a great lady at whose castle I recently spent a few days, is considered here a great musician. One day, after I have played to them and some of the Scottish ladies have sung their songs, they brought out a kind of accordion and she began playing on it the most dreadful tunes with the utmost gravity. . . . Another lady who accompanied her own singing, did so standing up while playing, no doubt to be original, and then sang French romances in an English accent, *J'aie aiimaiie* [*j'ai aimé*] which sounded like jay-ay-may!!! The Princess of Parma told me there is a lady here who whistles to her own guitar accompaniment. Those who know some of my works say to me in French: please play me your Second Sigh [The English edition of the Two Nocturnes Op. 37 was entitled *Les Soupirs*, The Sighs; No. 2 is the one in G major]; I love your bells. And every comment ends with the words *leik water*, which means that my music flows like water. I have never played to an Englishwoman without her saying *leik water*. And they all look down at their hands while playing and play the wrong notes with feeling. What characters, God help them.[14]

It was autumn and plans had to be made for the winter ahead. Staying on in Scotland meant living off other people's hospitality and, although this was convenient in view of his impecunious situation, it also had its disadvantages. He was never allowed to stay long in any one place. No sooner did he get used to being in one great house than Jane Stirling would point out the need to go somewhere else. In less than three months he changed hosts as many as ten or eleven times. After Calder House he stayed at Johnstone Castle as the guest of Mrs Houston; at Stachur, near Loch Lyne, as the guest of Lady Murray; at Keir House in Perthshire as the guest of William Stirling-Maxwell, chief of the Stirling clan; at Lady Belhaven's at Wishaw; at the Duke of Hamilton's in his sumptuous palace sixty miles from Edinburgh. He never had a corner he could call his own.

Jane Stirling could hardly have failed to notice that the

constant jolting in a carriage or train was sapping the life out of him, but she was too obsessed with her own matrimonial ambition to alter course. Having brought Chopin all the way from Paris to Scotland to meet her kinsmen, she could not stop short when the goal seemed so near. Relatives and friends accepted her claim to him and expected, as she did, that a proposal would soon be made. When, in spite of the family's affability and his own manifest gratitude to Jane, Chopin failed to ask for her hand in marriage, she put it down to his reserve. She could not, and would not, see that if he allowed her to drag him from one castle to another, it was not because he wanted to meet prospective in-laws but because he was too weak and dependent to do otherwise. Sometimes he managed to escape for a few days to Dr Lyszczynski's in Edinburgh, where the Polish atmosphere did more to revive him than the doctor's course of treatment. Jane Stirling and Mrs Erskine would follow him like two furies, insinuate themselves into his haven and fetch him away in their carriage. He felt suffocated under their benevolent tyranny; trapped.

Society watched and speculated. Rumours of an imminent marriage trickled to Paris and both Gutmann and Grzymala, independently of each other, wrote to enquire if they were true. 'I am nearer a coffin than a bridal bed,'[15] he told Grzymala; and 'She might just as well marry death,'[16] he said to Gutmann. But it was not the thought of death which kept him off marriage; it was the thought of Jane Stirling as a wife. He had no love for her. She filled him with boredom, not desire. 'There must be some physical attraction,' he explained to Grzymala. 'The unmarried one is too much like me. How can I bring myself to kiss myself?'[17] Deep down there was another reason which stifled any faint temptation he might have felt to accept the offer of home and comfort. He had not forgotten the painful lesson he had learnt at the hands of the Wodzinskis and had no reason to suppose that the Scottish gentry would welcome him as a son-in-law any more than the Polish aristocracy had. 'A rich woman needs a rich man,'[17] he wrote to Grzymala, tactfully substituting wealth for class so as not to offend his old friend, who was a count.

It was easier to explain his feelings to Grzymala than to the expectant lady; nor would he have ever broached the subject had it not been forced on him by some of Jane Stirling's kinsfolk, no doubt at her own request. The discussion took place some time in October, shortly after the Edinburgh recital, either with Mrs Stirling of Keir House or old Lord Torpichen of Calder House. Chopin was courteous but unequivocal. 'Friendship is friendship,' he said. 'It gives no claim to anything else.'[17]

Jane Stirling took her defeat gallantly, but Chopin felt he could no longer trespass on the family's hospitality. Besides, he could not face the prospect of the harsh Scottish winter. As always, chance came to the rescue. A letter from London asked him to play at a charity function in aid of Polish exiles. He had never refused a call to help needy compatriots and the opportune request gave him an excuse to leave without embarrassment. He bade farewell to his many Scottish friends and together with Daniel took the train back to London, where he arrived on the last day of October.

The early part of November was not cold, but Chopin had caught a chill and could hardly breathe or sleep. His new lodgings, at 4 St James's Place, Piccadilly, became like a hospital room. Doctors came and went, visitors tiptoed to ask how he was, Princess Czartoryska, back in London, called every day. He never left his bed. The loving furies, whom he thought he had shed in Edinburgh, came down after him and began busying themselves with his welfare. Jane Stirling pressed delicacies on him and cut short friends' visits; Mrs Erskine, good Protestant that she was, arrived Bible in hand to prepare him, non-practising Catholic that he was, for the joys of the next world. 'My goodly Scottish ladies are getting on my nerves,'[18] he complained to Grzymala.

The charity function which had brought him back to London was a grand annual affair in aid of the Polish Literary Association of the Friends of Poland, sponsored by Lord Dudley Coutts Stuart. It was basically a fancy dress ball preceded by a cultural programme for which, apart from himself, sixteen 'vocalists' and two conductors had volunteered their services. There was no question in Chopin's mind but that he would keep his undertaking to play for his compatriots. His instructions to his doctors were to do what magic they could to set him on his feet for just as long as he needed to play his few pieces. On 16 November he was lifted from his bed, dressed, put in a carriage and driven to the Guildhall, where the function was being held.

Guildhall looked magnificent that night. The elegant decorations from the recent Lord Mayor's Day had been purposely left on for the occasion, and the building was brilliantly illuminated. But the cultural part of the evening was clearly an encumbrance. Impatient patrons in resplendent costumes strolled in and out, letting the draught in, taking little notice of the frail figure by the piano. The Poles present applauded warmly, but by nine o'clock everything was over and the dancing began, to be continued unabated until the small hours of the morning. Chopin was driven straight back to his lodgings and put to bed with a violent headache and a swollen face. He spent the whole night gasping for breath. A day later hardly a soul remembered what he had played and how he played it; the *Illustrated London News*, the only paper which mentioned his participation, did so in the same paragraph which singled out Messrs Younghusband and Son for the excellence of their catering arrangements.

That was his swan song. The barely-noticed appearance in London's Guildhall on 16 November 1848 was Chopin's last public performance before his death.

It was also the last of his English venture. From his sickbed he vowed to stay in 'that beastly London'[19] for only as long as it needed to make him fit enough to brave the crossing. Sometimes, thinking of his recent experiences and frustrations, he felt like putting the blame on George Sand, whom he now called Lucrezia. In his moments of indecision he still wondered whether it was wise to return to Paris, but the aimlessness of his London existence was driving him mad. The furies must have helped to make up his mind for him. 'My Scottish ladies pester me so,' he cried out to Grzymala. 'God help them. They have fastened themselves to me so tightly, I cannot shake them off.'[19] Distance was his only salvation.

To Marie de Rozières, the former pupil turned a serviceable friend, he explained his decision to return to Paris more gallantly. 'The English climate this time of year is absolutely unbearable for me,'[20] he wrote. He asked her and Grzymala to prepare his old apartment at Square d'Orléans for himself and

Daniel, remove the dustsheets, hang the curtains, light fires, scatter about fresh-smelling pine cones, buy violets for the drawing-room and tell Pleyel to send over a piano to await his arrival.

He left London on 23 November and after an uneventful crossing in the company of a compatriot and Daniel, stayed the night at Boulogne. On the afternoon of the 24th he was back in Paris, which to him was home and hope. He had been away seven months.

Not alone

'How awful to die far away from where one has lived. How terrible it will be to see some cold-hearted doctor or servant by my death bed instead of my own family,'[1] Chopin wrote at the age of twenty, when he was miserably putting off his departure from Warsaw. The fear of dying among strangers was deeply ingrained and his recent visit to England made it all the more real. Once he was back at Square d'Orléans he could lean back on his pillows with the reassuring knowledge that he was being looked after by friends of his own choice.

He was surrounded with love and attention. Franchomme managed his finances; Mlle de Rozières ran errands; Princess Czartoryska, back in Paris, looked into his household arrangements; Gutmann, Grzymala, Delacroix and a host of aristocratic friends called to offer help. The best doctors were sent for. There was little they could do but the complete rest and relative peace of mind slowed down the process of deterioration. Within weeks he was giving lessons again, partly driven by his fear of becoming destitute and partly by the instinctive feeling that activity was the best palliative.

With the approach of spring he felt sufficiently strong to hold two musical evenings in his drawing-room, one on 30 March and the other on 11 April. He was too far gone to play, but his works were played by Countess Kalergis, a former pupil. Another former pupil who performed on both occasions was Countess Delphina Potocka whose repertoire included songs based on his piano works, operatic arias and Neapolitan romances. He and the Countess now addressed each other only by their surnames, but underneath the formality there was a bond based on youthful memories which time had not soured. Life had not been kind to the Countess; in her only extant letter to Chopin, dated that same year, she told him that she had had many disappointments. Their enduring friendship was a source of comfort to both.

During the first half of 1849 he clung to his self-prescribed activity even though the slightest exertion made him suffocate. With the help of the indispensable Daniel he dressed as meticulously, and as expensively, as ever and had himself driven in his carriage just for the sake of getting out of his sickroom. Once he had himself dressed in the grey winter coat he had brought from England and posed in it for a photograph commissioned by his music publisher Schlesinger. He tried to work. Miraculously he recaptured some of his lost inspiration and sketched two mazurkas which were posthumously published as Mazurka in G minor Op. 67, No. 2 and Mazurka in F minor Op. 68, No. 4. In mid-April he dragged himself to the first night of Meyerbeer's opera *Le Prophète* only to return to his sickbed as disgusted with the music as he was exhausted with the effort of sitting up. At the beginning of May he heard from Delacroix that George Sand had paid a three-day visit to Paris to hear Pauline Viardot sing in Meyerbeer's opera. She had enquired after his health, as she had been doing since their separation, but made no attempt to see him. She still expected him to make the first move.

The halt in his physical decline was temporary. At the beginning of summer he had a relapse and from then on his deterioration was rapid. His friends moved him to Chaillot, on the heights of Passy, which had open spaces and fresh air. He had to have a night-nurse and, when she proved unreliable, Princess Czartoryska sent over her Polish maid. He spent much of his time propped up in a chair by the window, or writing letters. The physical effort was agony, but the agony of the soul was worse. 'I cannot compose,'[2] he cried to Grzymala.

Even though Chaillot was then outside Paris, he had plenty of company. The drive was hardly long enough to accommodate the carriages which brought and fetched countesses and princesses who had come to cheer up their beloved patient. He was visited one day by Countess Potocka, her sister the Princess de Beauvau and Mme Rothschild, when Jenny Lind flitted in and delighted them with her singing. Another day a striking-looking old lady had herself announced and took his hands in hers with emotion. It was the sixty-nine-year-old singer Angelica Catalani who had heard him in Warsaw when he was nine or ten and who was one of the first non-Polish musicians of note to recognize his budding genius. A few weeks later he heard that she was carried off by cholera. So was his old friend Kalkbrenner.

Cholera and the heat of summer drove many of his friends out of Paris. Countess Potocka, before her departure for the south of France, made him promise that he would soon come to convalesce at her villa in Nice. Other close friends, like Franchomme, Delacroix, Gutmann and Marie de Rozières, were also away. On the other hand the Scottish ladies were about again. Jane Stirling had put aside the memory of her disappointment and together with her sister returned to Paris. Somewhat intimidated, but driven by her compulsive need to be near him and serve him, she renewed her calls. In June she and the inseparable Mrs Erskine drove to Chaillot. 'The Scottish ladies have just arrived,' an unrepentant Chopin informed Grzymala. 'Among other bits of news they tell me that the Duke of Noailles is better. So I told them King Charles Albert had just died in Lisbon. They bore me so much they will be the end of me.'[3]

While Franchomme was away, he tried to manage his finances by himself. The savings he had brought back from England had all gone and nothing else was coming in. He was worried about the rent of the elegant summer residence at Chaillot. To set his mind at rest he was given to understand that it was much lower than it was, the difference being discreetly made up by a generous princess. Even so he had to borrow from the Rothschilds and other well-to-do friends. His family in Warsaw must have realized that his financial resources had come to an end, for in July his old mother wrote him the following letter, the last he was to receive from her:

My dear Frederick,
  On the 16th I received your letter in which you say you are better; that was a real name-day present for me.
9

How I wish I could be with you and look after you the way I used to. But since that cannot be, we must bow to the will of God who in His mercy will send you friends to take my place. Put your trust in Him and be not afraid, my dearest. I expect you could do with some money, so I am sending you what I can for the time being, two thousand francs. Our good Barcinski [Isabel's husband] will explain what you must do should you need some more. May God bless you and give you health, this prayer goes to Him from

Your loving mother[4]

His rescue came from another quarter. When Jane Stirling and Mrs Erskine called on him in June at Chaillot, they were astonished to see him so worried about his financial situation. On their return to Paris they went to see Grzymala and revealed that some time in March they had anonymously sent Chopin the vast sum of 25,000 francs to Square d'Orléans, where he was living at the time. The gift had clearly been mislaid. Instead of alerting the police, Grzymala and the other intimates put the delicate matter into the hands of a fashionable clairvoyant. The latter immediately deduced that the thick, tempting-looking envelope had been kept back by the *concierge* of Square d'Orléans but, not to let the profession down, indulged in an extraordinary display of hocus-pocus. The upshot of it was that the frightened *concierge* produced the envelope from behind the mantelpiece clock in her lodge and claimed that she had forgotten to deliver it. The seal had not been broken. No charges were preferred but when the envelope was triumphantly taken to Chaillot and the seal broken in the presence of Chopin, he pushed the money away. He felt more offended than touched by the nature of the gift and explained to Mrs Erskine, the eternal go-between, that if he ever accepted money from a woman it would have to be from no lesser a person than Queen Victoria herself. It took all Gutmann's tact and common sense to persuade him to keep at least half the sum. Generous, well-intentioned, besotted Jane Stirling sighed with relief.

He was sinking fast. His breathing came with difficulty and he could hardly move without help. All he could do was to clutch a pen between his fingers and write to absent friends. The never-forgotten Titus Woyciechowski was taking the waters at Carlsbad that summer and there was some talk of his coming to Paris to see Chopin. They had not seen each other since their interrupted holiday in Vienna some eighteen years earlier. When Titus wrote that he had been refused a French visa and had to stop short at Ostend, Chopin wrote to apologize for not being well enough to rush to Belgium.

One night in June he had two haemorrhages. On the 25th he wrote to his sister Louisa in Warsaw:

> My dearest, if you possibly can please come. I am very weak and no doctor will do me half as much good as you will. If you are short of money borrow some. When I am better I shall easily make enough to pay back whoever will have lent it to you.[5]

In order not to alarm his family he added with a touch of his old humour: 'I don't really know why I want to see Louisa so much. I expect it is like the fancy of a pregnant woman.' His family, however, were in no way deceived about the gravity of his condition, having had reports from other sources. Money was borrowed, strings were pulled to hasten the granting of passports and travel permits, and on 9 August Louisa, together with her husband and young daughter, arrived at Chaillot. She immediately took things firmly into her hands, organized the household and gave her brother that taste of family life he had so much missed. With the first touch of autumn chill the entire household moved back to Paris to a large family apartment at Place Vendôme. Jedrzejewicz had to return to his academic duties at the Institute of Agronomy near Warsaw but Louisa and her young daughter stayed on.

The news that Chopin did not have long to live spread fast. George Sand, always at Nohant, heard that Louisa had arrived from Poland to look after her sick brother and wrote to ask for news of him; unfortunately her manner of writing was not calculated to disperse the bitterness accumulated in Louisa's heart against a woman who had forsworn her vows of everlasting loyalty. 'Please drop me a line,' Mme Sand irritatingly wrote, 'I venture to ask this of you, for one can be misunderstood and abandoned by one's children without ceasing to love them.'[6] Louisa did not reply. Presumably she never mentioned the letter to her brother so as not to upset him.

By the end of September it was clear that he was dying. Acquaintances swarmed in, the ante-chamber was full of visitors who clamoured for the honour of hearing Chopin's last words. He had a kind word for each and every one of them. 'All the great ladies of society felt duty-bound to come and swoon in his bedroom,' Pauline Viardot indignantly recalled. 'His room was crammed full of artists making hasty sketches of him. There was even a photographer who wanted the patient's bed pushed towards the window so that he would have more light for his daguerrotype.'[7] In the end, Gutmann chased them out.

Solange and her husband had returned from Gascony and rarely left his side. A thoughtful friend sent a telegram to Countess Delphina Potocka in Nice to tell her that the end was near; she rushed back and reached Place Vendôme on 15 October, two days before his death. 'God has spared me so that I might see you again,' he said, according to handed-down tradition. He then asked her to sing for him. The drawing-room piano was rolled into the bedroom and the Countess, fighting back her tears, began to sing. In the middle of the second song he had a violent fit of coughing. The singing was discontinued, Gutmann lifted the frail body of the patient in order to prop him into a less agonizing position, the other people in the room knelt down in prayer.

One of Chopin's most assiduous visitors during the last weeks of his life was a childhood friend who had become a priest. Alexander Jelowicki spent long hours by the sick man's bed, begging him to confess and take the sacrament. Chopin consistently refused. He had not been a practising Catholic for many years and could not bring himself to follow the rites of a faith he had neglected. But Jelowicki was determined to save a Christian soul from perdition and four days before the end his prayers were answered. Chopin confessed, accepted the last sacrament and pressed a relic to his lips, seeking in the frequent incantation of the names of God and the Virgin the strength to overcome the fear of death. Pauline

Viardot, who was not present, later gave a hearsay account. 'He died a martyr at the hands of the priests who forced him to kiss relics for six whole hours until his last breath.'[7]

He died on 17 October 1849 at two in the morning. Before he died he asked for his heart to be returned to Warsaw for burial. The brief note, written in a barely recognizable hand, asking friends to make sure he was dead before committing him to his grave, is now thought to have been written not by him but by his father in Warsaw before his own death; and the much-quoted deathbed saying about George Sand—'She promised I would die in her arms'—seems decidedly apocryphal.

The funeral was held on 30 October, the unseemly delay resulting from the chief mourners' insistence that the service at the Church of the Madeleine should include a performance of Mozart's Requiem with female singers, which was contrary to canonical regulations. It had taken all of thirteen days to obtain a special dispensation from the Archbishop of Paris and then only with the proviso that the female singers, Pauline Viardot and Mme Castellan, would remain concealed behind a screen, heard but not seen.

On the day, the great door of the Church of the Madeleine was hung with black drapes emblazoned with the initials F. C. in silver. In the space between the nave and the choir, a lofty mausoleum had been erected, also draped in black with the initials F. C. in silver. The Conservatoire orchestra and chorus, with the conductor and four soloists, were discreetly seated at the extreme end of the church. Mourners filled the nave and aisles, the choir, the galleries above the porticos, the spaces behind and between the columns of the porticos, the organ gallery, the gallery that ran round the choir. There were 3,000 of them, each and every one admitted strictly by a personal letter of invitation.

The service started at noon. To the sound of the funeral march from Chopin's Sonata in B flat minor, which had been orchestrated specially for the occasion, the coffin was solemnly carried through the church and placed on the mausoleum. Then Mozart's Requiem was performed. During the service Chopin's Preludes Nos. 4 and 6 were played on the organ. When it was over the coffin was carried to the cemetery of

Père Lachaise, three miles away, with the chief mourners including Prince Czartoryski, Franchomme, Pleyel, Gutmann, Delacroix and Meyerbeer, walking bare-headed all the way. A vast number of carriages followed behind, hundreds of simple Parisians stopped to gaze at the princely cortège. As the coffin was lowered into the grave, ladies in deep mourning threw garlands and flowers. No obituaries were said; the whole ceremony was conducted in silence.

George Sand had not been invited to the church service. Perhaps she found some wry consolation in the knowledge that one of the Preludes which were played during the service, Prelude No. 4 in E minor, had been composed during their stay in Majorca, when she so valiantly fought to save his life. Shortly afterwards she devoted to him some of the most beautiful pages in her *Histoire de ma vie*.

'Chopin's music', she wrote, 'is emotionally the richest and most profound that ever existed. He made one single instrument speak the language of the infinite. In ten simple lines which even a child could play he often created poems of immense sublimity, dramas of incomparable force. He never required large material means to give expression to his genius. He needed neither saxophone nor bass trumpet to fill the soul with terror, neither church organ nor human voice to infuse it with faith and exultation. The general public did not know him well during his lifetime and perhaps does not even now. . . . One day his music will be orchestrated and then the whole world will realize that his genius, as vast, comprehensive and erudite as that of the masters he had absorbed, has preserved an individuality more exquisite than Bach's, more powerful than Beethoven's, more dramatic than Weber's. He is all three put together, yet he is himself, more subtle in his taste, more austere in his grandeur, more heart-rending in his anguish.'[8]

Time has proved that Chopin's music did not need to be orchestrated to be loved and enjoyed. With that one reservation, George Sand's appraisal was a beautiful tribute to a genius who needed no epitaph.

Epilogue

Today, when the cult of Chopin has adherents all over the world, a thought might be spared for the woman who began it.

After his death, when he was no longer there to discourage her with his reluctant acquiescence, Jane Stirling's devotion blazed out like a sacred flame. She paid the cost of the funeral as well as Louisa's return fare to Warsaw, making out it was a loan; and when Louisa's husband sent instructions to put up Chopin's effects for sale, she bought up the entire contents, even the linen. She could not bear anything which he had touched to go to strangers. She gave some of the knick-knacks to his closest friends as mementos, sent his Pleyel to Louisa in Warsaw and had the bulk of the furniture transported to Calder House in Scotland. There she had it displayed in a special room and, together with a death-mask of Chopin by Clésinger and her own mementos, she started what she called the Chopin Museum.

She spared no effort or expense to build him a shrine in people's hearts. The Polish artist Kwiatkowski having made several sketches of him during the last weeks of his life, she commissioned an oil painting of Chopin on his death-bed and gallantly rose above her disappointment when she saw that the artist had painted in Louisa, Princess Czartoryska, Grzymala and himself, but not her. She often called at Clésinger's studio to see the progress of the monument which the Chopin Committee had commissioned from him. As the first anniversary of the death was approaching, she kept thinking of what might have given him most pleasure and came up with a gesture which has since become legend. 'My dear,' she wrote to Louisa on 12 June 1850, 'could you please send me some soil?'[1] On 17 October 1850, when a group of friends assembled at the Père Lachaise cemetery for a memorial service and the unveiling of Clésinger's monument, Jane Stirling scattered a handful of Polish soil over the grave. For the rest of her life she busied herself with keeping his memory alive, answering queries about his career and concerning herself with the difficult decision about the posthumous publication of manuscripts which by his own demanding standards would have still needed perfecting. She never forgot. Jane Carlyle flippantly named her Chopin's Widow.

Louisa Jedrzejewicz died in Warsaw in 1855. On her own death, in 1859, Jane Stirling willed her Museum to old Justina Chopin and it was accordingly shipped to Warsaw. When Justina died in 1861, it passed into the guardianship of the youngest sister Isabel. Two years later, furniture, piano, letters and documents perished during a Russian military action. Fortunately many other documents and mementos survived in other hands, and the work of collecting, preserving and reconstructing was soon under way, to be systematically and tirelessly continued until the present day. A lock of auburn hair, reverently removed after Chopin's death, is nowadays preserved at the Frederick Chopin Society in Warsaw, one of the few surviving personal mementos which Jane Stirling had collected for love and posterity.

References

Foreword
1. Huneker, J., *The Greater Chopin*, Mezzotints in Modern Music, p. 223

Chapter 1: A Frenchman in Warsaw
1. Coxe, W., *Travels in Poland*, Vol. I, p. 156
2. Sydow, B. E., *Correspondance de Frédéric Chopin*, Vol. I, pp. lv–lvi
3. Kobylanska, K., *Chopin in His Own Land*, p. 5

Chapter 2: Child prodigy
1. Kobylanska, K., *Chopin in His Own Land*, p. 11
2. Ibid., p. 12
3. Ibid., p. 17
4. Ibid., p. 41
5. Ibid., p. 44
6. Opienski, H., *Listy Fryderyka Chopina*, No. 4, p. 1
7. At the museum of the Frederick Chopin Society, Warsaw

Chapter 3: Adolescence
1. Kobylanska, K., *Chopin in His Own Land*, p. 43
2. Ibid., p. 61
3. Opienski, H., *Listy Fryderyka Chopina*, No. 7, pp. 3–4
4. Kobylanska, K., *Korespondencja Fryderyka Chopina*, No. 2, p. 33
5. Ibid., No. 7, p. 39
6. Ibid., No. 6, p. 37
7. Ibid., No. 5, p. 36
8. Ibid., No. 7, p. 39
9. Ibid., No. 4, p. 36
10. Coxe, W., *Travels in Poland*, Vol. I, p. 237
11. Kobylanska, K., *Korespondencja Fryderyka Chopina*, No. 8, pp. 39–40

12. Ibid., No. 7, p. 38
13. Kobylanska, K., *Chopin in His Own Land*, p. 73
14. Opienski, H., *Listy Fryderyka Chopina*, No. 9, p. 5
15. Ibid., No. 10, p. 6
16. Ibid., No. 12, pp. 7–9
17. Ibid., No. 11, p. 7

Chapter 4: Branching out

1. Opienski, H., *Listy Fryderyka Chopina*, No. 14, p. 11
2. Ibid., No. 14, p. 11
3. Ibid., No. 15, p. 12
4. Ibid., No. 16, p. 14
5. Ibid., No. 19, p. 18
6. Ibid., No. 28, p. 31
7. Ibid., No. 18, p. 17
8. Ibid., No. 20, p. 20
9. Binental, L., *Chopin*, plate 10 & p. 126
10. Sydow, B. E., *Correspondance de Frédéric Chopin*, Vol. I, No. 28, p. 65
11. Opienski, H., *Listy Fryderyka Chopina*, No. 21, p. 33
12. Kobylanska, K., *Chopin in His Own Land*, p. 115
13. Kobylanska, K., *Korespondencja Fryderyka Chopina*, Aneks I, No. 2, p. 195
14. Karasowski, M., *Friedrich Chopin*, p. 23
15. Murdoch, W., *Chopin: His Life*, p. 24
16. Opienski, H., *Listy Fryderyka Chopina*, No. 35, p. 41
17. Ibid., No. 14, p. 25
18. Ibid., No. 26, p. 28
19. Ibid., No. 26, p. 27

Chapter 5: Enter Chopin

1. Kobylanska, K., *Korespondencja Fryderyka Chopina*, No. 11, p. 45
2. Ibid., No. 12, p. 47
3. Ibid., No. 11, p. 46
4. Ibid., No. 12, p. 47
5. Pereswiet-Soltan, S., *Listy Fryderyka Chopina do Jana Bialoblockiego*, XI (12), pp. 64–5
6. Ibid., XI (12), p. 65
7. Binental, L., *Chopin*, plate 27, p. 137
8. Opienski, H., *Listy Fryderyka Chopina*, No. 38, p. 40
9. Kobylanska, K., *Korespondencja Fryderyka Chopina*, No. 17, p. 53
10. Ibid., No. 15, p. 50

11. Opienski, H., *Listy Fryderyka Chopina*, No. 38, p. 47
12. Kobylanska, K., *Korespondencja Fryderyka Chopina*, No. 16, p. 52
13. *Wiener Theaterzeitung*, August 1829
14. Kobylanska, K., *Korespondencja Fryderyka Chopina*, No. 16, p. 52
15. Ibid., No. 18, p. 54
16. Ibid., No. 16, p. 52
17. Ibid., No. 18, p. 54
18. *Allgemeine musikalische Zeitung*, 18 November 1829

Chapter 6: Emotional gropings
1. Smoter, J. M., *Spor o 'listy' Chopina do Delfiny*, No. 112
2. Sydow, B. E., *Correspondance de Frédéric Chopin*, Vol. I, No. 37, p. 92
3. Opienski, H., *Listy Fryderyka Chopina*, No. 26, p. 26
4. Ibid., No. 26, p. 29
5. Ibid., No. 30, p. 34
6. Ibid., No. 38, p. 48
7. Ibid., No. 49, p. 74
8. Ibid., No. 40, p. 52
9. Ibid., No. 26, p. 28
10. Ibid., No. 39, p. 48
11. Ibid., No. 39, p. 50
12. Kobylanska, K., *Chopin in His Own Land*, p. 238
13. Ibid., p. 238
14. Ibid., p. 242
15. Opienski, H., *Listy Fryderyka Chopina*, No. 43, p. 58
16. Ibid., No. 42, p. 56
17. Ibid., No. 42, p. 55
18. Ibid., No. 44, p. 60
19. Ibid., No. 44, p. 62
20. Ibid., No. 46, p. 65
21. Ibid., No. 47, p. 67
22. Ibid., No. 50, p. 74
23. Ibid., No. 43, p. 60
24. Ibid., No. 48, p. 69
25. Ibid., No. 49, p. 72
26. Ibid., No. 52, p. 80
27. Ibid., No. 52, p. 81
28. Ibid., No. 53, p. 82
29. Binental, L., *Chopin*, plate 32
30. Kobylanska, K., *Chopin in His Own Land*, p. 204
31. Kobylanska, K., *Korespondencja Fryderyka Chopina*, No. 45, p. 91

Chapter 7: On his own

1. Kobylanska, K., *Korespondencja Fryderyka Chopina*, No. 24, p. 65
2. Opienski, H., *Listy Fryderyka Chopina*, No. 60, p. 97
3. Ibid., No. 60, p. 95
4. Kobylanska, K., *Korespondencja Fryderyka Chopina*, No. 25, p. 85
5. Opienski, H., *Listy Fryderyka Chopina*, No. 60, p. 97
6. Ibid., No. 60, p. 98
7. Ibid., No. 60, p. 94
8. Kobylanska, K., *Korespondencja Fryderyka Chopina*, No. 27, p. 71
9. Opienski, H., *Listy Fryderyka Chopina*, No. 60, p. 96
10. Kobylanska, K., *Korespondencja Fryderyka Chopina*, No. 27, p. 71
11. Opienski, H., *Listy Fryderyka Chopina*, No. 99, p. 100
12. Ibid., No. 60, p. 97
13. Kobylanska, K., *Korespondencja Fryderyka Chopina*, No. 27, p. 70
14. Smoter, J. M., *Album Chopina*, p. 33
15. Kobylanska, K., *Korespondencja Fryderyka Chopina*, No. 26, p. 69
16. *Allgemeine musikalische Zeitung*, 21 September 1831, in *Chopin*, Vol. I, p. 189, Niecks, F.
17. Karasowski, M., *Life and Letters of Chopin*, p. 224
18. Sydow, B. E., *Correspondance de Frédéric Chopin*, Vol. I, No. 84, p. 286
19. Smoter, J. M., *Album Chopina*, pp. 8, 36–7
20. Brown, M., *Chopin: An Index of his Works*, p. 74

Chapter 8: A Pole in Paris

1. Opienski, H., *Listy Fryderyka Chopina*, No. 70, p. 113
2. Ibid., No. 69, p. 112
3. Ibid., No. 72, p. 122
4. Sydow, B. E., *Correspondance de Frédéric Chopin*, Vol. II, No. 92, p. 19
5. Opienski, H., *Listy Fryderyka Chopina*, No. 69, p. 112
6. Kobylanska, K., *Korespondencja Fryderyka Chopina*, Aneks I, No. 2, p. 195
7. Opienski, H., *Listy Fryderyka Chopina*, No. 70, p. 115
8. Ibid., No. 70, pp. 115–16
9. Kobylanska, K., *Korespondencja Fryderyka Chopina*, Aneks I, No. 3, p. 197
10. Ibid., Aneks I, No. 3, p. 198
11. *Revue musicale*, 3 March 1832
12. Kobylanska, K., *Korespondencja Fryderyka Chopina*, Aneks I, No. 3, p. 198
13. Opienski, H., *Listy Fryderyka Chopina*, No. 69, p. 111
14. Ibid., No. 74, p. 124

15. Marmontel, A., *Les Pianistes célèbres*, p. 3
16. Opienski, H., *Listy Fryderyka Chopina*, No. 73 p. 119.
17. Niecks, F., *Frederick Chopin as a Man and Musician*, Vol. II, Appendix
18. Sydow, E. B., *Correspondance de Frédéric Chopin*, Vol. II, No. 152, p. 115

Chapter 9: Delphina

1. Opienski, H., *Listy Fryderyka Chopina*, No. 69, p. 112
2. Bory, R., *La vie de Frédéric Chopin dans l'image*, p. 85
3. Sydow, B. E., *Correspondance de Frédéric Chopin*, Vol. II, No. 117, p. 81
4. Opienski, H., *Listy Fryderyka Chopina*, No. 70, p. 114
5. Smoter, J. M., *Spor o 'listy' Chopina do Delfiny*, No. 49
6. Opienski, H., *Listy Fryderyka Chopina*, No. 4, p. 1
7. Smoter, J. M., *Spor o 'listy' Chopina do Delfiny*, No. 72
8. Ibid., No. 29
9. Ibid., No. 21
10. Ibid., No. 10
11. Ibid., No. 54
12. Ibid., No. 10
13. Sydow, B. E., *Correspondance de Frédéric Chopin*, Vol. II, No. 129, p. 92
14. 'Norwid' may be the copier's misreading; see Foreword
15. Smoter, J. M., *Spor o 'listy' Chopina do Delfiny*, No. 45
16. Sydow, B. E., *Correspondance de Frédéric Chopin*, Vol. II, No. 165, p. 129
17. Smoter, J. M., *Spor o 'listy' Chopina do Delfiny*, No. 69
18. Ibid., No. 108
19. Ibid., No. 96
20. Wodzinski, A., *Les trois romans de Frédéric Chopin*, p. 217
21. Smoter, J. M., *Spor o 'listy' Chopina do Delfiny*, No. 26
22. Ibid., No. 86
23. Ibid., No. 41
24. Brown, M., *Chopin, An Index to his Works*, No. 42, p. 54
25. Smoter, J. M., *Spor o 'listy' Chopina do Delfiny*, No. 78

Chapter 10: The rise and fall of a matrimonial project

1. Liszt, F., *F. Chopin*, p. 73
2. Ibid., p. 75
3. Opienski, H., *Listy Fryderyka Chopina*, No. 83, pp. 131–2
4. Prochazka, J., *Frédéric Chopin et la Bohême*, pp. 148–50

5. Sydow, B. E., *Correspondance de Frédéric Chopin*, Vol. II, No. 174, p. 140
6. Brown, M., *Chopin: An Index of his Works*, No. 62, p. 68
7. Sydow, B. E., *Correspondance de Frédéric Chopin*, Vol. II, No. 156, p. 120
8. Brown, M., *Chopin: An Index of his Works*, No. 95, p. 99
9. Smoter, J. M., *Spor o 'listy' Chopina do Delfiny*, No. 18
10. Niecks, F., *Frederick Chopin as a Man and Musician*, Vol. I, p. 292
11. Sydow, B. E., *Correspondance de Frédéric Chopin*, Vol. II, No. 83, p. 157
12. Smoter, J. M., *Spor o 'listy' Chopina do Delfiny*, No. 62
13. Niecks, F., *Frederick Chopin as a Man and Musician*, Vol. II, Appendix IV, p. 337
14. Lissa, Z., *The Book of the First International & Musicological Congress*, p. 676
15. Sydow, B. E., *Correspondance de Frédéric Chopin*, Vol. II, No. 222, p. 201
16. Ibid., Vol. II, No. 224, p. 205
17. Ibid., Vol. II, No. 242, p. 219

Chapter 11: Preludes

1. Sydow, B. E., *Correspondance de Frédéric Chopin*, Vol. II, No. 226, p. 208
2. Niecks, F., *Frederick Chopin as a Man and Musician*, Vol. II, p. 8
3. Liszt, F., *F. Chopin*, p. 169
4. Denis, F., *Journal 1829–1848*, p. 69
5. Lubin, Georges, *Correspondance de George Sand*, Vol. III, No. 1377, p. 699
6. Ibid., Vol. III, No. 1418, p. 765
7. Ibid., Vol. III, No. 1421, p. 769
8. Ibid., Vol. III, p. 807, note 5
9. Sydow, B. E., *Correspondance de Frédéric Chopin*, Vol. II, No. 243, pp. 220–1
10. Sydow, B. E., *Korespondancja Fryderyka Chopina*, Vol. I, No. 217, p. 306
11. Smoter, J. M., *Spor o 'listy' Chopina do Delfiny*, No. 34
12. Mirska, M. & Hordynski, W., *Chopina na Obczyznie*, p. 126
13. Lubin, Georges, *Correspondance de George Sand*, Vol. IV, No. 1728, p. 395
14. Ibid., Vol. IV, No. 1728, pp. 437–8
15. Sydow, B. E., *Korespondencja Fryderyka Chopina*, Vol. I, No. 236, p. 325

16. Lubin, Georges, *Correspondance de George Sand*, Vol. IV, No. 1785, pp. 482–3

Chapter 12: Like a family

1. Facing p. 193. Hitherto unpublished
2. Lubin, Georges, *Correspondance de George Sand*, Vol. IV, No. 1811, p. 519
3. Sydow, B. E., *Korespondencja Fryderyka Chopina*, Vol. I, No. 243, pp. 327–8
4. Sydow, B. E., *Correspondance de Frédéric Chopin*, Vol. II, No. 277, p. 270
5. Ibid., Vol. II, No. 277, p. 271
6. Sydow, B. E., *Korespondencja Fryderyka Chopina*, Vol. I, No. 246, p. 330
7. Ibid., Vol. I, No. 256, p. 341
8. Sand, George, *Histoire de ma vie*, Vol. IV, p. 439
9. Ibid., Vol. IV, pp. 439–40
10. Lubin, Georges, *Correspondance de George Sand*, Vol. IV, p. 559 footnote, from the original edition of *Hiver à Majorque*, Vol. I, pp. 308–9
11. Sydow, B. E., *Correspondance de Frédéric Chopin*, Vol. II, No. 290, p. 292
12. Sydow, B. E., *Korespondencja Fryderyka Chopina*, Vol. I, No. 255, p. 339
13. Ibid., Vol. I, No. 267, p. 349
14. Lubin, Georges, *Correspondance de George Sand*, Vol. IV, No. 1906, p. 726
15. Sydow, B. E., *Korespondencja Fryderyka Chopina*, No. 271, pp. 354–5
16. Lubin, Georges, *Correspondance de George Sand*, Vol. IV, No. 1925, p. 754
17. Sydow, B. E., *Korespondancja Fryderyka Chopina*, Vol. I, No. 275, p. 357
18. Ibid., Vol. I, No. 277, pp. 358–9
19. Ibid., Vol. I, No. 279, p. 363
20. Ibid., Vol. I, No. 280, p. 364
21. Ibid., Vol. I, No. 275, p. 357

Chapter 13: Years of glory

1. Moscheles, Charlotte, *Aus Moscheles Leben*, Vol. I, p. 271
2. Ibid., Vol. I, p. 294
3. Ibid., Vol. II, p. 39
4. Ibid., Vol. II, p. 59

5. Ibid., Vol. II, p. 60
6. Hallé, C. E. & M., *Life and Letters of Sir Charles Hallé*, pp. 31–32
7. Smoter, J. M., *Spor o 'listy' Chopina do Delfiny*, No. 1
8. Ibid., No. 82
9. Lubin, Georges, *Correspondance de George Sand*, Vol. IV, No. 1949, p. 792
10. Ibid., Vol. IV, No. 2002, p. 858
11. Sydow, B. E., *Correspondance de Frédéric Chopin*, Vol. II, p. 374, No. 343
12. Ibid., Vol. II, No. 348, pp. 377–8
13. Lubin, Georges, *Correspondance de George Sand*, Vol. IV, No. 2008, p. 867
14. Ibid., Vol. V, p. 88
15. Ibid., Vol. IV, p, 615
16. Sand, George, *Histoire de ma vie*, Vol. II, p. 464 and p. 547
17. Lubin, Georges, *Correspondance de George Sand*, Vol. IV, No. 2005, p. 861
18. Ibid., Vol. V, p. 183
19. Ibid., Vol. V, p. 182
20. Marix–Spire, Thérèse, *Lettres inédites de George Sand et Pauline Viardot*, p. 108
21. Kobylanska, K., in *Muzyka Kwartalnyk*, No. 1–2, 1958, p. 91
22. Lubin, Georges, *Correspondance de George Sand*, Vol. V, No. 2207, p. 275
23. Ibid., Vol. V, No. 2213, p. 282
24. Ganche, E., *Frédéric Chopin*, p. 254
25. Ibid., pp. 255–6
26. Ibid., p. 258
27. Ibid., p. 259
28. Wierzynski, C., *The Life and Death of Chopin*, p. 307
29. Lenz, W., *Die Grossen Pianoforte-Virtuosen*, p. 36
30. Ganche, E., *Frédéric Chopin*, pp. 274–5
31. Ibid., p. 276
32. Lubin, Georges, *Correspondance de George Sand*, Vol. V, No. 2413, p. 607
33. Sydow, B. E., *Korespondencja Fryderyka Chopina*, Vol. II, No. 359, pp. 54–5
34. Lubin, Georges, *Correspondance de George Sand*, Vol. V, p. 683
35. Ibid., Vol. V, p. 653
36. Sand, George, *Impressions et Souvenirs*, pp. 80–81

Chapter 14: The glory and the agony

1. Lubin, Georges, *Correspondance de George Sand*, Vol. V, p. 783
2. Ibid., Vol. V, p. 763

3. Sand, George, *Lucrezia Floriani*, chapter 28, para. 1
4. Smoter, J. M., *Spor o 'listy' Chopina do Delfiny*, No. 46
5. Lubin, Georges, *Correspondance de George Sand*, Vol. VI, p. 285
6. Lenz, W., *Die Grossen Pianoforte-Virtuosen*, pp. 34–5
7. Ibid., p. 36
8. Denis, F., *Journal 1829–1848*, p. 124
9. Ganche, E., *Frédéric Chopin*, p. 340
10. Smoter, J. M., *Spor o 'listy' Chopina do Delfiny*, No. 31
11. Cortot, Alfred, *Aspects de Chopin*, p. 64
12. Ganche, E., *Frédéric Chopin*, p. 343
13. Hallé, C. E. & M., *Life and Letters of Sir Charles Hallé*, pp. 33–4
14. Lenz, W., *Die Grossen Pianoforte-Virtuosen*, pp. 45–7
15. Marix–Spire, Thérèse, *Lettres inédites de George Sand et Pauline Viardot*, p. 174

Chapter 15: Parting

1. Kobylanska, K., *Korespondencja Fryderyka Chopina*, No. 88, p. 148
2. Ibid., No. 89, p. 153
3. Ibid., No. 87, p. 145
4. Lubin, Georges, *Correspondance de George Sand*, Vol. VII, p. 97
5. Sand, George, *Lucrezia Floriani*, pp. 246–8
6. Ibid., p. 249
7. Arnold, Matthew, *Mixed Essays*, p. 318
8. Kobylanska, K., *Korespondencja Fryderyka Chopina*, No. 92, p. 160
9. Ibid., No. 92, p. 160
10. Sydow, B. E., *Correspondance de Frédéric Chopin*, Vol. III, No. 664, pp. 295–6
11. Lubin, Georges, *Correspondance de George Sand*, Vol. VIII, pp. 54–5
12. Ibid., Vol. VIII, pp. 112–13
13. Kobylanska, K., *Korespondencja Fryderyka Chopina*, No. 95, pp. 172–3
14. Hallé, C. E. & M., *Life and Letters of Sir Charles Hallé*, p. 36
15. Sydow, B. E., *Correspondance de Frédéric Chopin*, Vol. III, No. 689, p. 321
16. Hallé, C. E. & M., *Life and Letters of Sir Charles Hallé*, p. 36
17. Sydow, B. E., *Correspondance de Frédéric Chopin*, Vol. III, No. 702, pp. 331–2

Chapter 16: A London season

1. Kobylanska, K., *Korespondencja Fryderyka Chopina*, No. 94, p. 170
2. Sydow, B. E., *Correspondance de Frédéric Chopin*, Vol. III, No. 716, p. 340

3. Sydow, B. E., *Korespondencja Fryderyka Chopina*, Vol. II, No. 624, p. 244
4. Kobylanska, K., *Korespondencja Fryderyka Chopina*, No. 100, p. 183(g)
5. Sydow, B. E., *Korespondencja Fryderyka Chopina*, Vol. II, No. 625, p. 245
6. Kobylanska, K., *Korespondencja Fryderyka Chopina*, No. 100, p. 177
7. Ibid., No. 100, pp. 176–7
8. *The Illustrated London News*, 20 May 1848
9. Kobylanska, K., *Korespondencja Fryderyka Chopina*, No. 100, p. 178
10. Sydow, B. E., *Korespondencja Fryderyka Chopina*, Vol. II, No. 627, p. 249
11. Ibid., Vol. II, No. 645, p. 282
12. Smoter, J. M., *Spor o 'listy' Chopina do Delfiny*, No. 65
13. Kobylanska, K., *Korespondencja Fryderyka Chopina*, No. 100, p. 177
14. Sydow, B. E., *Korespondencja Fryderyka Chopina*, Vol. II, No. 627, p. 249
15. *The Athenaeum*, 1 July 1848
16. *The Illustrated London News*, 15 July 1848
17. *The Daily News*, 10 July 1848
18. *The Musical World*, 8 July 1848
19. Sydow, B. E., *Korespondencja Fryderyka Chopina*, Vol. II, No. 631, p. 253
20. Ibid., Vol. II, No. 631, pp. 254–5
21. Ibid., Vol. II, No. 627, p. 248
22. Ibid., Vol. II, No. 631, p. 253
23. Ibid., Vol. II, No. 630, p. 253
24. Ibid., Vol. II, No. 632, p. 255

Chapter 17: In Scotland and England

1. Sydow, B. E., *Korespondencja Fryderyka Chopina*, Vol. II, No. 636, p. 260
2. Sydow, B. E., *Correspondance de Frédéric Chopin*, Vol. III, No. 730, p. 361
3. Sydow, B. E., *Korespondencja Fryderyka Chopina*, Vol. II No. 639, p. 274
4. Brookshaw, Susanna, *Concerning Chopin in Manchester*, facing p. 22
5. Sydow, B. E., *Korespondencja Fryderyka Chopina*, Vol. II, No. 639, p. 275
6. *The Manchester Guardian*, 30 August 1848
7. *The Manchester Courier and Lancashire General Advertiser*, 30 August 1848
8. Hallé, C. E. & M., *Life and Letters of Sir Charles Hallé*, p. 111

9. *The Glasgow Herald,* 28 September 1848
10. *The Glasgow Courier,* 28 September 1848
11. *The Edinburgh Evening Courant,* 7 October 1848
12. *The Edinburgh Advertiser,* 6 October 1848
13. *The Scotsman,* 7 October 1848
14. Sydow, B. E., *Korespondencja Fryderyka Chopina,* Vol. II, No. 645, pp. 282–3
15. Ibid., Vol. II, No. 646, p. 284
16. Niecks, F., *Frederick Chopin as a Man and Musician,* Vol. II, p. 292
17. Sydow, B. E., *Korespondencja Fryderyka Chopina,* Vol. II, No. 646, p. 284
18. Ibid., Vol. II, No. 648, p. 287
19. Ibid., Vol. II, No. 651, p. 289 (top; bottom)
20. Sydow, B. E., *Correspondance de Frédéric Chopin,* Vol. III, No. 745, p. 401

Chapter 18: Not alone
1. Sydow, B. E., *Korespondencja Fryderyka Chopina,* Vol. I, No. 60, p. 135
2. Ibid., Vol. II, No. 668, p. 299
3. Ibid., Vol. II, No. 668, p. 299 bottom
4. Kobylanska, K., *Korespondencja Fryderyka Chopina,* No. 102, p. 186
5. Ibid., No. 101, p. 184
6. Lubin, Georges, *Correspondance de George Sand,* Vol. IX, pp. 255–6
7. Sydow, B. E., *Correspondance de Frédéric Chopin,* Vol. III, No. 788, p. 450
8. Sand, George, *Histoire de ma vie,* Vol. IV, pp. 440–2

Epilogue
1. Ganche, E., *Dans le souvenir de Frédéric Chopin,* p. 114

Bibliography

Arnold, Matthew, *Mixed Essays*, London 1879
Audley, Mme. A., *Frédéric Chopin*, Paris 1880
Balzac, Honoré de, *Lettres à l'étrangère*, 4 vols, Paris 1899–1950
Binental, L., *Chopin, Dokumente und Erinnerungen*, Leipzig 1932;
   Chopin, Paris 1934
Bone, Audrey E., *Jane Wilhelmina Stirling 1804–1859*, Gerrards
   Cross, 1960
Bory, R., *La Vie de Frédéric Chopin dans l'image*, Geneva 1951
Branson, D., *John Field and Chopin*, London 1972
British contemporary press
   Athenaeum, The, 1848
   Caledonian Mercury, The, 1848
   Daily News, The, 1848
   Edinburgh Advertiser, The, 1848
   Edinburgh Evening Courant, The, 1848
   Glasgow Constitutional, The, 1848
   Glasgow Courier, The, 1848
   Glasgow Herald, The, 1848
   Illustrated London News, The, 1848
   Manchester Courier & Lancashire General Advertiser, The, 1848
   Manchester Guardian, The, 1848
   Musical World, The, 1837, 1838, 1839, 1840, 1841, 1843, 1847,
      1848, 1849
   Scotsman, The, 1848
   Times, The, 1848
Brookshaw, Susanna, *Concerning Chopin in Manchester*, Manchester
   1951
Brown, Maurice J. E., *Chopin: an index of his works*, London 1972
Carrère, C., *George Sand amoureuse*, Paris and Geneva 1967
Chainaye, Suzanne and Chainaye, Denise, *De quoi vivait Chopin?*,
   Paris 1951
Chodzko, L., *La Pologne historique, littéraire, monumentale et pittoresque*,
   Paris 1835–6

Clavier, A., *Emilia Chopin*, Liège 1975
Cortot, A., *Aspects de Chopin*, Paris 1950
Coxe, W., *Travels into Poland*, Vol. I, London 1802
Czarkowski, A. and Jezewska, Z., *Fryderyk Chopin*, Warsaw 1967
Davison, J. W., *An Essay on the Works of Frederick Chopin*, London 1843
Delacroix, see Joulin
Denis, F., *Journal 1829–1848*, Fribourg and Paris 1932
Eigeldinger, J. J., *Chopin vu par ses élèves*, Neuchâtel, Switzerland 1970
Ganche, E., *La Vie de F. Chopin dans son oeuvre*, Paris 1909; *Frédéric Chopin*, Paris 1923; *Dans le souvenir de Frédéric Chopin*, Paris 1925; *Voyages avec Frédéric Chopin*, Paris 1934; *Souffrances de Frédéric Chopin*, Paris 1935
Gavoty, B., *Chopin*, Paris 1973 (see also Vuilermoz, E.)
Glinski, M., *Chopin the Unknown*, Windsor, Ontario 1963; *Letters to Delfina*, Windsor, Ontario 1961; *Chopin—Listy do Delfiny*, Toronto 1973
Godeau, M., *Le Voyage à Majorque de George Sand et Frédéric Chopin*, Paris 1959
Hallé, C. E. & M., *Life and Letters of Sir Charles Hallé*, London 1896
Harasowski, A., *The Skein of Legends round Chopin*, Glasgow 1967; 'Fact or Forgery', *Music and Musicians*, London, (I) March and (II) May 1973
Hedley, A., *Chopin*, London 1974; *Selected Correspondence by Frederick Chopin*, London 1962
Hensel, S., *Die Familie Mendelssohn 1729–1847*, 3 vols., Berlin 1879
Hipkins, Edith J., *How Chopin played: from notebooks of Alfred James Hipkins 1826–1903*, London 1937
Hoesick, F., *Chopiniana*, Warsaw 1912; *Slowacki i Chopin*, Warsaw 1932; *Chopin*, 3 vols., Cracow 1965
Huneker, James, *Chopin, the man and his music*, 1900; repr. New York 1966; *The Greater Chopin*, in *Mezzotints in Modern Music*, New York 1899
Joulin, A. (ed.), *Journal d'Eugène Delacroix, 1822–1852*, Vol. I, Paris 1932; *Correspondance générale d'Eugène Delacroix*, 5 vols., Paris 1936–8
Karasowski, M., *Friedrich Chopin*, Berlin 1914; *Frederick Chopin* (tr. Emily Hill), London 1938
Karénine, W., *George Sand, sa vie et ses oeuvres*, 4 vols., Paris 1899
Karlowicz, M., *Souvenirs inédits de Frédéric Chopin*, Leipzig 1904
Kleczynski, J., *Chopin's Greater Works* (tr. Nathalie Janotha), London 1912; *Chopina, Biblioteka Chopinowska I*, Cracow 1960
Kobbé, G., *The Loves of Great Composers*, London 1912

Kobylanska, Krystyna, *Chopin in his own land*, Warsaw 1955; *Korespondencja Fryderyka Chopina z Rodzina*, Warsaw 1972; *Nieznane Listy Chopina*, in *Muzyka Kwartalnyk*, Nos. 1–2, Warsaw 1958

Krakowski, E., *Trois destins tragiques*, Paris 1931

Lednicki, W. (ed.), *Zygmunt Krasinski*, New York 1964

Legouvé, E., *Soixante ans de souvenirs*, 2 vols., Paris 1886–7

Lehman, H., *Une correspondance romantique: Mme d'Agoult et Liszt*, Paris 1947

Lenz, W., *Die Grossen Pianoforte-Virtuosen*, Berlin 1872

Lissa, Zofia (ed.), *The Book of the First International Musicological Congress* (1960) *devoted to the works of Chopin*, Warsaw 1963

Liszt, F., *F. Chopin*, Paris 1852

Lubin, Georges, *Correspondance de George Sand*, 11 vols., Paris 1962–1975; *Oeuvres autobiographiques*, 2 vols., Paris 1970

Marix-Spire, Thérèse, *Un Polonais à Paris en 1836*, *Lettre inédite du compositeur Joseph Brzowski*, Paris 1954; *Les Romantiques et la musique: le cas George Sand*, Paris 1954; *Lettres inédites de George Sand et de Pauline Viardot*, Paris 1959

Marmontel, A., *Les pianistes célèbres*, Paris 1878

Maurois, André, *Lélia ou la vie de George Sand*, Paris 1953

Mendelssohn, Felix Bartholdy, *Briefe aus den Jahren 1833 bis 1847*, Leipzig 1864

Michalowski, K., *Bibliografia Chopinowska*, Warsaw 1970

Mirska, M. and Hordynski, W., *Chopina na Obczyznie*, Cracow 1965

Mizwa, S. P., (see Sydow, B. E.)

Moscheles, Charlotte, *Aus Moscheles Leben*, 2 vols., Leipzig 1872

Murdoch, W., *Chopin: His Life*, London 1934

Niecks, F., *Frederick Chopin as a Man and Musician*, 2 vols., London 1888

Nowak-Romanowicz, A., *Josef Elsner*, Cracow 1957

Ollivier, D., *Mémoires*, Paris 1927; *Correspondance de Liszt et de la Comtesse d'Agoult*, 2 vols., Paris 1933 and 1934

Opienski, H., *Chopin's Collected Letters* (tr. E. L. Voynich), New York 1931; *Listy Fryderyka Chopina*, Warsaw 1937

Pereswiet-Soltan, S., *Listy Fryderyka Chopina do Jana Bialoblockiego*, Warsaw 1926

Pevsner, Nicholas, *The Buildings of England: London, Vol. I*, London 1973

Pourtalès, G. F., *Chopin*, Paris 1927

Prochazka, J., *Frédéric Chopin et la Bohème*, Prague 1969

Reiss, J., *Slazak Josef Elsner*, Katowice 1936

Sand, George, *Lucrezia Floriani*, Paris 1880; *Hiver à Majorque*,

Paris 1855; *Histoire de ma vie*, 4 vols., Paris 1902–04; *Impressions et souvenirs*, Paris 1873. (see also Lubin, G.)

Smoter, J. M., *Album Chopina 1829–1831*, Cracow 1975; *Spor o 'listy' Chopina do Delfiny Potockiej*, 2nd edn., Cracow 1976

Sowinski, A., *Les musiciens polonais*, Paris 1857

Starzynski, J., *Delacroix et Chopin*, Warsaw 1962

Stromenger, K., *Fryderyk Chopin*, Cracow 1959

Sydow, B. E., 'Ipse Dixit—Extracts from Unpublished Letters of Chopin to Delfina Potocka,' *Frederick Chopin* (ed. S. P. Mizwa), New York 1949; *Bibliografia F. F. Chopina*, Warsaw 1949; *Supplement*, Warsaw 1954; *Correspondance de Frédéric Chopin*, 3 vols., Paris 1953–1960; *Korespondencja Fryderyka Chopina*, 2 vols., Warsaw 1955

Vuilermoz, E. and Gavoty, B., *Chopin Amoureux*, Paris 1960

Walker, A., *Frederick Chopin—Profiles*, London 1973

Weinstock, H., *Chopin, the Man and his Music*, New York 1949

Wierzynski, C., *The Life and Death of Chopin* (tr. N. Guterman), London 1951

Wodzinski, A., *Les trois romans de Frédéric Chopin*, Paris 1886

Zebrowski, D. (ed.), *Studies in Chopin*, Warsaw 1973

Index